SPILLED WATER:
INSTITUTIONAL COMMITMENT
IN THE PROVISION OF
WATER SERVICES

Edited by William D. Savedoff
and Pablo T. Spiller

INTER-AMERICAN DEVELOPMENT BANK

Washington, D.C.
1999

Cataloging-in-Publication data provided by the
Inter-American Development Bank
Felipe Herrera Library

Spilled water : institutional commitment in the provision of water services /
edited by William D. Savedoff and Pablo T. Spiller.
  p. cm.
  Includes bibliographical references.
  ISBN: 1886938563
  1. Water supply—Latin America. 2. Privatization—Latin America.
3. Water utilities—Latin America. 5. Decentralization in government—Latin
America. 6. Public utilities—Latin America. I. Savedoff, William D.
II. Spiller, Pablo T. (Pablo Thomas), 1951– III. Inter-American Development
Bank.
363.61 S75—dc20

SPILLED WATER
Institutional Commitment in the Provision of Water Services

Table of Contents

Latin American Research Network
Inter-American Development Bank

The Inter-American Development Bank created the Latin American Research Network in 1991 in order to strengthen policy formulation and contribute to the development policy agenda in Latin America. Through a competitive bidding process, the Network provides grant funding to leading Latin American research centers to conduct studies on economic and social issues selected by the bank in consultation with the region's development community. Most of the studies are comparative, which allows the Bank to build its knowledge base and draw on lessons from experiences in macroeconomic and financial policy, modernization of the state, regulation, poverty and income distribution, social services and employment. The individual country studies are available as working papers and are also available in PDF format on the internet at http://www.iadb.org/oce/41.htm.

Acknowledgments

The studies in this book were financed by the Latin American Research Network of the Inter-American Development Bank and would not have been possible without the collaboration of many friends and colleagues. Ricardo Hausmann was instrumental in beginning the research project and providing many sparks for its original conception. The project benefited greatly from the participation of Mario Niklitschek, who collaborated in the selection and review of the case studies. Naoko Shinkai provided valuable research assistance for the first chapter whose ideas first coalesced in a paper by the editors and which was presented at the "IDB Conference on Private Investment: Infrastructure Reform and Governance in Latin America and the Caribbean" in September 1997. We would like to thank Ricardo Quiroga and Christopher Jennings for their participation in seminars, comments, and general encouragement. Thanks are due also to the following for their collaboration and comments on the case studies that appear in the book: Milagros Maraví, Irma Ugaz, Alejandro Molinari, and Hugo Oliveira. Norelis Betancourt, Graciela Thomen, Raquel Gomez, and Leticia Cuevas kept the machinery of the research endeavor humming smoothly, and Rita Funaro's editing helped us pull the final manuscript together.

Preface

Macroeconomic stabilization has topped the economic policy agenda in Latin America for many years now. However, increasingly stable policies have not spared the region from a volatile economic environment. Consequently, attention has turned to the underpinnings of economic progress in the microeconomic arena. New questions are being asked about the institutional frameworks that are conducive to investment and growth, the political economy of reforms, and the relationship between government, private firms, and the public.

These issues are particularly salient for public infrastructure —the roads, electricity plants, water networks, ports, and telecommunications that provide the support structure for economic activity. For decades, the provision and operation of this kind of infrastructure was viewed as the sole domain of the state. Governments used tax revenues to invest, maintain, and operate the systems, through direct administration or occasionally through parastatal companies. But this approach failed to keep pace with demand, and today the region is searching for new answers.

These political and economic crosscurrents have been nowhere more severe and problematic than in the potable water sector. For decades, the expansion of water systems in Latin America has lagged the expansion of its urban areas, and made only slow progress for the rural population. But the cause of this slow progress runs deeper than a simple lack of political will or insufficient public funds. Rather, the political-economy of the sector, as it is generally structured, works against adequate investment and quality service. Politicians accede to the public demand for low prices, so water companies remain dependent on public sector transfers. Ownership of physical capital is unclear so there is little incentive to properly maintain facilities. And those who are excluded pay prices that are several times the marginal cost of service provision but remain out of the reach of cash-starved water companies. This political stalemate hinders institutional reforms that would give water companies greater autonomy, allow them to charge fees that cover their expenses for operation and expansion, and subject them to external auditors in the form of regulatory agencies that would protect the public interest in quality service.

These questions of the political-economy of the sector and the way it influences the institutional framework of the sector are at the core of the studies in this Latin American Research Network project. They will be of value to policymakers and researchers who are concerned with the water sector. But they will also be of interest to those who recognize that Latin America's challenge in the next few decades is to design, promote, and establish new institutional frameworks —in many areas of the economy— that can break the strangleholds of the present and promote greater welfare in the future.

Ricardo Hausmann
Chief Economist
Inter-American Development Bank

CHAPTER 1:

Government Opportunism and the Provision of Water

Pablo T. Spiller and William D. Savedoff[1]

What happens to the provision of water services when institutional arrangements cannot restrain government opportunism? Even when utilities are in public hands, governments are tempted to keep prices below financially sustainable levels and thereby "expropriate" the public agencies as effectively as if they were private. In the resulting low-level equilibrium, low prices are reflected in low quality, limited service expansion, operational inefficiency, and corruption, which further erode public support. A number of alternative institutional arrangements have been tried without success, but others hold promise including fragmentation, competition, and privatization.

Lost Water

Latin America loses about 9 trillion cubic meters of water each year, about 33 percent of the water collected and treated for public consumption. While it is impossible for water systems to deliver 100 percent of their water to the household tap, Latin America could cut those losses by more than three quarters if it could reach international standards for properly managed and operated water systems.[2] If the costs to society are so great in terms of tax

---

[1] The authors are Joe Shoong, Professor of International Business and Public Policy, and Chair, Business & Public Policy Group, Walter A. Haas School of Business, University of California, Berkeley; and Senior Research Economist, Office of the Chief Economist, Inter-American Development Bank, respectively.

[2] Assuming water losses of 8 percent, similar to those of Singapore (World Bank 1994), losses could be cut by 6.8 trillion cubic meters per year, and to a mere 1.3 trillion cubic meters per year if the region could achieve the loss levels reached by U.S. water companies (only 4.7 percent). See American Water Works Association (1993).

revenues, environmental impacts, and reduced coverage, why is it so difficult to properly manage and operate water systems in the region, and more
generally in the developing world?

The problem is not related to project finance or lack of technical or
manpower capabilities, but rather to the political economy of the sector.
Indeed, the region has invested some 1 percent of GDP in water projects
every year for the past decade, and operating costs are at least as large. The
water sector employs tens of thousands of employees, with a ratio of employees per thousand connections more than three times the level considered efficient by privately managed firms. With these large resources devoted to the sector, why is it so difficult to expand coverage, improve quality,
and properly maintain water systems? The nature of the sector, coupled with
the nations' political institutions, create incentives for governments to behave opportunistically, for water companies to operate inefficiently, and for
the public to withhold support from the sector. Thus, the water sector, as
with other utilities in the region, has a tendency toward a *low-level equilibrium* from which it is difficult to escape. The problems of regulating the
water sector are not uniquely related to the recent efforts to involve the private sector through concessions,[3] but rather are an essential part of why
public enterprises in the region, and the developing world in general, have
had difficulty providing efficient services.

A useful framework for analyzing the constraints to improving water
services in Latin America begins with a discussion of the problems facing
the potable water and sanitation sector—most of which are shared with other
infrastructure and utility sectors. The problem of governmental opportunism is found to be the main reason for the poor performance of utilities, and
of water utilities in particular, whether they are public or private. This opportunism leads to a low-level equilibrium in which low prices are associated with low quality, limited pace of service expansion, operational inefficiency, and corruption, which further erode public support. The peculiar
characteristics of the water sector make this problem even more acute. The
framework is complete with a discussion of the institutional arrangements
that have been tried without success, and others that hold promise, such as
fragmentation, the introduction of competition, and privatization.

---

[3] See Willig et al. (1998).

When this framework is applied to case studies from throughout the region, Honduras and Peru stand out as clear examples of the stability of low-level equilibria that emerge when governments cannot develop a credible policy for the financial sustainability of the water sector. In these cases, efforts to increase coverage and service quality are regularly stymied. Consumers are unwilling to spend more on services they view as wastefully managed. Water authorities face perverse incentives as they are not allowed to raise sufficient tariff revenues, obtain adequate fiscal commitments for investment, or retain the funds they obtain from service improvements. Thus, they reasonably prefer to manage the system in ways that reduce effort, increase employment, or even allow them to privately appropriate resources. Finally, governments with relatively short time-horizons will prefer the status quo over costly political actions that might involve increased water rates in the short-run and yield diffuse benefits only in the longer term. Consumers are relatively dispersed and too disorganized to assume an active role in holding the water authority accountable. It is not surprising that in this political and social environment, private investment is not forthcoming without major regulatory and institutional changes. The government's lack of credibility to establish commercially independent and viable water systems is, then, the key to disentangling the low-level equilibrium.[4]

In Mexico, Chile, and Argentina, the analysis produces very different results. Mexico shows how changes within fully public institutions can lead to better performance, although the improvements from decentralizing to municipal authorities are only marginal. Chile shows decidedly strong performance among public institutions, particularly when they take advantage of private subcontracting; however, it also shows the continuing limitations of such a regulatory and ownership structure in terms of mobilizing sufficient investment. In Argentina—the country in the region that has proceeded most quickly toward extensive private participation in the sector—the interplay of two different concession arrangements with their respective institutional contexts has generated incentives for the achievement of public policy goals that are reasonable in Buenos Aires and problematic in Corrientes.

In analyzing the water sector, this book focuses primarily on issues related to the provision of potable water services. Issues related to efficient

---

[4] This does not mean, however, that private investors would not be willing to operate the system under a contract that assures their investment recovery in a very short period of time.

water resource management, which would require consideration of alternative water uses, are not encompassed. It is appropriate to bracket such concerns because potable water uses are very small relative to the volumes consumed by agriculture or required for maintaining natural habitats. Furthermore, efficient allocation of water for direct consumption by human populations can generally be more easily attained when the price of water charged to utilities reflects its opportunity cost for agricultural or environmental uses. Therefore, any recommendations for placing water utilities on commercial standards of operation are fully compatible with efficient water resource management.

This book concentrates on the issue of increasing coverage and quality in the provision of potable water. Although it does analyze the treatment of wastewater, this subject is given relatively less emphasis. To some degree this is justified by the growing recognition, as demonstrated in almost all new concession arrangements, that the provision of potable water and the treatment of wastewater must be addressed simultaneously in the investment and operational plans of water utilities. Nevertheless, the fact that the effects of contaminated water are not generally perceived directly by the same people who consume water effectively reduces the political support for recovering costs or allocating investments toward wastewater treatment. If anything, a separate analysis of wastewater treatment would show that the processes that lead to low-level equilibria in the provision of potable water are even more extensive and problematic in the case of adequate wastewater treatment.

Main Features of the Potable Water Sector

Potable water services are a critical part of the urban fabric of all societies as they influence health conditions, land prices, manufacturing costs, and daily comfort. Although Latin America has ample water supply in the aggregate, the process of capturing and distributing water has been deficient. Coverage has expanded over the past few decades but remains low in several countries. For those who receive water from public utilities, water quality and reliability of service are often poor. Almost without exception, the cost of providing the service is very high and prices are below cost. Latin America needs to invest on the order of $12 billion annually over the next 10 years to reach adequate levels of water service coverage and sanitation, and much of this may have to come from the private sector (World Bank 1995). Yet, despite the recent increases in investment in utilities and the rapid surge in private investment in these sectors, investment in the water sector has generally lagged. In the first half of the 1990s, the private sector committed some $35 million to Latin America's electricity sector in 50 projects and $22 million in 85 transportation projects, but only $10 million in 19 potable water and sanitation projects.[5] This lag in private sector interest parallels the lag in water sector reforms.[6] These numbers are evidence that the problems in attracting investment to water utilities are more acute than they are for the other utility sectors.

Potable water services have many of the characteristics of private goods that are bought and sold in any private market—a fairly homogeneous commodity, purchased for domestic or industrial consumption, with reasonable information about its quality and characteristics. It is a commodity for which demand is normal with fairly stable and predictable elasticities in prices and income. However, potable water services share three basic characteristics with other utilities that make it difficult to provide them through perfectly competitive markets: large sunk costs, economies of density and/or scale, and massive consumption.[7] The combination of these characteristics leads to significant politicization of the sector's pricing and operations.

In comparison with other utility sectors, these characteristics are more acute for potable water services, making for a higher degree of politicization of its pricing and operations. First, in the water sector, sunk costs are more significant because most of the sector's fixed assets have few alternative uses. In that sense, the sector resembles the gas and electricity distribution sectors. By contrast, telecommunications assets are substantially more mobile than water sector assets thanks to computer technology. Furthermore, the ratio of operating to total costs for efficient water firms is much lower than for gas or electricity. For example, in the United States, this ratio is about 10 percent for water companies, while it is 32 percent for gas utilities and over 57 percent for electric utilities.[8] In the cases of gas and electricity, the energy

---

[5] Estimated from data in *Public Works Financing* (October 1995).

[6] In Peru, Chile, and Argentina, water sector reforms were introduced much later than reforms in other utility sectors. See chapters 3, 5, and 6.

[7] See Spiller (1993) and Levy and Spiller (1994).

[8] These operation cost ratios were calculated from data in American Water Works Association (1993), EIA 1997, and Department of Energy annual reports.

component of total costs is higher than the expenditure for the actual water resource, and depreciation of capital may be relatively lower as well. This implies that the revenue needed to cover current cash expenditures as a proportion of total costs is smaller in water than in other utilities.

The water sector shares large economies of density with the electricity and gas distribution sectors. For a given distribution network, increasing the number of households connected or their consumption reduces the network's average costs.[9] This is especially true when alternative sources of water are not available. In such cases, retail competition may not be feasible even when using the same infrastructure for distribution as is increasingly common in the electricity and gas sectors. Thus, in a given locale, there will normally be a very small set of actual suppliers.[10]

Finally, water is the quintessential massively consumed product, and access to water is generally perceived to be more of a "social" and "basic" service than other utility services. In open political rhetoric, but alas not in public investment decisions, equitable access to potable water services is more strongly defended than access to services such as telephones or electricity. In Latin America, cultural attitudes toward paying the full cost of electricity and telephones have changed more rapidly than attitudes toward water rates. In Honduras and Peru, even the suggestion that reforms will increase rates has been sufficient to halt reform efforts. Similar consumer opposition to price increases associated with some water sector privatizations took place in Argentina.[11] In Chile, by contrast, substantial price increases have been readily accepted as a means for receiving improved services. A large part of this acceptance may be due to Chile's decision to establish a water bill subsidy targeted to poorer households, thereby defusing the political argument that the poor will be hurt by adequate rates.

These three characteristics—prevalence of sunk costs, economies of density and/or scale, and massive consumption—lead to the politicization of utility pricing. First, the fact that a large component of infrastructure

---

[9] For evidence of these economies in the United States, see Bhattacharyya et al., 1994; and for Mexico, see chapter 4.

[10] This, however, does not mean that competition has not developed in water sectors. Free entry into the potable water sector has created direct competition in Guatemala City. A similar process is beginning to develop in Colombia. In both cases, competition is developing where multiple water sources are available.

[11] See *Financial Times* (February 13, 1996).

investments is sunk implies that once the investment is undertaken the operator will be willing to continue functioning as long as operating revenues exceed operating costs. Since operating costs do not include a return on sunk investments (but only on the alternative value of these assets), the operating company—whether public or private—will be willing to operate even if prices are below total average costs.[12] Second, economies of density imply that in most utility services, there will be few network operators in each locality. Consumers will tend to view the service provider as a monopoly, presuming it will use its market muscle to extract higher prices. This will raise public concern about its pricing and operational practices. Finally, the fact that utility services tend to be massively consumed creates an opportunity for politicians to use pricing strategically as an instrument of political mobilization, and generates a large, potentially vocal group of consumers whose interests can be used to obstruct effective reforms. Thus, massive consumption, economies of density and/or scale, and sunk investments allow governments (whether national or local) to behave opportunistically vis-à-vis the investing company.[13] For example, after the investment is sunk, the government may try to lower prices, disallow costs,[14] restrict the operating company's pricing flexibility,[15] require the company to undertake special investments,[16] control purchasing or employment patterns, or try to restrict the movement or composition of capital.[17] All these are attempts by politicians (and those they represent) to capture the rents associated with the

---

[12] The source of financing does not change this computation. For example, if the company is completely leveraged, a price below average cost will bring the company to bankruptcy, eliminating the part of the debt associated with the sunk investments. Only the part of the debt that is associated with the value of the nonsunk investments would be able to be subsequently serviced.

[13] This incentive exists vis-à-vis both public and private companies and is discussed further below.

[14] This is possible under the current regulatory framework in Chile. See chapter 5 for a discussion of how the Chilean legislation limits the potential for opportunistic behavior by the regulator.

[15] Chapter 6 discusses how the government of Corrientes in Argentina successfully limited the pricing flexibility of the private operator, triggering a change of ownership.

[16] The first renegotiation of the Aguas Argentinas concession was associated with a new government's desire to change the investment plan detailed in the concession agreement (see chapter 6).

[17] For example, the latest water sector legislation in Chile limits the ownership of water companies by other utility operators (see chapter 5).

company's sunk costs by administrative measures. This political capture of rents is equivalent to asset expropriation, as the company— whether public or private—will be unable to reap the rewards associated with those sunk assets. Thus, expropriation may be indirect and undertaken subtly. While the government may uphold and protect traditionally conceived property rights, it may nonetheless attempt to expropriate—i.e., capture rents— through regulatory procedures.

The Political Profitability of Government Opportunism

Governments may find it advantageous to expropriate sunk assets if the direct costs are small compared to the (short-term) benefits of such action and if the indirect institutional costs are not too large. The direct costs of expropriation—either directly or through administrative measures—include reduced investment by other operators in the infrastructure and utilities sectors who will, as a result, consider further commitments as increasingly risky. The institutional costs of such expropriations are to undermine the effectiveness of basic rules and norms of governance by disregarding judicial findings or evading proper, or traditional, administrative procedures. Meanwhile, the government may anticipate short-term benefits in electoral gains or winning parliamentary debates by mobilizing the public around the issues of reducing operators' prices or attacking monopoly suppliers.

Thus, incentives for expropriating the quasirents associated with the existence of sunk assets will be largest in countries where direct costs are small, indirect institutional costs are low, and the government's horizon is relatively short. Direct costs will be smaller when there are fewer private operators in the infrastructure sector; when the sectors do not, in general, require massive investment programs; and when technological change is not an important factor in the sector. Institutional costs will be low in countries where formal or informal governmental regulatory procedures—checks and balances—are weak or absent; where regulatory policy is centralized in the administration; and where the judiciary has little tradition, or authority, to review administrative decisions. Perhaps most important, the government's time horizon is strongly affected by the periodicity of elections, and whether or not the government faces highly contested elections and a need to satisfy key constituencies. Private operators will recognize and evaluate these factors, often choosing not to undertake investments in the first place. Thus, direct government provision of infrastructure may become the default mode of operation.

Credibility and Regulatory Frameworks

Clearly, the three basic structural features of utilities have important implications for the development of regulatory structures. In particular, it is important to link regulatory reform to a country's institutional environment in a discriminating fashion.[18] Moreover, regulatory structures cannot be directly copied from one country to another, and regulatory reforms that attempt to improve upon current regulatory structures have to pass the acid test of implementability.

But in every case, regulatory designs have to confront the inexorable tradeoff between flexibility and credibility. On the one hand, regulations must be sufficiently fixed and rigid to provide investors and managers with the certainty they need regarding future terms and profitability. Without the credibility provided by this rigidity, investment decisions will be biased toward shorter-term gains or investment will dry up all together. On the other hand, governments need to have sufficient flexibility to adjust to changing conditions. Surprises can come in the form of windfalls for the utility companies, through technological advances or unforeseen cost-savings, and the public interest demands that these savings be shared with consumers. Most countries, then, develop institutions that create a mixture of flexibility and credibility that is strongly conditioned by the strength and effectiveness of other institutions, such as parliaments, courts, and regulatory agencies. In other words, a first best solution is seldom achievable.

The particular features of utility sectors make regulatory credibility a necessary ingredient for managing public or private investment in a socially efficient manner. The regulatory proposals that attempt to grant regulators substantial discretion to reform and correct perceived market imperfections adversely affect investment incentives and explain much of the lagging performance for infrastructure in Latin America. This paradox is at the essence of the tradeoff between credibility and flexibility developed in Levy and Spiller

---

[18] See, for example, Guasch and Spiller (1995), Levy and Spiller (1994 and 1996), and Spiller (1993 and 1996a).

(1994). Indeed, this tradeoff reflects a more general problem inherent to commitment in governments. As Weingast's (1995) opening paragraph excellently exemplifies: "A government strong enough to protect property rights and enforce contracts is also strong enough to confiscate the wealth of its citizens."

The government opportunism that lies at the root of the low-level equilibrium can only be made transparent and confronted directly when the operator has some autonomy from the executive branch. Such an arrangement can range from arms-length relationships among governments and public water agencies—as is the fashion currently in Brazil—to concessions designed to attract private investors—as actively pursued by Argentina. In either event, a government that wants to address the problems of service coverage and quality will have to design institutional arrangements that limit its own ability to behave opportunistically toward the water company—be it public or private. Such institutional arrangements are nothing more than the design of a credible regulatory framework.

A credible regulatory framework has to stipulate the procedures and policies for price setting, conflict resolution (arbitration or judicial) between the parties, consumer rights, quality standards, and investment, among other things. In other words, regulation, if credible, solves a key contracting problem between the government and the utilities by restraining the government from opportunistically expropriating the utilities' quasirents.[19] This, however, does not mean that the utility has to receive assurances of a rate of return or exclusive licenses.[20] In some countries, however, such assurances may be the only way to limit the government's discretionary powers.

The absence of a credible regulatory framework is most apparent when looking at efforts to attract private investment in the sector. A first order effect is that, without a credible regulatory framework, investments may never take place. In countries where the government's commitment not to expropriate investments explicitly or implicitly is very weak, private investors will

[19] See Goldberg (1976) for one of the first treatments of this problem. See also Williamson (1976).
[20] Indeed, when Colombia's initial reform of telecommunications deregulated value added networks, it specifically stipulated that the government could not set its prices nor did it allow exclusivity provisions. Thus, the regulatory framework in this context meant a total restriction on governmental discretion.

simply not take the risk. Under such conditions, even public entities with any degree of decision-making autonomy will underinvest.[21]

A second effect of noncredible government policies is that operators may keep maintenance expenditures to a minimum, thus degrading quality and increasing water losses. This has been an important cause of the low quality of supply in the water sector across Latin America. For example, unaccounted water reached 50 percent in Honduras, Mexico, and Peru,[22] while in Argentina (prior to the privatization of the water sector in Buenos Aires and Corrientes) it was as high as 60 percent. In Chile, on the other hand, unaccounted water is much lower, averaging 17 percent among private companies. Quality can also be measured in terms of pressure and frequency of interruptions. In Argentina, prior to the privatization of Aguas Argentinas, the percentage of connections in the federal capital with reasonable water pressure (more than 8 meters) was only 15 percent. In three years, Aguas Argentinas was able to increase that percentage to 97 percent (see chapter 6 on Argentina). A high frequency of interruptions is also quite prevalent in the region. In Honduras, the average water system provides only 10 hours of service per day, with 70 percent of connections showing intermittent service (see chapter 2 on Honduras).

Third, operators may insist upon high up-front rents achieved through high prices. Although these may provide incentives for some investment, they may also be politically unsustainable. To privatize Argentina's telecommunications sector, prices were raised well above international levels, which allowed companies to reduce their exposure to regulatory risk. Subsequent to privatization, however, the government reneged on many other aspects of the license.[23] Prior to granting the Buenos Aires concession, the Argentine government increased the prices for water services in Greater Buenos Aires close to costs. Although the concession for Corrientes appears not to have

---

[21] As chapters 2 and 3 on Honduras and Peru make clear, this is the current situation in both countries. Chapter 6 on Argentina, on the other hand, shows this to be the case prior to the recent privatization. See Willig et al. (1998) for other examples.

[22] Some Peruvian companies have much higher percentages of unaccounted water (see chapter 3).

[23] License provisions such as indexation were initially not implemented—allegedly because of the passage of the Convertibility Act that prohibited indexation. Later, indexation and other provisions were modified by the government. The initially high prices, though, allowed the companies to remain profitable even when the government deviated from the license provisions. See Spiller (1993).

followed this rule—since the winning bid proposed a price reduction of 17 percent below then current rates—most of this price reduction was planned to take place after the fifteenth year of the concession. Generous price increases, however, may turn out to be politically infeasible, as demonstrated by the water service concession of Tucumán. In that case, the price increases triggered a customer revolt, which led to substantial nonpayment problems, and the eventual revocation of the license (see chapter 6 and Artana et al., 1997).[24]

A fourth effect of noncredible regulatory frameworks is to push the financing of sunk costs to users through relatively high connection charges. This has occurred in various sectors, from telecommunications to water, where high connection charges are used by investors to offset the risk to their sunk assets. For example, the World Bank estimates the long-run incremental cost of a water connection in Greater Buenos Aires to be approximately $2,500. Connection charges under the current concession agreement with Aguas Argentinas vary from $400 to $600 (see chapter 6). Although these hook up charges do not reach the full connection cost, they do substantially reduce the payback period for the investor, partially protecting the utility from governmental opportunism. Other water systems expand only when users or third parties commit full funding for the investment. Bolivia has several examples of this practice. The Santa Cruz water company expands only when all potential users in a particular expansion zone have committed to pay the related expansion costs. In El Alto, expansion of the system has been contingent on community mobilization of resources with matching grants from exter-

---

[24] Another effect that may not be directly applicable to the water sector, is that investment may be undertaken with technologies that have a lower degree of sunk investments, even at the expense of reducing the quality and increasing the cost of services. In this regard, it is not surprising that private telecommunications operators have rushed to develop cellular rather than fixed link networks throughout Eastern Europe. While cellular technology has a higher long-run cost than fixed link, and on some quality dimensions is also an inferior product, the magnitude of investment in specific assets is much smaller than in fixed link networks. Furthermore, a large portion of the specific investments in cellular telephony are undertaken by the customers themselves who purchase the handsets. In the solid waste sector, too, private haulers will use general purpose trucks or handcarts rather than invest in specialized compacting equipment, even though the latter may be more profitable and environmentally sound, simply because it is more difficult to resell or convert them to other uses (see Cointreau 1994).

nal funding agencies.[25] In water systems that combine low prices and low hookup charges, it is difficult to attract operators who might otherwise be willing to face regulatory risk in return for the ability to exploit particularly profitable service segments.

By strongly encouraging inefficiency and poor performance, a non-credible regulatory framework eventually creates the conditions for a direct government take-over. Thus, the government eventually becomes owner and operator by default. Government ownership, then, represents neither the best way to promote the public interest nor the most efficient way to provide services, but simply the failure to develop institutions that limit the temptation for opportunistic governmental behavior.

The Emergence and Stability of Low-level Equilibria

While much of the literature demonstrates the importance of government credibility and the effects of regulatory frameworks on *private* participation, credibility and regulatory frameworks are also critical to effective provision of water and other utility services *when they are in government hands.* The relationship between the executive arm of government and the agencies or semiautonomous authorities that operate and manage publicly owned water systems illustrates the same range of incentive problems as those that arise with private sector participation. The manifestations of these incentive problems are generally similar—low coverage, limited investment, and poor quality service. They differ, however, in other ways. Private operators will respond to regulatory frameworks and incentive structures in ways that maximize their return and minimize their risk. By contrast, public operators—who do not directly realize returns from asset ownership—are more likely to dissipate rents through excessive employment and other forms of inefficient resource utilization, creating indirect ways to capture those rents privately. If it were easy to limit governmental opportunism and develop workable frameworks for private operation, these would have been more

---

[25] In numerous cases, mobilizing communities to finance expansion costs, in full or in part, has been a successful tool for reaching areas that lack water service for several reasons. Community mobilization can create a lobby to voice demands for adequate water service to the relevant political authorities; provide the marginal funds necessary to initiate a project; perform formal or informal supervision of public works to assure quality; and establish support for continuing maintenance and proper operation.

common in the region. Given the difficulties in limiting governmental opportunism, public ownership becomes the predominant mode of provision by default, nowhere more so than in the water sector.

Government opportunism, in its basic form, implies low prices: prices so low that they fail to provide the operator—public or private—with the ability to finance its business expansion, whether current or past (i.e., servicing the debt). Lowering prices, however, is not simply a one-time reversible action. Rather, once the short-term political interest in lower prices is seized upon, the low prices trigger a downward spiral in which mutually reinforcing factors make low prices and low quality a stable equilibrium. This downward spiral is depicted in Figure 1.1.

Politicians, in their clamor for lower prices—or delayed billing, or performance of unprofitable activities—can claim social consciousness while blaming the operator, whether public or private, for inefficient performance.[26] But low prices imply that the public operator will depend on government transfers for expansion and investment. In Peru, for example, the average return on equity of the water operators is a startling 0 percent. Similarly, in Honduras the average revenue per connection reaches only 50 percent of operating costs, while the Buenos Aires water operator reached profitability only

Figure 1.1

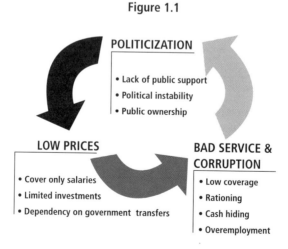

<hr>

[26]Low prices fit the perfect "credit claiming—blame shifting" strategy discussed in Fiorina (1982).

following its privatization. The need for government transfers, in turn, limits the operator's ability to expand, as investments are not evaluated relative to their own profitable returns but against the competing uses of funds in the national budget. In Chile, for example, one of the key restrictions on expanding water services or treatment is the fact that the water companies remain public entities whose expenditures form part of the national budget (see chapter 5). Despite the fact that these investments might easily be recovered through rates and, therefore, would represent no net claims against future tax revenues, the investment budgets are restricted by competition with other sectors, such as education, for which little or no cost recovery can be anticipated.

A cash-poor company that needs direct government transfers to finance its investment program will also be subjected to substantial scrutiny and intervention, thus limiting its autonomy in matters of personnel, allocations among inputs, and areas for expansion. Once it becomes politically convenient for the polity to set opportunistic prices, the maintenance and investment budget may disappear, leaving only the minimum required to cover salaries (which themselves are protected by a strong lobby).[27,28] Under such scrutiny, a cash-poor company also loses much of its ability to protect its autonomy by strategically manipulating its information. Consequently, the company will find its asset base depreciating, its maintenance program will suffer, and its service quality will deteriorate. These factors will further tighten its investment capabilities, making its expansion programs sporadic, generating low coverage levels, and probably shortages and rationing as well (see Table 1.1).

Although public enterprises usually require the Finance Ministry to approve investment programs, some cash-rich companies may protect their autonomy by utilizing their information advantage, forestalling close government scrutiny. This is where the reinforcing dynamics start to make this

---

[27] In SAANA's Tegucigalpa operation, the union effectively co-administers the enterprise. One effect is a pattern of excessive employment in Tegucigalpa, even in comparison to the inefficient employment levels in other parts of Honduras (see chapter 2).

[28] For example, in Honduras, labor costs exceed 50 percent of current revenues, while in Buenos Aires prior to the privatization, labor costs hovered between 30 percent and 64 percent of total revenues. By contrast, efficient operators in countries with higher unit labor costs have much lower shares. For example, in a sample of over 1,000 water companies in the United States between 1989 and 1992, the American Water Works Association estimates that labor costs averaged 20 percent of revenues (AWWA 1995).

Table 1.1 Measures of Efficiency for Selected Water Utilities in Latin America

Country/Company	Revenues/ Oper. Costs	Wage Bill/ Revenues	Coverage	Hours of Operation	Employees Per 1000 Connections	Water Losses
Chile (1995)						
Public Enterprises (avg.)	1.27	0.15	99%	23	2.5	31%
Private Enterprises (avg.)	1.21	0.12	100%	24	4.9	17%
Honduras (1994)						
SANAA – Tegucigalpa	0.36	0.25	53%		13.6	50%
SANAA – Other	0.48	0.43	77%	10	5.0	
Municipal Authorities	0.41	0.29	67%	11	4.0	
DIMA	1.67	0.21	65%	22	6.0	37%
Mexico (1994)			85%			
Auton. Municipalities				14	6.3	47%
Regulated Municip.				15	5.8	46%
Auton. States				15	5.7	49%
Regulated States				16	5.5	46%
Peru (1993/1994)			72%	14		
SEDAPAL	1.17	0.19	75%	14	2.1	38%
SEDAPIURA	0.86	0.35	81%	18	7	55%
Admin. Sullana	0.97	0.32	70%		4.4	49%
SEDAQOSQO	1.16		55%		5.7	46%
Argentina						
OSN (1985)	0.89	0.57	72%		9.6	
Aguas Argentinas (1994)	1.22	0.39	77%		3.6	
Aguas de Corrientes (1991)	0.01	0.37	66%		7.4	61%
Aguas de Corrientes (1995)	0.99	0.35	73%		2.6	45%
Brazil (1995)						
SANEPAR	1.08	0.70	99%		2.8	28%
CASAN	0.99	0.72	88%		3.3	35%
CESAN	1.13	0.67	95%		3.6	28%
SABESP	0.99	0.39	94%		2.5	36%
CAESB	0.70	0.63	90%		3.2	24%
SANESUL	0.71	0.44	94%		4.3	47%
EMBASA	1.01	0.61	100%		4.2	54%
CAEMA	0.82	0.78	78%		8.0	59%
CAGECE	0.84	0.58	74%		2.9	39%
CAER	0.40	0.25	99%		7.4	43%

Sources: Chapters 2–6, and for Brazil, SNI 1997.

a low-level equilibrium. As the company is stripped of cash, the management and the union have a clear incentive to engage in "cash hiding." That is, since extra cash cannot be used for investments without government authorization, it will be used to increase employment, whether permanent (if the company has the ability to do so) or temporary. Corruption can then become endemic. Corruption, bad service, and low quality make the company a public eyesore, reinforcing the public perception of bad management and reducing general support for continuing fiscal transfers. For example, households in the marginal neighborhoods of Honduras were willing to pay about twice as much for service improvements in privately or cooperatively managed systems than in those operated by the national water company or municipal water authorities due to the poor reputation of the latter. Clearly, in such contexts, there is successively less political incentive for elected officials or the Finance Minister to support government transfers.

Thus, a stable low-level equilibrium is achieved in which prices are kept low, government transfers are limited, service quality and coverage are low, and no one—whether the service operator, the government, consumers, or constituents—has an interest in changing their position. Although attempts at reform may occur, they commonly fail. Low-level equilibria, then, are stable because: (a) there is no public support for increasing government transfers or raising prices to adequate levels; (b) the government has little incentive to spend scarce investment funds on a mismanaged organization; and (c) attempts to improve management fail, unless there is basic institutional change.

Failed Strategies

Clearly, low-level equilibria have high social costs.[29] Specific calculations for Honduras conservatively estimate that raising prices to cover incremental costs of expansion and increasing coverage to 93 percent of the population would increase national welfare by some 2 percent of GDP (see chapter 2). In addition to the social costs of not providing water to people who are willing to pay for it, lack of potable water has a negative impact on health conditions. Unreliable water service prompts firms to invest in generating

---

[29] For further discussion on the importance of the infrastructure sector on a nation's wellbeing, see Spiller and Savedoff (1998).

their own supplies, increasing their costs and reducing their international competitiveness. Furthermore, it degrades the environment by diverting too much water from aquifers and streams. A well-developed potable water sector has, then, a direct impact on the wellbeing of a nation. It improves health, reduces the cost of urban development, and increases the available time for market and nonmarket activities. It also reduces the cost of water-dependent industries (e.g., food processing).

Thus, moving out of a low-level equilibrium should be an important government priority. But as the previous discussion suggests, low-level equilibria are stable—simple fixes will not do the job. Past efforts include the standard set of international agency recommendations including price increases, performance contracts, or other types of temporary performance improvements, and even hiring private firms under Build-Own-Transfer (BOT) contracts.

A standard international agency recommendation is that prices should cover operating and investment costs. When prices are raised to cover operating costs and finance investment, they are rarely raised enough because the low efficiency of the system means that actual costs are much higher than long-run marginal cost. Consumers resist the hike in prices and will not accept them until service is first improved. As a result, the cash generated by a price increase is easily dissipated by the existing management structure and eventually eroded by inflation or repealed. Even pressure from international agencies may not work. In negotiations on a particular sector development loan, a government may agree to a price increase. Once that price increase is introduced, however, the political forces that triggered opportunistic price setting will kick in again—slowly or rapidly—depending on the extent to which inflation erodes the imposed price increase. In the longer run, the price increase will be nothing more than a blip in the chart.[30] As a result, reforms that introduce price changes without making an institutional change in the way prices are set are not sustainable.

---

[30]Between 1979 and 1989, electricity rates fell by an average of 1.5 percent after IDB loan approvals in the electricity sector compared to an average increase of 7.2 percent before, despite contractual clauses requiring that rate levels be maintained. This applies to 23 loans in 12 countries for which data was available in "Evaluation Report on Electric Power Sector, Tariff Policy and Lending," ORE, RE-187, Inter-American Development Bank, Washington, DC (March 1993).

A second type of improvement exercise is to introduce performance contracts. These contracts are effected between management and government, where management will receive some part of the expected increased profit. In general, such contracts have failed in their effort to improve public sector performance as demonstrated by Shirley and Xu (1996). The reason is quite simple. On the one hand, these contracts do not change the basic discretionary power of the government nor do they alter the degree of asymmetry of information between management and government. Since managers know that the government or consumers will eventually appropriate any surplus or profits, they will operate the firms to redistribute cash to themselves and their workers, rather than to increase efficiency. These performance contracts often fail because the government lacks credibility—it can neither establish hard budget constraints nor effectively monitor management's actions. Hence, the use of management contracts as a solution to a credibility problem is ultimately self-defeating. Similarly, introducing new management is also generally inadequate for sustainable changes because the new management faces exactly the same incentives as the old guard. Although not necessarily corrupt, the new management will find that it is better to keep any excess cash in the company rather than transfer it (directly or indirectly) to the government.[31] Since there are no effective incentives to expand or improve service, the cash is used in ways that are not perceived by consumers as better service. Thus, a basic implication of this analysis is that public companies subject to governmental opportunism will rotate management without substantive operational improvements.

A third strategy aims to decentralize the service provider, either by reorganizing administratively or transferring responsibility to subnational political entities. For example, Peru drastically decentralized its water services at the end of the Alán García administration with no significant impact on service quality because the incentives faced by the operator remained the same (see chapter 3). The debate in Honduras over whether to "regionalize" the national water company or "municipalize" water services risks ignoring the more fundamental incentive problems (see chapter 2).

A final strategy is to use BOTs to expand systems. BOTs are attractive because they promise to add capacity without disturbing the existing bal-

---

[31] An indirect transfer back to the government means that excess cash crowds out government transfers, probably on a one-to-one basis.

ance of political interests. They require no fundamental change in the way the company operates or is managed, nor do they require any direct transfer from the government. BOT's, however, require substantial governmental guarantees, very high initial prices, and relatively inflexible contract terms. Since the overall credibility problem is not resolved, BOTs are appropriately perceived as "very expensive," further reinforcing the public impression of corruption and favoritism that encircles the company.

Complementary Mechanisms for Success

The basic question remains: what will succeed? In other words, what set of changes could move a water sector away from its low-level equilibrium? The key to escaping the low-level equilibrium is to develop a process that limits government discretion in price setting. Once such limits are in place, attempting to improve management and to set prices at reasonable levels may actually succeed because they will take place within a context of incentives compatible with improving coverage and service quality.

For a process to be effective in limiting government discretion, the operator must have substantial financial and managerial autonomy and three complementary mechanisms must be in place.[32] First, substantive restraints on regulatory discretion must be embedded in the regulatory framework; second, formal or informal constraints must limit the ability of the polity to change the regulatory framework itself; and finally, institutions must be in place that enforce those substantive or procedural constraints. These three mechanisms are easier to implement in countries where decision making is naturally decentralized. In countries where decision making is heavily centralized, regulatory credibility requires more rigid institutions and restraints.

Regulatory commitment has generally been introduced in three different forms: through specific legislation, "hard wiring," or license terms (i.e., contracts). In the first case, governments can enact specific legislation and delegate its implementation to a regulatory agency whose decisions, on both substance and process, are subject to review by the judiciary. Such legislation seeks to establish the conditions for investment and operation of companies in the particular sector and endows the regulator with substan-

---

[32] See Levy and Spiller (1994).

tial discretion in pursuing the objectives as set out by law. In the second case, regulatory credibility can be achieved by designing the decision-making process ("hard wiring") so that the interests of the regulated companies are safeguarded against administrative expropriation.[33] In these cases, the regulatory agency is tied to specific, predetermined procedures for supervising the industry. In the case of pricing, this can involve specifying the exact method to calculate and determine acceptable adjustments. Here again, the courts may review agencies' decisions, both on substantive and procedural considerations. Finally, regulatory credibility can be achieved by granting the operator a license or contract that specifies the regulatory process through which its prices will be determined. Deviations from the license could then be challenged through the courts.

These three regulatory instruments have different implications for both regulatory credibility and flexibility and perform differently depending upon the context.[34] To show the difficulties in building commitment, consider the United States, which enjoys a relatively propitious political environment with fragmented political structures, decentralized decision making, and multiple checks and balances. The United States has a government structure that fragments power among a directly elected president, a legislature composed of two chambers elected under different rules and at different times, and electoral rules designed to tie legislators to their local constituencies which limits—but does not eliminate—the power of political parties. The United State's judiciary is reasonably well respected by the population and its decisions are widely accepted and implemented. In such a case, specific legislation may be difficult to introduce, as the political fragmentation inherent to the political system increases legislative costs. Thus, a policy problem must be a priority before legislators will spend time drafting—and negotiating—very specific legislation.[35] Hard-wired decisions, that is, very specific decision-making procedures are, on the other hand, easier to draft and adopt, but are, as everything, potentially imperfect. In particular, they run the risk of being diverted by future judicial interpretation. Finally, although contractual arrangements such as licenses are feasible in the United

---

[33] See McCubbins, Noll, and Weingast (1987). On hard-wiring, see Hamilton and Schroeder (1992) and Macey (1992).

[34] For an in-depth discussion, see Spiller (1996a).

[35] See Schwartz, Spiller, and Urbiztondo (1996).

States, they may be too rigid given the nature of the U.S. political system. Thus, the commitment potential of U.S. regulatory structures is quite strong and allows most of these mechanisms to function much better than in less propitious environments. It is, then, not surprising that hard-wiring solutions are the regulatory norm for the United States.[36] Hard-wiring solutions provide politicians with the necessary political flexibility while at the same time the credibility of the judiciary and their traditional protection of property and contract rights provide investors with some assurances against opportunistic behavior.[37]

On the other hand, in nations with centralized decision-making processes, the first two approaches do not provide much regulatory credibility. Nations with centralized political decision making can change laws relatively easily; hence, very specific laws (in substance or in process) will not effectively constrain governmental decision making. Indeed, it is quite interesting to observe that while in the United States the evolution of the electricity sector was undertaken almost without federal legislation, in the United Kingdom, a highly centralized system, most major regulatory changes occurred via legislative action.[38] Similarly, in centralized political environments, courts are less likely to challenge administrative decisions.[39]

Various countries have attempted different approaches to limit governmental discretion when privatizing infrastructure sectors. Chile, a country with substantial checks and balances, introduced very specific legislation to regulate price setting in electricity, telecommunications, and water. Similarly, Chile's antitrust legislation limits political interference through a very complex decision-making process.[40] On the other hand, Argentina, a country with substantial credibility problems, privatized its water and electricity distribution utilities with a very specific regulatory framework embedded

---

[36] See McCubbins, Noll, and Weingast (1987).

[37] This does not mean, though, that U.S. utilities have not had their share of regulatory difficulties. In the 1970s, higher inflation, the increase in the real price of oil, and the emergence of environmental concerns required substantial changes in the regulatory process (Joskow 1974), costing electric utilities substantial market value. One of the lasting effects of this period is an increase in the perception of regulatory risk because capacity additions (mostly nuclear) that were undertaken during the oil shock period were challenged in courts by environmental groups and eventually were withdrawn from the rate base.

[38] See Spiller and Vogelsang (1996).

[39] See Spiller (1996a) for a theory of the evolution of independent courts.

[40] See Corbo, Luders, and Spiller (1997).

in their operating licenses. These licenses, themselves, substantially limit the ability of the regulatory agency to deviate from the prescribed price setting process. Bolivia, almost alone, has maintained private ownership of electricity through the use of very specific concessions since the turn of the century.[41] Mexico, which until recently had a highly unified political system, chose to reform the utility sector through decentralization. This decentralization has had limited effects on performance, largely because responsibilities have been devolved to states that recreate the low-level equilibrium problem at the subnational level. Peru and Honduras, both countries with very few checks and balances, have systems that grant substantial discretion to the regulatory authorities,[42] which limit their ability to escape from low-level equilibria.

Table 1.2 provides a summary of the relation between the extent of flexibility of the regulatory systems chosen by various nations and the extent of checks and balances in their political decision-making process. It shows that among the countries with extensive checks and balances, the United States chose a flexible regulatory system, while Chile chose a more rigid one. Both, though, have succeeded in reaching a higher level equilibrium. The Aguas Argentinas concession and the U.K. concessions are examples of rigid regulatory structures in environments with fewer checks and balances. The cases where low-level equilibria remain stable are those in which the regulatory regime provides ample flexibility with few checks and balances. These are the cases of Honduras, Peru, and Argentina prior to the recent wave of privatizations. Mexico, on the other hand, is still in transition. There, the price setting process remains too discretionary. In an environment with few checks and balances, this creates serious concerns about the country's ability to sustain a higher level equilibrium.

Given the scarce administrative law tradition in the developing world, it is not surprising that few countries have experimented with administrative procedures as ways to provide regulatory credibility. But regulatory structures by themselves may not be enough. Ancillary structures may have to be developed.

---

[41] The other long-lasting, private electric company in Latin America is the Caracas Electricity Company, which has had no regulatory structure in place but has had widely diffused local ownership. The impact of diffused local ownership is discussed further below.

[42] In the case of Honduras, the regulator is the largest operator, further eroding any regulatory credibility (see chapter 2).

Table 1.2 Checks and Balances of Regulatory Systems

Checks and Balances	Regulatory Scheme	
	Flexible	Rigid
Extensive	United States	Chile
	Argentina prior to privatization	Argentina after privatization
Limited	Mexico	
	Peru	U.K.
	Honduras	

Maintaining a High-Level Equilibrium (or Remaining on Higher Ground)

An implication of this analysis is that high-level equilibria are inherently unstable unless there are institutional restraints to governmental opportunism. In their absence, a political shock may call for a price freeze, for a change in the company's investment pattern, or any other operational change that has the effect of expropriating the sunk investments of the public company. Indeed, the movement down from a high-level equilibrium could be stochastic—precipitated by random political and economic shocks, like high inflation, political and social unrest, and so on.[43]

Once a high-quality equilibrium is achieved, the design emphasis should shift toward how to sustain it. Sustaining it means providing political support to maintain a process that limits governmental opportunism. Such support must come from interested parties. Thus, a polity interested in preserving a high-level equilibrium will need to design an industry structure that increases the number of interest groups supporting such a high-level equilibrium.

A basic strategy to increase political support is to fragment the industry. Fragmentation can take many forms, but in every case it generates multiple actors with competing interests. The most common form of fragmentation in infrastructure is by geographic area; for example, national water or telecommunication enterprises can be broken up into many smaller independent firms that retain responsibility for service provision in a particular

---

[43] It is in this sense that some of the reforms in Mexico may not be sustainable because the transfer of operational and regulatory responsibilities to some municipalities may create incentives for utilizing the water companies' resources for short-term political gain.

area. In some cases, fragmentation takes place by subdividing the sector, as when electric generation is separated from transmission and distribution. Occasionally fragmentation creates firms that directly compete with one another, as is increasingly the case in telecommunications. Fragmentation of ownership can even be achieved by selling shares to the public or directly distributing shares in public enterprises to citizens.

Fragmenting the industry has the advantage of creating multiple sources of political support for proper governmental behavior. Similarly, fragmenting the industry and creating—at least potential—competition limits the informational advantage enjoyed by each company. This, in turn, makes it possible for the regulatory agency to learn much more about developments in the industry with regard to cost structures and strategic behavior by comparing and contrasting the performance of different firms. It also makes it more difficult for a single firm to "capture" the regulatory agency, i.e., bias agency findings in its favor, because competing firms have an interest in exposing the kind of cozy relationships that would put them at a relative disadvantage. At the same time, fragmenting the industry reduces the appearance of monopoly and makes it less attractive as a target of politicians seeking to garner political support against the operator.

The Argentine reformers have extensively utilized fragmentation. A clear example is the privatization of the electricity sector in Argentina, where today the Argentine wholesale electricity market has more than 600 players.[44] Although not as extensively as the Argentine case, Chile has also fragmented many of its utility sectors, including the water sector. Chile has sought to depoliticize pricing through the use of a formula whose parameters are negotiated every five years on the basis of technical cost studies. The existence of multiple operators provides substantial information to both the regulator and to the experts who may be called to arbitrate conflicts between an operator and the regulator.

Fragmentation and operational or regulatory decentralization may go hand in hand. Indeed, the federal nature of Argentina has generated a fragmented structure for utilities and regulators.[45] While fragmentation is a key

---

[44] See Spiller and Torres (1996) for a discussion of the Argentine electricity reforms.

[45] Argentina also has regulatory fragmentation, as each province has its own set of regulatory agencies, to the point that, as in the United States, there is now a National Association of Regulatory Agencies in Argentina.

feature of Colombia's utility sector, along with operational decentralization among more than 1,000 water service companies, regulatory policy is centralized in a single regulatory agency. Several other countries have decentralized the provision of water services, such as Brazil, Peru, and Mexico.[46] Other countries, like El Salvador and Uruguay, retain centralized operational and policy schemes. Countries with fragmented water sectors have an advantage in undertaking successful reforms because they can create a regulatory environment that separates the regulated from the regulator and generate multiple sources of support for proper regulation, at the same time that fragmentation limits the informational advantage of each supplier.

A second basic strategy is the elimination of exclusive franchises. Granting exclusive supply rights limits potential competition and increases the informational advantage of the concessionaire. Consequently, it increases the leverage of the operator vis-à-vis the government, and may create a more acrimonious negotiating environment. This, in turn, increases the potential for negotiation breakdowns.[47]

Exclusive concessions also generate regulatory frameworks that are specific to the concessionaire. These specific regulatory frameworks—usually in the form of a concession rather than a public law—are then more easily renegotiated. Indeed, most water concessions granted since 1990 have been renegotiated in their first two years.[48] While there could be good reasons for renegotiations to take place (e.g., the concession may have been granted under substantial uncertainty about asset valuation), renegotiations are unavoidable in the granting of exclusive concessions. Once an exclusive concession has been granted, the regulator and the concessionaire will always find an amendment that will make both of them better off. The reason for this is twofold: first, as time passes political interests change, providing the regulator with an incentive to modify the concession; second, even if political interests remain constant, once the management of the concession is transferred to the regulator, the regulator's own interests are likely to differ in some way from the agreement reached among the groups that origi-

---

[46] Honduras has a partly decentralized sector and has resisted recent efforts to introduce generalized decentralization.

[47] The case of Tucumán's water concession is particularly illuminating, where a negotiation breakdown motivated the operator to leave the concession.

[48] See Willig et al. (1998).

nally granted the concession. Both factors were at work in Argentina and are best exemplified by the concession for Buenos Aires. While this concession was designed by the federal government, its regulation was granted to a regulatory authority that had local representation as well. In this case, the concession was renegotiated two years after the granting of the concession. The renegotiation allowed the governor to get credit for expanding the service towards previously unserved areas, at the cost of a general rate increase. Following that rate increase, the operator's average rate was above the rate offered by the second lowest bid. Knowledge that renegotiation is unavoidable tilts the granting of the concession away from the most efficient operator towards the operator who is the best negotiator, thus reducing the welfare improvement associated with potential privatization of the water utility.

When exclusive licenses are granted, there are institutional designs that can offset, although not eliminate, the problem of renegotiation. In particular, the regulatory framework can preserve a degree of flexibility yet guard against abuse by involving more actors in decisions regarding modification of the contract. A particularly interesting case can be found in the United Kingdom, where the regulator and the company may modify the license by mutual agreement, thereby creating some flexibility in the regulatory framework.[49] This flexibility, however, is checked by the ability of the Secretary of State of Trade and Industry to refer such a license modification to the Monopolies and Mergers Commission (MMC). The MMC must, in such cases, assess whether or not such a license modification is in the public interest, and the modification will not occur without the MMC's ratification. Thus, having multiple decision makers involved in modifying concessions may limit the potentially perverse incentives for "insiders" to benefit from renegotiations at the public's expense.[50]

Introducing multiple and independent decision makers in ratifying a concession amendment does not mean that the same decision makers should be involved in the granting of the concession. Indeed, in the United Kingdom, the MMC is not involved at all in the granting of licenses, but is involved in the license modification process. Limiting the set of decision mak-

---

[49] See Spiller and Vogelsang (1997).

[50] In Argentina, renegotiation of the Aguas Argentinas' concession required the approval of the Ministry of Economics, as it had to approve the company's estimate of extra costs associated with the change in the investment plan.

ers that participate in granting licenses reduces potential rent seeking by various parties, thereby providing some assurances that the initial regulatory framework can enhance efficiency.

A third basic strategy for maintaining the high-level equilibrium is to privatize the sector. Privatization creates a group with a clear interest in limiting the government's opportunistic behavior and the will to spend substantial resources to this end. At the same time, privatization provides an opportunity to grant large segments of the population direct interest in the profitability of the operator. Various forms of popular capitalism have been successful in this regard. For example, investments by private pension plans in Chile and Bolivia have given large segments of the population direct interest in protecting these plans from being raided to fund other public activities—a common problem under the prior publicly owned and managed arrangement. Similarly, the sale of large shares of utility companies to widespread groups of individual citizens can help shield these companies from direct or indirect expropriation, as has been the case with the Caracas Electricity Company, and the public enterprises privatized in the United Kingdom and the Czech Republic. Since widespread ownership deters governmental opportunism by affecting the domestic political process, popular capitalism that is directed toward citizens will be, in that sense, superior to selling the company to a foreign investor. The lack of direct political support for foreign investors may well increase the risk of governmental opportunism.[51] The experience of the concession in Corrientes—discussed in chapter 6—illustrates how a conflict between the governor and the foreign operator was readily resolved once the company was sold to a local group.[52] In the Tucumán case, though, the conflict was not resolved, and the concession was cancelled.

It is important to reiterate that each of these strategies will have a limited effect if the mechanisms for establishing prices are not insulated from governmental opportunism. The more fragmented and competitive is the market, the less justification for government involvement in price determination at all. But when fragmentation is limited and operators are private, the need to protect consumers against rent seeking provides fertile ground

---

[51] Nevertheless, foreign investors from large and politically strong nations may also have recourse to their countries' influence to restrain some acts of governmental opportunism.
[52] See chapter 6 and Artana et al., 1997.

for governmental opportunism in price setting. Under precisely such conditions, price setting mechanisms are critical because they must fulfill their legitimate functions of protecting consumers while establishing the credibility and certainty required by investors. All too often, the screen of consumer protection is used to shield opportunistic behavior by the government. Hence, when fragmentation is limited, the mechanisms of independent price-setting boards with explicit procedures and formulaic price-setting—or very specific contractual licenses that are difficult to change—need to be considered as a way to institutionalize credible government policy toward pricing in the sector.

Although various pricing models may work well, others do not. Chile's negotiation method that relies on firm, specific, long-run average cost calculations works like a price cap and has proven effective, as is also the case with the Aguas Argentinas pricing scheme. By contrast, the pricing arrangements in Honduras, Peru, and to a lesser extent in Mexico, have proven ineffective. However, the key point is that the actual pricing scheme comes to play only in the presence of a credible regulatory framework. Without credibility, even putatively efficient pricing schemes (e.g., that of Corrientes) will generate few investment incentives.

Conclusions

The efficient expansion and provision of high quality water services is important to the economic development of Latin America. Nevertheless, the potential for government opportunism inhibits the expansion of coverage and the provision of adequate services because it hinders the government's ability to build a credible regulatory framework.

While the potable water sector may be constructed of concrete, it is nonetheless quite fragile. The water sector suffers acutely from the implications of three essential features: large sunk costs, economies of scale and density, and massive consumption. Because of these features, the sector is prone to government opportunism, triggering a downward spiral of low prices, low investment, low quality, low coverage, and high levels of corruption. To avoid such a downward spiral, escape a low-level equilibrium, and maintain high quality levels, several basic design features should be introduced. First and foremost, countries must establish enterprises that are financially and managerially autonomous. Second, industries should be frag-

Table 1.3

Institutional Design	Institutional Framework	
	Supportive	Difficult
Promising	Chile Argentina – Bs. As.	Argentina – Corrientes
Problematic	Mexico	Peru Honduras

mented to the greatest extent possible and exclusive rights of supply should be eliminated whenever possible so as to promote competition. Third, a regulatory framework should be created with procedures for determining prices that drastically limit governmental discretion. Finally, utilities should be privatized, with an emphasis on achieving widespread domestic participation in ownership of assets.

The case studies analyzed in this book deepen the understanding of the characteristics of the potable water sector, the political institutions that lead to a low-level equilibrium and create obstacles to reform, and the three basic design features necessary for improvement (see Table 1.3). The cases of Peru and Honduras demonstrate clearly the emergence and stability of low-level equilibria. In those two countries existing institutions are characterized by weak checks and balances that preserve extensive governmental discretion. Coupled with a problematic institutional design for operating and regulating the sector, this weak institutional framework tends to obstruct investment and service improvements while resisting change. Mexico, an intermediate case, is characterized by a somewhat supportive institutional framework, but also suffers from a problematic institutional design. Because regulatory and operational functions are not always separated, the Mexican reforms may recreate the same tendency toward low-level equilibrium that characterized the national and centralized system. The increasing fragmentation of politics in Mexico could either strengthen the institutional framework by developing stronger checks and balances or lead to autarchic, and problematic, institutional frameworks at subnational levels. On the other hand, Chile's relatively strong institutions and positive regulatory design have helped it maintain a high-level equilibrium. The remaining problems in that country are related to restrictions on the composition of capital, implementation of the arbitration process, and obstacles to investment in sanitation as a consequence of continuing public ownership. In Argentina, two concession arrangements whose designs were both promising provide a basis for comparison. One experience developed fairly positively due to the compatibility of the design with the institutional framework. In the other case, the basic incompatibility between design and context led to a breakdown in the original arrangement. In each case, it is evident that the three basic design features described above are promising avenues that may allow countries to break out of the low-level equilibrium—and make a serious start toward reducing the loss of water.

References

Artana, D., Navajas, F. and Urbiztondo, S. 1997. "Argentina: La Regulación Económica en las Concesiones de Agua Potable y Desagues Cloacales en Buenos Aires y Corrientes." Serie de Documentos de Trabajo R-312. OCE, Inter-American Development Bank. Washington DC.

Corbo, V., Luders, R., and Spiller, P.T. 1997. *The Foundations of Successful Economic Reforms: The Case of Chile.* Universidad Católica de Chile. Santiago, Chile. Mimeographed document.

Cointreau-Levine, Sandra. 1994. "The Formal Sector." In: *Private Sector Participation in Municipal Solid Waste Services in Developing Countries.* Urban Management Program Series. 13. The World Bank. Washington, DC. 1: 47–52.

Fiorina, Morris P. 1982. "Legislative Choice of Regulatory Forms: Legal Process or Administrative Process?" *Public Choice,* 39: 33–66.

Goldberg, Victor. 1976. "Regulation and Administered Contracts." *Bell Journal of Economics.* 7(2) 426–452.

Grupo Macroconsult, S.A. 1997. "Retos de Economía Política en Agua Potable: El Proceso de Reforma en Perú." Serie de Documentos de Trabajo R-311. OCE, Inter-American Development Bank. Washington, DC.

Guasch, J.L. and Spiller, P.T. 1995. *The Path Towards Rational Regulation in Latin America and the Caribbean: Issues, Concepts and Experience.* World Bank Directions in Development Series. Washington, DC.

Hamilton, J.T. and Schroeder, C.H. 1994. "Strategic Regulators and the Choice of Rulemaking Procedures—The Selection of Formal vs. Informal Rules in Regulating Hazardous Waste." *Law and Contemporary Problems.* 57(1–2): A111–A160.

Joskow, P.L. 1974. "Inflation and Environmental Concern: Structural Change in the Process of Public Utility Price Regulation." *Journal of Law and Economics.* 17: 291–327.

Levy, B. and Spiller, P.T., eds. 1996. *The Institutional Foundations of Regulatory Commitment: A Comparative Analysis of Telecommunications Regulation.* Cambridge: Cambridge University Press.

Levy, B. and Spiller, P.T. 1994. "The Institutional Foundations of Regulatory Commitment: A Comparative Analysis of Five Country Studies of Telecommunications Regulation." *Journal of Law, Economics, and Organization.* 10(2):201–46

Macey, Jon. 1992. "Organizational Design and Political Control of Administrative Agencies." *Journal of Law, Economics, and Organization.* 8(1): 93–110.

McCubbins, M.D., Noll, R.G. and Weingast, B.R. 1987. "Administrative Procedures as Instruments of Political Control." Working papers in economics. Hoover Institution on War, Revolution, and Peace. Domestic Studies Program. Stanford University. Palo Alto, California. E-87-36.

Morandé, F. and Doña, L. 1997. "Los Servicios de Agua Potable en Chile: Condicionantes, Institucionalidad y Aspectos de Economía Política." Serie de Documentos de Trabajo R-308. OCE, Inter-American Development Bank. Washington DC.

Instituto Tecnológico de Estudios Superiores de Monterrey. 1997. "Regulation, Organization and Incentives: The Political Economy of Potable Water Services in Mexico." Serie de Documentos de Trabajo R-326. OCE, Inter-American Development Bank. Washington, DC.

Perotti, E.C. September 1995. "Credible Privatization." *American Economic Review.* 85(4): 847–59.

Schwartz, E.P., Spiller, P.T. and Urbiztondo, S. 1993. "A Positive Theory of Legislative Intent." *Law and Contemporary Problems.*(1–2): 51–74.

Shirley, M. and Xu, L. Colin. 1996. "Information, Incentives and Commitment: An Empirical Analysis of Contracts Between Government and State Enterprises." World Bank Work Paper 1769. Washington, DC.

Spiller, P.T. September 1992. *Institutions and Regulatory Commitment in Utilities' Privatization.* Institute for Policy Reform. IPR51. Washington, DC.

Spiller, P.T. 1996. "A Positive Political Theory of Regulatory Instruments: Contracts, Administrative Law or Regulatory Specificity?" *Southern California Law Review.* 69(2):477.

Spiller, P.T. and Torres, C. 1996. *Argentina's Electricity Regulation: Its Performance, Credibility and Options for the Future.* The World Bank. Washington, DC. Mimeographed document.

Spiller, P.T. and Vogelsang, I. 1996. "Regulations, Institutions and Commitment: The Case of British Telecom." *In*: B. Levy and P. Spiller, eds. *The Institutional Foundations of Regulatory Commitment.* Cambridge: Cambridge University Press.

Spiller, P. and Savedoff, W. 1998. "Commitment and Governance in Infrastruture." *In*: Willig, Uribe, and Basañes, eds. *Can Privatization Delivery Infrastructure for Latin America?* Baltimore, Maryland: Johns Hopkins University Press.

Willig, R., Uribe E. and Basañes, C. F., eds. 1998. *Can Privatization Deliver Infrastructure for Latin America?* Baltimore, Maryland: Johns Hopkins University Press.

Walker, I., Velásquez, M., Ordoñez, F. et al. 1997. "Regulation, Organization and Incentives: The Political Economy of Potable Water Services. Case Study: Honduras." Serie de Documentos de Trabajo R-314. OCE, Inter-American Development Bank. Washington, DC.

Weingast, Barry R. 1995. "The Economic Role of Institutions: Market Preserving Federalism and Economic Development." *Journal of Law, Economics, and Organization.* 11(1):1–31.

Williamson, O.E. 1976. "Franchise Bidding for Natural Monopolies: In General and With Respect to CATV." *Bell Journal of Economics.* 73–104.

CHAPTER 2

Reform Efforts and Low-Level Equilibrium in the Honduran Water Sector

Ian Walker, Max Velásquez, Fidel Ordóñez, and Florencia María Rodríguez[1]
Fundación Centroamericana para el Desarrollo Humano (FUMANITAS)

The water sector in Honduras has performed poorly and a "low-level equilibrium" is maintained by keeping rates too low to finance efficient service expansion. A comparison of the performance of the national water authority (SANAA) with various municipal services provides a useful context for reviewing the current reform debate over regionalization and municipalization. The key issue is not municipal versus national control of service provision, but whether the system operates free of direct political control and whether all types of service providers are adequately regulated. The sector continues to depend on external funds to support investment and its operations are grossly inefficient. Consumers are relatively less willing to accept higher rates in return for promises of improved performance when dealing with public entities that lack credibility, than they are with private or community controlled entities. A stakeholder analysis suggests ways to break out of the low-level equilibrium and establish a more efficient sector.

---

[1] Ian Walker is director of ESA Consultores; Max Velásquez and Florencia María Rodríguez are senior consultants on urban development at ESA Consultores; Fidel Ordóñez is chief of the statistics division of ESA Consultores.

The urban water and sanitation sector in Honduras suffers from the perplexing phenomenon of a low-level equilibrium, in which poor quality public services are sustained indefinitely, avoiding corrective pressures. This low-level equilibrium is reflected in the sector's performance and is perpetuated by flawed arrangements for sectoral governance, organization of service delivery, and regulation. Why is it so difficult to escape from a low-level equilibrium? An analysis of the failure of recent reform efforts using political economy techniques provides insight into this question.

The performance indicators for the state-owned *Servicio Nacional de Agua y Alcantarillado* (SANAA) and for municipal providers show that their poor record is rooted in their exposure to political capture and in the lack of adequate regulation rather than in the degree of centralization or decentralization. Supporting econometric evidence on the credibility of different sorts of service providers, using willingness to pay data from a recent nationwide survey, suggests that public providers lack credibility and are more exposed to rent-seeking behavior than are private providers. A financial analysis of SANAA shows that it could quickly become self-financing if it reached reasonable goals for cost effectiveness and rate levels, which would produce very large welfare gains indeed. The case for reform is overwhelming, but the political task of organizing reform is considerable.

The political economy of reform can be traced back to the failed Water and Sanitation Sector Structural Adjustment Credit, which was supported by the World Bank and the Inter-American Development Bank (IDB) during 1994–96. A stakeholder analysis shows how the proponents of reform failed to mobilize potential sources of support and how the government itself was divided, while critics exploited weaknesses in the proposal to mobilize opposition. Two weaknesses in the adjustment effort were particularly damaging. First, the reform proposal made municipalization a central principle but failed to address the poor performance and low credibility of existing municipal systems. A review of recent efforts at municipalization in Honduras concludes that the strategy is feasible but not a panacea for all of the sectors' ills. There is a need to develop a credible model of municipal water system operation that is free from political interference. Second, the reform proposal did not adequately address the issue of a regulatory guarantee for users. These lessons have been incorporated into the current reform strategy and have thus strengthened the prospects for success in the coming years.

Box 2.1 Organization of the Water and Sanitation Sector in Honduras

The *Servicio Autónomo Nacional de Agua y Alcantarillado* (SANAA) was formed in 1961 as an autonomous state enterprise, to serve as the leading institution in the water and sanitation sector, responsible for setting and enforcing service delivery norms and for operating services in all urban communities with populations above 500.

The law that created SANAA specified that it would gradually assume control of all existing municipal water and sewerage systems in Honduras. However, the law stopped short of creating a legal monopoly, and at present in Honduran towns with populations of 2,000 or more, there are 74 municipal water systems (including that of the second largest city, San Pedro Sula), compared with 23 SANAA systems. All towns with fewer than 2,000 people have either municipal or community based systems.

Municipal utilities supply around 65 percent of urban water connections, covering some 54 percent of the urban population, while SANAA supplies 35 percent of connections, covering 29 percent of the urban population; the only sewerage system run by SANAA is in Tegucigalpa.

In 1990, municipal development legislation established water and sanitation as municipal competencies; however, the law that created SANAA was neither repealed nor reformed, so the existing statutes are contradictory.

Performance of the Water and Sanitation Sector

The performance of the water and sanitation sector over the last 20 years has not been good. Coverage of piped potable water services in the urban sector has stagnated since 1973 at just over 80 percent (Table 2.1); the water networks have expanded only fast enough to keep abreast of population growth. In contrast, in the rural areas (communities with fewer than 500 inhabitants), coverage of piped water has grown sharply, from 21 percent in 1973 to 40 percent in 1993, but is still very low. Including nonpiped sources such as wells, some 53 percent of rural dwellers were estimated to have access to potable water in 1993.

Within these totals, SANAA is directly responsible for only 23 percent of all connections, covering just 14 percent of the population of Honduras (Table 2.2). However, SANAA has also been involved in the construction of rural systems supplying water to an estimated 440,000 people, now administered by local *juntas de agua* (water committees).

Table 2.1 Water and Sanitation Coverage in Honduras

| | Water | | | | | Sanitation | | | |
| | Piped | | | Total | | Sewerage | | Total incl. latrines | |
	1973	1988	1993	1988	1993	1988	1993	1988	1993
				Millions of people covered					
Urban	0.76	1.4	2.05	1.51	2.22	0.93	1.24	1.54	2.25
Rural	0.41	0.97	1.09	1.12	1.45	0.20	0.14	0.95	1.23
National	1.17	2.38	3.12	2.64	3.64	1.15	1.3	2.51	3.43
				Percentage of population covered					
Urban	81	80	83	86	90	53	50	88	91
Rural	21	39	40	45	53	8	5	38	45
National	43	56	60	62	70	27	25	59	66

Source: PAHO, WHO (1993), and authors' calculations.

Table 2.2 Population with Coverage by Type of Provider, 1993

	Persons (million)	Population (percent)	Connections (percent)
Urban	**2.05**	**83**	**10**
SANAA	0.71	29	35
Municipal	1.34	54	65
Rural	**1.09**	**40**	**100**
SANAA	0.02	1	2
Other[1]	1.08	39	98
National	**3.12**	**60**	**100**
SANAA	0.73	14	23
Municipal	1.34	26	43
Other[1]	1.05	20	34

Note: 1/ Many of the rural systems were constructed by SANAA but then handed over to a water committee. SANAA estimates that 440,000 persons living in rural areas are covered by such systems.

Sources: Calculated from SANAA and PAHO data.

Only 29 percent of the urban population is covered by SANAA (Table 2.2). Municipalities are responsible for 65 percent of urban connections, which supply around 54 percent of the urban population.

The Metropolitan Systems

Honduras has two major cities: the capital, Tegucigalpa, in the center of the country, with a population of 800,000; and the industrial center, San Pedro Sula, on the north coast, with a population of just under 500,000. The water and sewerage system of Tegucigalpa is run by SANAA; that of San Pedro Sula is run by the municipality.

The Tegucigalpa system dominates SANAA's operations, accounting for more than half of the company's 140,000 connections. Water coverage in Tegucigalpa, at 85 percent, is scarcely better than the national urban average of 83 percent, and much of that coverage is due to private systems that have been created to fill the vacuum left by SANAA. According to SANAA's commercial cadastre there are 72,000 domestic connections in the city; this represents fewer than half the city's households. The cadastre is known to be very inadequate, but even supposing the existence of a further 38,000 illegal or unregistered connections to the SANAA system, this still leaves 30 percent of Tegucigalpa's dwellings uncovered by the SANAA system (Table 2.3).

This high percentage of uncovered dwellings reflects SANAA's failure to expand services to the marginal *barrios*, mainly located on high ground, to which it is relatively costly to deliver water supplies due to the need for pumping stations. The unresolved tenure status of many of these settlements also creates problems for their formal incorporation into the public service.[2] About a third of the dwellings in these settlements have piped water from private distribution systems administered by *barrio* committees. Some have

---

[2] In Central America, contractual rights to public services are attributions of individuals, not of their property, and are in principle transferable between properties, but not between persons. Public utility companies will not normally extend service contracts to individuals whose tenure status is contested, since this may expose them to legal action on the part of the legal owner of the property. This contrasts with many countries in South America where the service is attributable to the property and is automatically extended to whomever occupies the property, so that tenure is not an issue in extending service coverage to marginal areas.

Table 2.3 Tegucigalpa: Piped Water Coverage by Type of Provider, 1996

	No. Connections (thousands)	Share (%)
SANAA—cadastre	72.0	46
SANAA—illegal	38.0	24
Private networks	24.5	16
Without domestic connection	22.5	14
Total	157.0	100

Sources: Based on data from DGEC for the total number of dwellings and for the percent without a connection; from SANAA for the number of formal domestic users in the cadastre; SANAA for the number of marginal *barrio* users in private systems that receive water from SANAA; and Walker and Ordóñez (1995) for marginal *barrio* users of private systems with an independent supply. The estimate for illegal connections to the SANAA system is then calculated as a residual. SANAA's own estimate of illegal connections is much lower, at 15,000.

Table 2.4 SANAA: Annual Costs per Connection, 1993[1]

	Tegucigalpa	Other	Total[2]	
	L	L	L	US$[3]
Labor costs	140	77	181	26.6
Energy	61	87	74	10.9
Chemicals	87	6	49	7.3
Depreciation and provisions	0	0	74	10.8
Other operating costs	17	12	35	5.2
Total	305	181	414	60.8

Notes: 1/ Excludes debt interest, which is absorbed by the central government.
2/ Including the costs of central administration.
3/ Exchange rate of 6.8 lempiras per U.S. dollar.
Source: Aquagest (1995) and authors' calculations.

their own wells; others receive water from SANAA's network, either illicitly or on the basis of the block rate[3].

Many bilateral lenders and NGOs support the development of water systems in marginal *barrios*; most notably, UNICEF has a project with SANAA to finance the construction of distribution systems in such barrios. However, these systems usually offer inferior service. *Barrios* with their own wells tend to have poor quality water with high salinity. Those whose water is supplied in block by SANAA usually face infrequent service and low pressure. Meanwhile, some 22,500 dwellings—almost 15 percent of the city's total—are altogether without piped water.

SANAA's failure to expand coverage is rooted in poor cost performance and a weak rate effort. The metropolitan system of Tegucigalpa has an estimated 13.6 staff per 1,000 connections—at least three times the necessary level.[4] These high staffing levels are attributable mainly to a rigid labor agreement that prevents multitasking.[5] Detailed data for SANAA's cost structure (Tables 2.4 and 2.5) show that the main problems are rooted in labor costs in Tegucigalpa and in the central administration. Labor costs per connection in Tegucigalpa in 1993 stood at L 140 per year, almost double the L 77 incurred in the rest of the country (Table 2.4). Additionally, there is a very large labor cost in the central administration, representing 17 percent of SANAA's total costs (Table 2.5).

The performance of SANAA's Tegucigalpa system contrasts poorly in many respects with that of the *División Municipal de Aguas* (DIMA) in San Pedro Sula. Formed in 1976, DIMA is part of the municipality but is admin-

---

[3] The block rate is a wholesale rate for the sale of water to independent distribution systems. It is set well below the normal commercial rate in order to reflect only production costs and not distribution and commercial costs.

[4] Author's estimate, including a share of SANAA's central administrative employment in proportion to the number of connections in the city. Estimates for SANAA's staffing levels vary considerably, in part due to the practice of including many employees on the payroll of investment projects, which are not consolidated into the company's accounts. This estimate for Tegucigalpa is derived from data on labor costs, and is probably conservative. The overall number of SANAA employees per thousand connections was estimated in January 1995 at 14.7, which would imply a higher ratio for Tegucigalpa.

[5] During 1997, SANAA has made some headway in negotiating with the union to increase flexibility and reduce staffing levels. However, few redundancies have been implemented. In January 1997, SANAA had a total staff of 1,809, which is 13 per 1,000 connections, compared with 1,936 staff a year earlier (13.8 per 1,000).

Table 2.5 SANAA's Cost Structure, 1993[1]
(percent)

	Central admin.	Tegucigalpa	Other systems	Total
Labor costs	17	18	9	44
Energy	0	8	10	18
Chemicals	0	11	1	12
Depreciation and provisions	18	0	0	18
Other operating costs	5	2	1	8
Total	40	39	20	100

Note: 1/ Excludes debt interest, which is absorbed by the central government.
Source: Authors' calculations from data in Aquagest (1995).

Table 2.6. Performance Indicators for SANAA's Metropolitan System and DIMA, 1994

	SANAA (Tegucigalpa)	DIMA (San Pedro Sula)
Legal individual connections	76,050	59,794
Domestic	71,713	54,064[1]
Other	4,337	5,730
Coverage of legal domestic connections	46%	84%[2]
Percent of all connections with meters	64%	43%
Unaccounted for water	50%	48%
Employees per 1,000 connections	13.6	6.5[3]
Total billings, L million/year	38.6	46.3
Billings per connection, L/month	42	64
Income from billings, L million/year	26	31.4
Collection rate	67%	68%
Income per connection, L/month	28	44

Notes: 1/ The figure for DIMA includes projects and special connections.
2/ Percent of households in the city legally connected to the system; authors' estimate.
3/ The figure for Tegucigalpa, including a share of central administrative posts in proportion to connections, is the authors' estimate.

istratively independent. In spite of the rapid growth of San Pedro Sula (7 percent annually in recent years), it has achieved coverage of 84 percent. In 1994, DIMA reported 6.5 employees per 1,000 connections (Table 2.6).

The SANAA system in Tegucigalpa also shows a much weaker income performance compared with that of DIMA. In 1994, average billings per connection stood at L 42 per month in Tegucigalpa and L 64 in San Pedro Sula, and income per connection was, respectively, L 28 and L 44. In this context, it is striking to note that in 1994, DIMAs annual revenues (L 31.5 million) were scarcely below SANAA's total revenue for the entire country (L 35.8 million).

However, DIMAs operation is not superior to SANAA's Tegucigalpa system in all aspects of performance. DIMAs metering coverage in 1994 was 43 percent compared to 64 percent for Tegucigalpa; its level of unaccounted-for-water[6] stood at 48 percent, scarcely better than Tegucigalpas 50 percent; and the collection rates of the two systems are very similar, with income totaling just under 70 percent of billings (Table 6). And, most importantly, both have exhibited serious problems with political interference in their management of water rates.

Nonmetropolitan Systems

The performance of seven nonmetropolitan SANAA systems and nine municipal systems[7] were analyzed to see if there are any systematic differences in performance that might be attributable to the system's administration, rather than to other characteristics. As described in Table 2.7, the systems have broadly matching characteristics in relation to size, type of water source, poverty levels in the corresponding community, and geographical location.

---

[6] This is the difference between the total volume of potable water produced by the system and the total amount billed to users. It is composed of physical losses due to leaks in the distribution system, plus water that is undercharged to the users (i.e., where estimated billing is used, rather than metering), or that is simply stolen from the system by illegal users.

[7] This section is based on a survey carried out in mid-1995 by FUNDEMUN for the World Bank, and on data on municipal performance collected by FUNDEMUN and AHMON. FUNDEMUN, AMHON, and the World Bank gave permission to use these data sources, but responsibility for the analysis of the data and for the conclusions is the authors' alone.

Table 2.7 Characteristics of the Nonmetropolitan and Municipal Systems Studied

	System Type	Urban population	Type of source	Poverty index (higher = poorer)	Area
Choluteca – Municipal	Mun	70,585	P	34	South
Choloma	Mun	70,200	P	33	North
Sta. Rosa de Copán	Mun	24,356	P	44	West
Olanchito	Mun	24,000	G	28	North
Tocoa	Mun	18,916	G	26	Atl. coast
El Paraíso	Mun	16,613	G	34	Center-east
Nacaome	Mun	15,304	P	53	South
Ocotepeque	Mun	11,166	G	25	West
Azacualpa	Mun	5,100	G	34	West
Choluteca—SANAA	SANAA	70,585	M	34	South
Comayagua	SANAA	52,355	G	32	Center-west
Danlí	SANAA	38,088	M	40	Center-east
Juticalpa	SANAA	28,700	P	39	Center-east
La Entrada	SANAA	18,412	M	33	West
Intibucá	SANAA	10,088	G	53	Center-west
Sn. Marcos de Colón	SANAA	7,966	M	43	South

Note: G = gravity, P = pumped, M = mixed.

Table 2.8 presents a summary of indicators of physical efficiency for the two types of systems. While there are considerable variations within each group, it is striking that the averages are very similar. Each group has achieved coverage of only 68 percent of the urban population. Service frequency averages 11 hours a day in the municipal systems and 10 in the SANAA systems; 67 percent of municipal users and 77 percent of SANAA users face intermittent service. And most strikingly, both groups have very low staff levels: four per 1,000 connections for the municipal systems and five for the SANAA systems. This serves once more to show that overstaffing in SANAA is concentrated in Tegucigalpa.

The similarities between municipal and SANAA suppliers are again evident in the indicators of financial performance, which are presented in Table 2.9. Operating cost per connection averaged L 252 per year in the municipal group and L 225 in the SANAA group. Labor cost per connection

Table 2.8 Indicators of Physical Efficiency in Nonmetropolitan Systems: 1994

	Clients	Water coverage (percent)	Sewerage coverage (percent)	Hours of service (average)	Intermittent service (percent of users)	Staff/ 1,000 connections
Municipal systems						
Azacualpa	850	100	0	24	0	2
Choloma	4,771	41	25	14	60	5
Choluteca—Municipal	1,100	n.a.	n.a.	n.a.	n.a.	15
El Paraíso	2,300	83	33	n.d	n.a.	2
Nacaome	1,113	44	10	11	100	6
Olanchito	3,184	53	54	6	85	2
Ocotepeque	1,846	89	n.a.	8	70	2
Sta. Rosa de Copán	2,254	50	40	6	60	4
Tocoa	2,650	84	8	5	95	4
Totals and averages [1]	20,068	68	24	11	67	4
SANAA systems						
Comayagua	6,402	73	69	17	30	3
Choluteca—SANAA	6,709	n.a.	n.a.	n.a.	n.a.	8
Danlí	3,344	53	54	n.a.	90	2
Intibucá	1,220	73	30	18	50	4
Juticalpa	3,500	73	59	8	100	6
La Entrada	1,968	64	8	3	100	9
San Marcos de Colón	998	75	26	6	94	4
Totals and averages[1]	24,141	68	41	10	77	5

Note: 1/ Reported is the weighted average for staff per 1,000 connections; the other averages are
simple.

is L 72 in the municipal group and L 97 in the SANAA group, reflecting the
latter's slightly higher staffing levels; wage levels appear to be similar between the two groups.

The municipal systems studied registered better pricing, billing an average of L 189 per connection, compared with L 125 for SANAA. However,
this is offset by a much lower collection rate of 55 percent for the municipalities compared with 85 percent for SANAA. As a result, income per connection is similar between the two groups (L 103 and L 107, respectively). It
is also striking that SANAA registered zero income for the Juticalpa system,

Table 2.9 Indicators of Financial Efficiency in Nonmetropolitan Systems: 1994

	Operat-ing cost per conn.[1]	Labor cost per conn.	Billings per conn.	Col-lection rate[2]	Income per conn.	Total profit[3]	Profit per conn.[3]	Profit as % of expenses	Policy of service suspen-sion?	% with meter
Municipal systems	L/yr.	L/yr.	L/yr.	%	L/yr.	L/yr.	L/yr.	%		%
Azacualpa	27	n.a.	n.a.	n.a.	23	−3,185	−4	−14%	NO	0
Choloma	437	67	230	68	157	−1,335,864	−280	−64%	YES	0
Choluteca— Municipal	609	169	250	n.a.	n.a.	n.a.	n.a.	n.a.	YES	n.a.
El Paraíso	148	n.a.	n.a.	n.a.	120	−63,882	−28	−19%	YES	0
Nacaome	301	47	121	92	112	−211,000	−190	−63%	YES	0
Olanchito	75	n.a.	68	89	61	−45,550	−14	−19%	NO	0
Ocotepeque	19	n.a.	n.a.	n.a.	58	71,266	39	203%	NO	0
Sta. Rosa de Copán	484	46	279	47	131	−796,429	−353	−73%	YES	0
Tocoa	91	n.a.	189	99	187	253,154	96	105%	NO	0
Totals and avs.[4]	252	72	189	54	103	−2,801,594	−140	−55%		0
SANAA systems										
Comayagua	96	n.a.	167	89	149	339,696	53	55%	YES	8
Choluteca—SANAA	272	130	138	98	136	−916,714	−137	−50%	YES	n.a.
Danlí	205	49	125	99	124	−272,066	−81	−40%	YES	0
Intibucá	91	n.a.	150	79	119	33,703	28	30%	YES	0
Juticalpa	447	80	0	0	0	−1,564,884	−447	−100%	n.a.	0
La Entrada	203	123	122	87	122	−159,597	−81	−40%	YES	1
San Marcos de Colón	223	49	157	64	101	−121,932	−122	−55%	YES	0
Totals and avs.[4]	225	97	125	85	107	−2,661,794	−110	−49%		1

Notes: 1/ Defined as total expenditure on water and sewerage per water system connection.

2/ System income from water and sewerage as a percent of billings.

3/ Negative sign indicates a deficit.

4/ Weighted averages for operating expenditure per connection and for operating profit. Other averages are simple.

which had recently received significant new investments under the IDB's Four Cities project. As a condition of this investment, the system was transferred from municipal control to SANAA ownership, but at the time of this study SANAA had not yet organized a commercial system.[8]

The data on operating profits show that, on average, the municipal and SANAA nonmetropolitan systems are equally incapable of covering their costs. There is little here to support the hypothesis that municipal politicians are in general less prone to undercharging than their counterparts in central government. In fact, the loss per connection in the municipal systems averages L 140 per year compared to L 110 for the SANAA systems. Losses averaged 55 percent of expenses in the municipal group and 49 percent in the SANAA systems. Nevertheless, two of the municipal systems studied, Tocoa and Ocotopeque, registered a tidy profit, showing that municipal operators in some circumstances may overcharge for water, generating surpluses that can be used to fund other projects.

How Governance and Regulation Contribute to Poor Performance

The analysis above places in doubt the thesis that centralized organization is the sector's main problem. Both the centralized (SANAA) and the decentralized (municipal) systems exhibit serious weaknesses in their performance. All the nonmetropolitan systems studied appear to be undercapitalized and poorly administered and all are in need of investment resources and technical assistance for both their physical and organizational development. Rather, the sector's poor overall performance is rooted in the weakness of the existing structure of sectoral governance and regulation, which fails to comply with most of the internationally established norms.[9]

----

[8] Data for the SANAA system as a whole for 1994 show billings per connection outside Tegucigalpa of L 134, very close to the L 125 found in the sample. Income per connection was L 148, implying a collection rate of 110 percent, presumably due to the charging of arrears. In 1995, the situation changed radically. SANAA billed L 234 per connection, but collected only L 86, a collection rate of 37 percent. It is also striking that although 46 percent of SANAA's connections are outside Tegucigalpa, only 22 percent of billings and 15 percent of income arose outside Tegucigalpa in 1995 (Source: SANAA).

[9] A summary of good practice for water sector organization can be found in Foster (1996).

Sectoral Governance and Resource Allocation

Water sector strategy is formally a matter for the Ministry of Health, but is effectively delegated to SANAA, which submits investment proposals for the approval of the Finance Ministry.[10] However, SANAA also acts as the single largest service producer, concerned with procuring resources for its own investments. There is a clear conflict of interest between these functions, the more so because capital resources are supplied as grants (not loans) to SANAA.

SANAA's conflict of interest in acting as strategic planner for the sector and simultaneously as a service provider is clearly reflected in how it skews the distribution of capital resources in its own favor. Although it supplies only 23 percent of the connections in Honduras, between 1989 and 1993 SANAA received 66 percent of Honduras' water sector investments (Table 2.10). SANAA's investments were heavily concentrated in urban projects (73 percent), with much less (27 percent) designated for rural systems. Other agencies important in investment finance in the sector are the Ministry of Health, which finances small rural systems (17 percent of the total); the Honduran Social Investment Fund (FHIS), which finances both rural systems and urban marginal systems (8 percent) and San Pedro Sulas *División Municipal de Aguas* (DIMA) (9 percent).

SANAA's failure to expand coverage at an adequate rate is rooted in its inefficient use of capital rather than in the lack of resources; during 1989–93, the investment assigned to the sector averaged 1.2 percent of GDP (Table 10). As long as system operators receive capital free of charge as grants from the central government, and with no other accountability mechanism, they cannot be expected to use it efficiently. It is hardly surprising, for example, that SANAA has no preventive maintenance program, or that it seeks to disguise a large part of its revenue costs as capital expenditures.

---

[10] The Finance Ministry has a directorate responsible for monitoring the performance of public service providers; it publishes reports on performance, but this is not functionally important. In 1995-96, the Planning Ministry had an important role in approving public investment proposals; it has since been closed (in 1997) and its functions in this regard were transferred to the Finance Ministry.

Table 2.10 Honduras Water and Sanitation Sector: Distribution of Investment Resources by Agency: 1989–93

	1989	1990	1991	1992	1993	Total	Total (percent)
			L (millions)				
SANAA, Total	86	139	106	119	149	599	66
of which, rural	17	28	34	51	38	167	18
Ministry of Health	17	20	39	44	36	156	17
DIMA	4	6	8	11	50	79	9
FHIS	0	8	23	17	23	71	8
Total	107	173	176	190	258	905	100
Total (% of GDP)	1.0	1.4	1.1	1.0	1.3	1.2	
Total (US$ millions)	38	58	44	33	38	211	
Exchange rate (L/US$)	2.8	3.0	4.0	5.8	6.8	n.a.	

Source: IDB/World Bank/PAHO 1994.

Political Control of System Operation and Rent Seeking

In addition to the inefficient use of capital, the operation of all systems both SANAA and municipal is usually subject to political interference. There is a general belief that water services are a social good that should be subsidized, and nowhere in Honduras does a water system operate with fully independent finances. The result is the capture of system rents by users through generalized under-charging. However, the benefit to users is ambiguous because this practice results in low-quality provision.

Users are not necessarily the main beneficiaries of political interference in the operation of water systems. In SANAA, the workforce captures a large proportion of system rents through a union that has established very high staffing levels in Tegucigalpa. According to a study commissioned by the IDB, the World Bank, and the Pan-American Health Organization, the union has acquired such strength and predominance in the company that the nomination of technical, administrative, and manual staff requires union approval, as do decisions related to operations and control" (IDB/World Bank/PAHO 1994, p.14). The involvement of the union in SANAA's admin-

Box 2.2 DIMA: A Case Study in Political Interference in Pricing Decisions

From 1984 on, to fund the implementation of a water and sanitation master plan, San Pedro Sula took on debt from the World Bank and the Commonwealth Development Corporation, with central government guarantees. It also has outstanding loans from the IDB and USAID. In contrast to the SANAA, DIMA is required by the government to cover the debt service out of its operating revenues. However, the execution of the projects was delayed, in part due to the political problems of the 1980s, and in part due to disputes with principal contractors. As a result, the grace periods on the loans ran out before the works were completed and could begin to generate income. In addition, the lempira cost of the dollar-denominated loan service was inflated by currency depreciation from 1990 onward, while increased reliance on subterranean sources of water, coupled with increased electric rates, led to a tenfold increase in DIMA's electricity bill.

DIMA needed to double its rates to get over the problem—but the municipality refused to approve such a sharp increase. As a result, from 1993 onwards, DIMA faced a cash crunch and the central government had to cover part of the debt service due to the World Bank, to the tune of US$7 million between 1993 and 1995. Although rates were finally adjusted in 1995, the agreed increase was much less than the necessary 100 percent, and DIMA hoped to close the gap by shifting away from its heavy dependence on subterranean sources. These problems have tarnished DIMA's image as a model for the municipal administration of water systems and have generated pressure for increased private sector participation in order to depoliticize rate setting and provide access to sources of capital.

istration also contributes to weak commercial performance. In late 1996, SANAA's commercial director was replaced at the request of the union when he alleged that union leaders in his department were involved in corrupt practices linked to the assignment of new connections.

Such problems are not limited to SANAA. The nonmetropolitan municipal systems show very similar patterns of water rate levels and service efficiency to those registered by SANAA's nonmetropolitan systems, and in recent years DIMA in San Pedro Sula has also experienced serious problems with political interference in its pricing decision (see Box 2.2).

Econometric evidence on willingness to pay for improved water services provides a measure of the extent to which the politicized control of system operation has undermined the credibility of public sector providers, both SANAA and municipalities. Willingness to pay for service improvements should be positively correlated with the supplier's credibility as a service provider. The evidence, summarized in Box 2.3 and detailed in Walker et al. (1997), suggests that once the effect of other relevant factors such as existing service cost and quality, income and education is controlled for there is little difference in the willingness of clients to pay between SANAA and the municipalities. However, in contrast, willingness to pay for service improvements is much higher among clients of privately administered systems. These results are consistent with the hypothesis that the latter have higher credibility.

Regulatory System

The regulation of the water sector is badly conceived and weakly implemented. It fails in what should be its central goal of defending the right of existing and potential users to receive good quality service at a reasonable cost. SANAA's users effectively have no enforceable rights, and municipal services are completely unregulated.

The principal regulatory agency for the water sector is the *Comisión Nacional Supervisora de Servicios Públicos* (CNSSP), which is responsible for the regulation of water rates. In addition, the ministries of Environment and Natural Resources and of Public Health have regulatory responsibilities regarding the use and protection of water sources, sanitary disposal of waste water, and norms for the quality of piped water supplies.

CNSSP was established in 1991, when, as part of Honduras first structural adjustment program, the IDB and the World Bank proposed the creation of an apolitical agency to set public service rates, including water, telephones, electricity, and transport. Previously, the National Congress set rates directly. CNSSP was given a general mandate to regulate water rates. However, this statute stands in direct conflict with the right of municipal operators to establish their own rates under the municipal legislation of 1990 and 1991 (articles 84, 85, and 86 with their corresponding regulations; Chama 1995). In practice, CNSSP has limited itself to regulating the SANAA rate.

CNSSPs structure strongly suggests that it was conceived as a body for the political negotiation of public service rates rather than as a technical body dedicated to the independent determination of the cost of services and of equitable mechanisms for their recovery. It is formally autonomous

Box 2.3 The Low Credibility of Public Providers Undermines Users' Willingness to Pay

Willingness to pay (WTP) for improved water services might be expected to vary under different conditions of system administration for two reasons, each related to the supplier's credibility:

- WTP for promised service improvements is a positive function of the confidence that the improved service will materialize (due to greater efficiency and/or less corruption).

- WTP is an inverse function of the perceived scope for rent seeking. If users believe they can improve services through political mechanisms, their WTP will be lower.

In a national survey of water demand conducted by the authors in 1995 (Walker and Ordoñez 1995), for SANAA and the World Bank households with a piped water connection and with service inferior to four hours per day were asked if they would be prepared to pay a given price for improved service, defined as: at least four hours a day of potable water with good pressure. System administration had a clear impact on the responses. When the system administration is private (via barrio committees called *patronatos,* or specialized barrio committees that only deal with water, called *juntas de agua*), the probability of acceptance is much higher. This effect is especially marked where the administrator is a *patronato*.

Willingness to Pay Estimates

Estimates were made of the average willingness to pay (WTP) for the improved system for each type of system administration. The analysis shows much higher WTP for improved water service among the users of services run by *juntas de agua* and *patronatos* in the marginal *barrios* of Tegucigalpa (L36.6/month and L44.8/month, respectively), compared with both clients of SANAA and municipal clients (with L18.7/month and L21.5/month, respectively). Within the public sector, WTP is higher when the administration is municipal than when it is SANAA. These findings support the hypotheses that

- the credibility of municipally administered systems is somewhat higher than that of SANAA; and

- private community-based administration leads to a higher willingness to pay for improved water services, presumably because there are fewer perceived opportunities for rent seeking.

The obvious policy conclusion is that the municipalized water systems should, wherever possible, be managed by enterprises at arms length from the local government in order to discourage rent-seeking activity by the systems' clients, and that private management can be expected to contribute positively to the improvement in system performance.

Note: For details on the econometric analysis reported here, see Walker et al. (1997).

but in practice is linked to the Ministry of Transportation. It has few resources at its disposal, with a budget of US $100,000 per year from the central government and only four professional staff, so it depends heavily on the regulated entities for information.

The fact that the director has remained unchanged since the CNSSP began operations, in spite of the change of government in 1994, suggests some degree of independence from the executive arm of government. However, the government has an effective majority on the CNSSP. Its 14 deliberative members include the minister of transportation, who chairs and has a vote, the ministers of finance and trade, the four professional staff of CNSSP (nominated by the government), two congressional representatives, two private sector representatives, two trade union representatives, and one representative of *barrio* organizations.

The rate setting process in CNSSP has always been politicized, with long intervals between revisions leading to severe erosion of SANAA's real income by inflation. The water rate had not been adjusted for five years between 1990 and 1995 when a 100 percent increase was authorized, but inflation since the previous increase had been 159 percent (Table 2.11). The interval between rate adjustments was similar when the Congress controlled rates directly.

The procedures followed for the negotiation of the 1995 increase highlight the politicized nature of the process. Before it was approved, the increase was discussed and informally approved by the government's economic cabinet, which simultaneously considered requests for rate increases by the electricity and telephone companies and decided to give priority to SANAA's request. It was thought politically untenable that more than one increase should be approved. The law that established CNSSP (Decreto 85–91) stipulates (Article 1) that rates should be based on "the real economic cost of providing services to each category of consumers" (Rendón Cano 1995). But in practice, rates have always been well below this level. The 1995 rate increase was based on a study of the income needed to cover annual operating costs.

Financing the Low-level Equilibrium

The government finances SANAA's deficits through a series of subsidies, most of which are not transparent. These include: capital grants for project finance, which in reality contain large elements of operational financing; the

Table 2.11 SANAA Water Rates and Inflation: 1990–1995

Residential Water Rate (Tegulcigalpa)	1990 (Aug)	1995 (Sept)	% Increase
Cost of 35 M³ (L)	14.9	30	101%
Consumer Price Index	286.5	741.7	159%

payment by the central government of all interest and amortization on the debt related to SANAA's investments; and the partial nonpayment of electricity charges and chemical costs.[11] In this context, SANAA's day-to-day financial management problem is reduced to the generation of sufficient cash from water rates to cover the payroll. This has provided an objective basis for alliances between the union leadership and successive SANAA managers, since the principal goal of each is to secure sufficient revenue. As a result, rate increases normally transmit rapidly into pay increases; this in turn has strengthened political resistance to rate increases.

Table 2.12 analyzes SANAA's 1994 financial balance, showing how different subsidy elements contributed to the company's operations.[12] Current revenue was L 55 million compared with current expenditure, which totaled L123 million, including an estimated L 50 million of interest charges on the US$160 million in external debt on SANAA projects. The resulting L 68 million deficit was financed by depreciation charges of L12 million and revenue subsidies of L 56 million, including: the partial nonpayment of energy and chemical bills, and the non-payment of loan interest. In addition, SANAA received L128 million in capital transfers from the central government budget. Total subsides to SANAA represented 0.68 percent of GDP and were the equivalent of 334 percent of the company's current revenue.

---

[11] In early 1997, the electric company, ENEE, adopted a policy of charging SANAA for power and began billing approximately L 2 million monthly. When SANAA fell into arrears, the power supply to the administrative offices was cut and SANAA had to install a generator. However, it was deemed politically unacceptable to cut power to the water production and distribution systems.

[12] The SANAA revenue account presented here is based on the official account, but supplemented by a series of expenses that are not normally registered by SANAA, most notably debt interest.

Table 2.12   SANAA's Income, Expenditures, and Subsidies: 1994

	L millions[2] amount	Share of revenue (%)	Share of GDP[2] (%)
Current revenue	55	100	0.20
Current expenditure	123	223	0.45
Labor	29	53	
Energy	10	18	
Chemicals	8	15	
Debt interest[1]	50	92	
Depreciation	12	22	
Other costs	14	25	
Current balance	**−68**	**−123**	**−0.25**
Financing			
Depreciation	12	22	
Operating subsidies	56	102	
Nonpayment of energy	4	7	
Nonpayment of chemicals	2	3	
Debt interest paid by government	50	92	
Total revenue subsidy	**68**	**123**	**0.25**
Capital transfers	**128**	**233**	**0.47**
Total subsidy	**184**	**334**	**0.68**

Notes: 1/ The 3.5 percent average interest rate for 1989-95 was applied to the outstanding stock of SANAA-related debt.

2/ Nominal GDP in 1994 was L 2.71 billion. The year-end exchange rate was L 9.00 = US$1.00.

Source: Authors' analysis of data from SANAA, SECPLAN, and the Ministry of Finance.

Table 2.13 projects SANAA's subsidy needs over the next decade, under three scenarios for system performance.[13] The baseline scenario supposes that performance on water rates, cost efficiency, and urban coverage remain unaltered at 1994 levels. In this scenario, the 100 percent rate increase that was authorized in late 1995 is quickly eroded by inflation, staffing levels remain persistently high, and labor and capital productivity remain unchanged.

---

[13] This section owes much to a study conducted for the World Bank and IDB by Ian Walker and Raimundo Soto of ILADES, Chile, on the fiscal and equity impacts of the proposed water sector adjustment program in Honduras (I. Walker and R. Soto 1995). The assumptions used in this exercise are described in full in Walker et al. (1997).

Table 2.13   Projected Performance of the SANAA System: Three Scenarios (millions of 1994 lempiras)

	1994 real	1995 estimated	2000 projected	2005 projected
Baseline: no improvement in performance				
Real water rate (% of 1994)	100	100	104	104
Unaccounted for water (% of production)	50	50	50	50
Coverage (% of urban households)	83	83	83	83
Current income	55	55	73	93
Current expenditure	123	151	321	370
Current balance	−68	−96	−248	−277
Current balance (% of GDP)	−0.3	−0.3	−0.7	−0.7
Optimistic scenario: rapid improvement in performance				
Real water rate (% of 1994)	100	100	317	496
Unaccounted for water (% of production)	50	50	38	25
Coverage (% of urban households)	83	84	88	93
Current income	55	55	264	625
Current expenditure	123	151	309	352
Current balance	−68	−96	−45	273
Current balance (% of GDP)	−0.3	−0.3	−0.1	0.7
Intermediate scenario: moderate improvement				
Real water rate (% of 1994)	100	100	317	317
Unaccounted for water (% of production)	50	50	45	40
Coverage (% of urban households)	83	83	86	88
Current income	55	55	237	324
Current expenditure	123	151	310	355
Current balance	−68	−96	−73	−31
Current balance (% of GDP)	−0.3	−0.3	−0.2	−0.1

The following general assumptions apply in all scenarios:

Real interest rate on sector debt	3.5%
Depreciation rate on net capital stock	2.5%
Urban population growth	5%
Total investment 1995–2005	US$197million

Source: Authors' calculations. See Walker et al. (1997) for further details on the assumptions used in preparing this table.

Based on these assumptions, both costs and income would rise in line with urban population growth (projected at 5 percent a year over the next decade) and the system would register operational deficits of around 0.3 percent of GDP, rising to 0.7 percent in 2005. However, SANAA's cash flow would continue to be viable as long as the government continued to absorb the debt service burden. Net of debt service and depreciation charges, the operational deficit would remain stable and only slightly negative.

These projections highlight the point that the existing situation is an *equilibrium*, in the sense that it could continue as long as the financial arrangements under which SANAA makes no debt service contribution are maintained. On the other hand, if either the government or the financial agencies that fund the capital program do not allow this, then the revenue and capital subsidies to SANAA would dry up, coverage would drop behind population growth, and service quality would deteriorate. In this way, a crisis could be precipitated by a political decision not to tolerate a continuation of SANAA's poor performance.

The second scenario in Table 2.13 shows that if the system's performance were improved to normal levels, the subsidy would not be necessary. If average water rates gradually increased fivefold to the still moderate level of L 2.0 (US$0.22) per M^3, labor costs were halved by implementing normal levels of efficiency, and programmed capital resources were used relatively efficiently to increase coverage levels from 83 percent to 93 percent, the system could eliminate its deficit by the end of the decade and generate an operational surplus of just under 1 percent of GDP by 2005, even after covering its debt service and financing the establishment of new planning, regulatory, and technical assistance functions.[14] The third, intermediate, scenario shows that a more moderate rate increase and more moderate productivity gains would enable the deficit to be stabilized at around zero by 2005.

---

[14] This scenario has a provision for the cost of closing SANAA's operating systems (including redundancy payments and writing off the accounts receivable in the balance sheet) for their transfer to new operators. This cost would be comfortably recouped within a decade, as a result of reduced operating costs and revenue increases.

The Political Economy of Low-level Equilibrium

The Honduran water sector shows the classic symptoms of a low-level equilibrium trap in which the systems are financially crippled by low rates and high costs. As a result, unless the water utilities can negotiate heavy subsidies, the quality of service provision must suffer. SANAA is the operator that has most successfully negotiated subsidies, mainly capital grants from the central government. However, since the subsidy flow does not automatically rise when the system expands, the company loses money by expanding. Therefore, coverage tends to stagnate.

This tendency is reinforced by the fact that many production systems are gravity fed, so that the marginal cost of water is usually above the average cost because the cheapest sources are exploited first. This implies that the subsidy required for each new connection is higher than that on the existing stock of connections.

This is the fundamental reason why SANAA has failed to expand services to cover Tegucigalpa's marginal barrios. In this context, the SANAA-UNICEF project to construct private systems, which SANAA then supplies with water at the block rate, is a second best solution, made necessary by SANAA's inability to set water rates to reflect the marginal cost of incorporating these barrios into the principal network.

Those who gain from this status quo are the households that already have connections and receive heavily subsidized water services and the employees of the staff-heavy SANAA system, concentrated mainly in Tegucigalpa. The principal losers are the households that cannot get into the system because it is unable to expand fast enough; these are mainly concentrated in the marginal *barrios* of the cities, especially Tegucigalpa.[15]

In recent years there has been greater awareness of the fundamental inequity of denying the poorest *barrios* access to urban water systems, and of the potential for realizing very large welfare gains by expanding water

---

[15] Households within the system are the principal gainers from the status quo when its redistributional impact is analyzed as a zero sum game. However, since rates are not even sufficient to provide for maintenance programs and there is a limit to the amount of subsidy that can be extracted from the political system, the quality of their service is often low. In this sense, the status quo is a negative sum game. It is possible that households in the system would be net gainers from a feasible combination of rate increases and service improvements.

Box 2.4. The Welfare Gains from Escaping Low-level Equilibrium

Increased coverage of piped water creates welfare gains for households that previously had to get their water from other (more expensive and/or lower quality) sources, while increased rates imply losses for households that previously received their service for less than marginal cost and now have to pay more. However, to the extent that existing users are currently being supplied with water at an economic opportunity cost that is higher than their marginal willingness to pay for it, the reduction of their consumption will add to net social welfare. This is likely to happen if the increased rate is implemented through billing for metered consumption. For the present study, these effects were quantified on the basis of survey data and SANAA data for water demand. The details of the estimates are explained in Walker et al. (1997).

Households without piped water in Tegucigalpa at present consume on average only 3.7 m^3 per month and pay L 27 per m^3. If they had access to the piped water system they would pay only L 2 per m^3 and would consume an estimated 33 m^3. The estimated net welfare gain per new client incorporated in the system is L 440 per month, which includes the benefit from the reduced cost of the water they already consume, coupled with the consumer surplus arising from the large expansion of their consumption, made possible by access to piped water. All of this gain is received by the new client. For existing clients, the net welfare gain is L 16 per month. This is the sum of a net welfare loss for the consumer (who must now pay the full cost of his water, which was previously subsidized) and a net gain for SANAA (which previously supplied the water below cost).

If urban coverage in the existing SANAA systems were increased to 93 percent by 2005 (as per the optimistic scenario in Table 2.13), an estimated 29,000 households would benefit by about L 440 a month. If coverage stagnated at 83 percent, there would be 243,000 households with coverage; the net gain for each of these would be L 16 per month. The total net annual welfare gain is estimated at L 201 million, equivalent to 0.7 percent of 1994 GDP. These results are not very sensitive to the shape of the demand curve.

The reform of the sector aims to transform the performance of all the urban water systems in Honduras—not just those run at present by SANAA. As documented in the main text, the systems already in municipal hands, which account for 65 percent of urban connections, exhibit similar weaknesses to those of SANAA. If reform were to produce similar improvements in all the urban systems of Honduras, then the annual welfare gain would be about 2.1 percent of GDP.

service to these communities. A formal estimate of the welfare gains that could result from breaking out of the low-level equilibrium is presented in Box 2.4 and detailed in Walker et al. (1997). However, it has proven difficult to organize the political and legislative changes needed to make this possible. The vested interests aligned in defense of the status quo have proven stronger than the forces in favor of reform.

Prospects for Reform

Not surprisingly, in the face of the social, economic, and fiscal costs identified above, the sector's performance has given rise to growing discontent among the agencies that provide the capital to the water and sanitation sector. As a result, during the Callejas administration (1990–94), discussions began between the World Bank, IDB, and the government about reform of the sector. During the Reina administration (1994–98) these discussions intensified, crystallizing in a proposal by the government's *Comisión Presidencial de Modernización del Estado* (CPME) to strip SANAA of the operation of water systems, pass SANAA's nonmetropolitan systems into municipal ownership, and establish a private management contract for the metropolitan Tegucigalpa system.

This proposal was supported by the offer of a US$65 million sectoral adjustment loan, to be cofinanced by the World Bank and the IDB. This would have been Honduras' fourth sectoral adjustment program, following operations in agriculture, energy, and public sector modernization. The proposal was also reinforced by the IDB's reluctance to finance further investments in the water and sanitation sector until it was reformed. In 1996, however, the adjustment operation was dropped due to the government's failure to pass the necessary legislation.

In tracing the gestation of the reform proposal, a stakeholder analysis shows why the reform effort stalled. The failure was not simply one of political management. The original proposal suffered from two weaknesses that undermined potential support. First, the reform centered on rapid municipalization without establishing convincing mechanisms for strengthening the institutional capacity of the municipalities. And second, although the reform promoted the separation of system administration from political control via the introduction of private and mixed capital service providers, the regulatory provisions in the early drafts of the reform legislation were weak, creating the fear that users might lose out when private service providers were introduced.

The Failure of Reform, 1994–96

In March 1994, the World Bank and the IDB agreed with SANAA on the broad outlines of a reform to separate the functions of operation and supervision through the municipalization of SANAA's systems. The government established a high-level commission to supervise the process. Soon afterward, the commission established a technical support group, comprising representatives of SANAA; the planning, health, and finance ministries; and the economic cabinet's economic policy analysis unit (UDAPE), which acted as a secretariat. This group supervised a series of World Bank and IDB-funded consultations to develop the reform proposal.

For the banks, the 1990 and 1991 local government legislation[16] provided a clear window of opportunity for the divestment of the SANAA systems, since it established the operation of water and sanitation systems as a local government function. In response, some municipalities had already requested the transfer of the systems from SANAA to municipal control. The SANAA manager, Jerónimo Sandoval, strongly supported the idea of transferring SANAA's systems to municipal control and by early 1994 had agreed to the transfer of San Lorenzo and Puerto Cortés. However, the local government legislation did not cancel SANAA's right to operate water systems, nor did it mandate the transfer of all systems. Therefore, further legislation was necessary.

The main elements of the legislative proposal that gradually emerged from this process over the following 12 months were: a framework law for potable water services that would close down SANAA and transfer all its systems to municipal control; the creation of a subsecretariat in the health ministry to handle sector planning and finance; the creation of a new national institute to supply technical assistance to the municipalities and to develop rural systems; and the creation of an independent regulatory agency to supervise both water quality and rate setting. Within this framework, municipalities would have been expected to join together in multicity water

---

[16] See Box 2.1.

companies in order to take advantage of scale economies in system administration (especially billing and financial management).[17]

However, in September 1994, just six months into the reform process, Sandoval was appointed head of the crisis-torn state electric corporation and was replaced at SANAA by Manuel Romero. Romero quickly made it clear that he was opposed to the disappearance of SANAA. He argued that SANAA's problems should be resolved though the development of an enterprise culture, and believed he could negotiate a radical reduction in staffing and more flexible work procedures with the union, and also persuade the political authorities of the need for a significant rate increase. The fact that SANAA's position could change so drastically following a change of manager reflects the lack of a national policy and the resulting personalization of sector strategy.

SANAA then proposed regionalization as an alternative to municipalization. The regionalization strategy was broadly similar to that being pursued by other water companies in Central America and the development of this strategy in Honduras was supported by Central America's regional body for cooperation among water companies, CAPRE, with technical assistance from the German development agency GTZ. Regionalization differs from municipalization in that it represents only an administrative decentralization of the national water company rather than passing ownership of the systems to other legal entities. In this context, SANAA began to resist the municipalization of the Puerto Cortés system and, as an experiment, opened a regional office in La Ceiba. As a result, from late 1994 onward, there were two reform strategies at work: the officially sponsored project, backed by the World Bank and the IDB, and SANAA's own regionalization strategy.

The conflict came to a head at a seminar held in mid-1995, where Romero showed considerable skill in lining up allies in support of his position. Among them were the Ministry of Planning, which was also slated for closure under the state modernization program and which headed the government's social cabinet; the mayor of Tegucigalpa, Oscar Acosta, who viewed the management of the metropolitan system as too big a task for the city government; and the existing body responsible for public service regu-

---

[17] The first and most general description of the proposed reform is laid out in the report by Chilean consultants Maximiliano Alvarez and Jorge Ducci (1994).

lation *(Comisión Nacional Supervisora de Servicios Públicos,* CNSSP*)*, which was reluctant to accept a reduced sphere of influence. The main supporters of the municipalization proposal were the Minister of the Presidency, Armando Aguilar Cruz (also secretary of the Presidential Commission for the Modernization of the State), and representatives of the mayors' association, AHMON. However, AHMON also expressed reservations about the reform proposal and demanded municipal control of the regulatory and sectoral planning agencies (AHMON 1995).

The opponents of the reform criticized the complexity of the proposed reorganization, questioned the wisdom of a rapid municipalization program, and argued that the closure of SANAA would damage rural water development and disperse a valuable central core of technical competence. They also highlighted the need for a two-thirds majority in Congress to close down SANAA, undermining the political viability of the scheme.

In the second half of 1995, the reform process entered a confused period as the different actors maneuvered for position and the government and the banks adjusted their proposal to take into account the issues that had been raised by critics of the original proposal. By the start of 1996, they had reached agreement on a significantly revised proposal under which the water systems would still be municipalized but SANAA would survive, assuming the function of policymaker for the sector and the responsibility for technical assistance and rural water development. This new scheme is outlined in Box 2.5.

The banks agreed with the government to accept just two conditions for the first tranche of the adjustment program: passage of the revised framework legislation, and the letting of a management contract for the Tegucigalpa system, where half of SANAA's connections and most of its worst inefficiencies were concentrated. The latter was a tactical move to side step Tegucigalpa's refusal to accept the system, with the intention of proceeding to a concession at a later date, following the Mexico City strategy (Foster 1996).

In early 1996, consultants were commissioned to redraft the reform legislation and analyze the financial feasability of a private management contract in Tegucigalpa. They concluded that such was the inefficiency in Tegucigalpa that a private manager could turn SANAA's existing US$1 million annual operating deficit for Tegucigalpa into a surplus of about the same amount, even after paying the contractor for his services and without raising rates. In May 1996, the government placed an advertisement in *The*

Box 2.5 Honduran Water Sector Reform Proposal, 1996

Organization of Service Delivery

- The water and sewerage systems owned by SANAA would be transferred to municipal ownership, free of debt, within two years.
- The law would explicitly permit and encourage the use of private agents and mixed companies to run the municipal systems through management contracts, leasing, or concessions. While it also allows for the direct operation of systems by municipal departments, it stipulates that provision should preferably be indirect.
- Transitional provisions would clear the way for a private management contract for the Tegucigalpa system, to be let directly by SANAA, subject to municipal approval

Regulation

- An independent regulatory commission would be created, with three commissioners nominated by the president. Two of the candidates would be taken from short lists provided by the colleges of civil engineers and economists. They would serve for five years (the presidential term is four years).
- There would be no national water rate, but the regulator would establish norms for calculating rates on a cost-plus basis using the model enterprise system, and no operator would be allowed a rate above full efficiency cost. The regulator would oversee contracts between municipalities and private agencies.
- Municipalities would be allowed to cross-subsidize within the water rates but not to use water revenues to fund other services.
- The regulator would be free to declare self-regulatory status for smaller systems.
- Access to public resources would be conditional on compliance with recommended practice on rate setting. This was conceived as a key regulatory mechanism to promote good performance and avoid undercharging by municipal operators.

Sector Strategy

- SANAA would become the agency responsible for strategic planning and technical assistance, and act as advisor to the Ministry of Finance on the allocation of public capital resources in the sector.

Rural Water

- SANAA would also retain responsibility for the development of rural water supplies and for the implementation of capital works on a regional scale.

Source: Authors' summary based on Rendon Cano (1996).

Economist magazine requesting expressions of interest from international firms.

Understandably, since most of the vested interests linked to the status quo were located in Tegucigalpa, the proposal to privatize the Tegucigalpa system provoked the strongest opposition yet to the reform project. SANAA manager Romero now publicly declared his hostility to the proposal (*El Heraldo*, June 17, 1996, and *El Nuevo Día*, June 21, 1996). He was supported by the leader of the SANAA staff union, Francisco Menjivar, who denounced privatization as a way to bring about enormous rate increases.

The SANAA union was able to make this claim because the reform camp had failed to state clearly at an early stage that the regulator's mandate was to control rates to efficiency levels. In fact, in early drafts of the proposed legislation, there was no provision at all for the regulatory control of water rates, due to the reluctance of the municipalities to be subjected to rate regulation (justified, spuriously, by the principle of municipal autonomy). This allowed opponents to scare-monger about the rate increases that would come with privatization. This was corrected in the July 1996 draft, summarized above, which was developed with the help of IDB regulation specialists. But by that time, the damage had been done.

Romero also produced a legal sophistry to block the idea of a private management contract for Tegucigalpa. He argued that SANAA's founding legislation does not allow the company to contract private agents to run its water services. This was debatable, since there is a general provision in Honduran law for administrative delegation, which includes delegation to private agents. Nevertheless, the banks accepted the idea that the management contract should be put on hold pending the passage of the framework legislation, which would make explicit the legality of management contracts, leasing arrangements and concessions, and allow SANAA directly to make management contracts during the transition period, with the agreement of the relevant municipality (see Box 2.5).

This episode was the *coup de grace* for the adjustment loan. The government's failure to replace Romero as the head of SANAA, even after he assumed a stance of public opposition, was the final blow to the credibility of Honduras commitment to sector reform. With other sector adjustment loans in jeopardy due to noncompliance with their conditionalities, Honduras IMF agreement in suspense due to missed fiscal targets, and an election year in the offing, the banks quietly deleted the Water and Sanitation

Sector Structural Adjustment Credit from their work programs and began to search for an alternative strategy to secure passage of the reform.

In the meantime, they focused their efforts on preparing future investment credits and technical assistance for municipally run systems. Although both banks continued to insist that the framework legislation was a sine qua non for future support to the sector, by the end of 1996 the legislation had still not been submitted to Congress, and the probability that it would be passed during the final year of the Reina administration seemed low.

A Stakeholder Analysis of the Failed Reform

Table 2.14 presents a stakeholder analysis, which identifies the forces in favor and against the reform. The analysis divides the actors into three groups: external actors, the government (including Congress), and other national actors. For each actor, the table shows their potential interest in the issue, the position they took, and the resources at their disposal to pursue their interest.[18] This analysis shows that support for the reform was weak and makes it clear why the adjustment operation failed to materialize.

Among the external actors, the government's failure to coordinate the external support to the sector allowed each development agency to promote its own line. There was strong support for the reform only from the two banks that proposed to cofinance the adjustment operation. USAID, which has long promoted municipalization, supported the transfer of SANAA's water systems to municipal control but had reservations about whether this should be mandatory rather than voluntary and opposed the idea of a national regulator nominated by the central government.

Other bilateral agencies such as GTZ and JICA effectively opposed the proposal, giving support to the alternative regionalization strategy promoted by SANAA. JICA provided grant funds to upgrade the La Ceiba system, giving credibility to the regionalization option and helping to dampen support for municipalization in that city. Since GTZ supports the association of Central American water companies, CAPRE, it has considerable moral authority in the field, so its absence from the reform camp was important. Similarly, although it cofunded the initial diagnostic study that set the stage for

---

[18] This analysis broadly follows the methodology developed by Crosby (1992 a, b, and c).

the reform, the Panamerican Health Organization, (PAHO) never declared its position.

The government itself was divided on the matter. The only government agency strongly committed to the reform was the Presidential Commission for State Modernization (CPME by its Spanish initials). It also enjoyed the support of the economic cabinet, which needed the balance of payments resources the operation would have released, and which subscribed to the general goal of improving the effectiveness of public infrastructure investment. But the reform was strongly opposed by SANAA, the Planning Ministry, and the existing regulatory agency, CNSSP, which wanted to defend its turf. The President of the Republic appeared to have no position on the issue and was known to have a high personal regard for the SANAA manager, Romero. When the President failed to intervene to resolve the differences of opinion within the government, the reform process simply disintegrated.

Table 2.14 also shows the weakness of national support for the project outside of government circles. In the preparatory phase of the reform, research studies were commissioned that underlined the inequity of the water situation. But in spite of the huge welfare gains that would have come from improving the sector's performance, no political entrepreneur emerged to mobilize support from households without water or with very poor service that suffer from the status quo. Instead, the *patronatos* (*barrio* committees) of the marginal urban sector remained indifferent to the debate on municipalization. Even the municipalities, purportedly the main gainers from the process, remained cautious, unsure of the consequences of taking on responsibility for their water systems, anxious about securing a guarantee of resources up front and reluctant to accept external regulation.

The leaders of the private sector (organized in the *Consejo Hondureño de la Empresa Privada*, COHEP), normally the most vociferous proponents of privatization initiatives, had nothing to say on the issue of water privatization. The SANAA employees' union, on the other hand, intervened effectively in the debate, persuading Congressional leaders that if they supported the privatization proposal they risked being held responsible for a drastic rate increase in an election year.

The absence of a strong national alliance in favor of the reform legislation was fatal. The only strong supporters of reform with real power were the banks because they held the purse strings on balance of payments sup-

Table 2.14   Stakeholder Analysis of the Reform of the Water Sector

Group	Interest in the issue	Position on reform	Resources available
External actors			
World Bank	Promotes reform in infra-structure sector; needs an adjustment operation for cash-flow reasons.	Strong support	Structural adjustment financing of US$30 million.
IDB	Finances the sector; needs adjustment operation for cash-flow reasons.	Strong support	Structural adjustment financing of US$35 million plus ability to withhold investment loans to sector.
International firms	Possible contracts for man-agement and concessions; contracts for consultants.	Support	Ability to offer technical assistance to reform planning process.
Bilateral lenders	Finance the sector.	No general position; USAID supports volun-tary transfer to munici-pal control but opposes both compulsion and the creation of a central government controlled regulatory agency. GTZ opposes; JICA has not declared	Financial resources and technical assistance.
CAPRE	Regional body for state water companies in C.A.	Opposed—promotes the alternative of regionalization	Technical assistance; capacity to legitimize the opposition to reform.
PAHO	Concerned with rural primary health.	None declared	Few

Table 2.14 (continued)

Group	Interest in the issue	Position on reform	Resources available
Government			
SANAA	Existing agency would lose operational functions, but would remain in charge of sector strategy.	Strong opposition—proposes alternative of modernization and regionalization.	Technical capacity; controls information; able to dedicate itself full time to maneuvering on the issue; strong personal relationship of manager Romero with the President; strong support from SANAA professional staff for Romero.
President	Ultimately responsible for defining government policy and for relations with the World Bank and the IDB.	Apparently not interested in the substance of the issue.	Ability to impose his decision within the Executive—but not on the Congress.
Presidential Commission for Modernization of the State (CPME)	Prime agency for modernization; sees sector reform as complementary to the general modernization program.	Strongly in favor—Secretary Armando Aguilar Cruz (also Minister of the Presidency) is reform's main public advocate.	Ability to influence the President; access to technical assistance from banks; but not influential with the majority Flores faction in Congress (linked to Reina faction).
Economic cabinet	Responsible for balance of payments management—needs adjustment loan to be approved. Also concerned with infrastructure efficiency	Though originally skeptical, coordinator Guillermo Bueso supported the reform, more to get the adjustment loan than because he supports the reform per se.	Ability to influence President.
Health Ministry	General responsibility for water and sanitation—special interest in rural systems and for technical norms.	No clearly defined position.	Presides in the SANAA board; moral authority on health-related impacts of sectoral reform.

Table 2.14 (continued)

Group	Interest in the issue	Position on reform	Resources available
Planning Ministry	The ministry responsible for public investment program at the time; since then, it has been abolished	Opposed—supported SANAA proposal for solidarity among bodies threatened with closure due to the adjustment program.	Presided in Social Cabinet which includes the Health Ministry, which in turn supervises the water and sanitation sector.
CNSSP	Existing rate regulator—defending its turf.	Opposed—supports SANAA proposal.	Technical capacity to question proposals.
Congress	Would have to pass framework law.	No declared position.	Can block the reform.
Other national actors			
Municipalities	Would take over system operation—potential for increased scope of activity, income, etc. But also high risks from taking over run-down systems that they are not well equipped to administer.	Diverse positions: AHMON broadly supports transfer of water systems to municipal control but wants a resource guarantee; would prefer that the transfer of systems were optional rather than compulsory; and opposes the creation of a national government-controlled regulator. The municipality of Tegucigalpa is not interested in taking over the capital's water and sewerage systems, which are half of SANAA's customers; many other municipalities are concerned about getting greater responsibility without resources.	Lobbying power; also, could block the reform by refusing to accept systems.

Table 2.14 (continued)

Group	Interest in the issue	Position on reform	Resources available
SANAA union	Loss of jobs and of opportunities for corruption.	Strong opposition to reform.	Lobbying power (influential with leading deputies in the controlling Flores faction of Congress); scare tactics on price rises; xenophobic rhetoric.
Users of SANAA system	Would face rate increases but could get improved service.	No clear public opinion on the matter.	If politicians fear that the measure is unpopular with existing users, who are relatively articulate with access to the media, this could cause a Congressional veto
Nonusers (marginal *barrios*)	Presently unable to get piped water due to low-level equilibrium trap.	No clear public opinion on the matter.	*Patronato* organizations have lobbying power.
National private sector (COHEP, *Cámaras de Comercio e Industrias*)	Fear of increased rates; opportunities for contracts.	No clear public opinion on the matter.	Very considerable lobbying power.
Political parties	Opportunity to win popularity / risk of losing popularity.	No important political group argued strongly for the reform because it was not viewed as a popular cause.	Influence of liberal and national parties is decisive in Congress.

port and on future loans to the sector. But recent experience has shown that the Honduran Congress will not automatically put the executive's macroeconomic needs above its own political expediency. Throughout 1996, Honduras' IMF agreement was in suspension following the Congressional decision to push through income tax cuts that increased the consolidated public sector deficit above the agreed upon ceiling. Inconvenient as it might seem, politicians, at the end of the day, are more interested in votes than in balance of payments support.

With this backdrop, the question is what should be done now to reform the sector? In the medium term, given the IDB's ability to offer large-scale finance for future water sector investments, its attitude will prove crucial. The IDB can insist on satisfactory progress in sector regulation, organization, and performance in return for new funding. In the past, when centralization was in fashion in the water sector, the IDB prevailed on SANAA to take over the systems of Tela, Juticalpa, and Ceiba in return for financial support.[19] By the same token, the bank could now force the transfer of systems to municipal control, if it chose to do so.

However, the prospects for reform would also be improved if the legitimate concerns expressed by some of the reforms' opponents were addressed. The two most controversial aspects of the reform were: the proposed rapid municipalization of all of SANAA's systems; and the absence of a sufficiently clear regulatory guarantee for the users (in the form of a rate ceiling).

The Debate over Municipalization

The rapid municipalization of service delivery is a central plank of the proposed reform. All of SANAA's water systems would be passed to the ownership of their respective municipalities within two years, free of debt (Rendón Cano1996, Articles 13, 14, and 15). However, the latest (July 1996) version of the draft legislation, summarized in Box 2.5, leaves open the possibility that in some cases this might not happen, in which case SANAA would continue to run the systems (Ibid. Article 16). The inclusion of this provision so late in the drafting process was a tacit acknowledgement of widespread skepticism about the capacity of many municipalities to manage their water systems.

Nevertheless, in recent years, most political mobilization still favors the organization of water sector reform around the demand that SANAA systems be transferred to municipal control. This has happened mainly where SANAA systems have been in a state of collapse and where local political leaders have seized on the resulting popular discontent. In two cases, San Lorenzo and Puerto Cortés, these mobilizations led to the transfer of system administration to municipal control. The results of these initiatives and

---

[19] Interview with Luis Moncada Gross (June 1995).

SANAA's establishment of a decentralized regional office in La Ceiba as an alternative to municipalization provide lessons on the problems and possibilities of a national decentralization process.

Recent Experiences in Municipalization

Since 1993, in the context of the political and administrative decentralization process that followed the municipal legislation of 1990–91, SANAA has delegated responsibility for management, operation, and maintenance of water networks to local governments in San Lorenzo, Puerto Cortés, and Tela. In each case, the ownership of the system remained with SANAA. The first two cases were piecemeal initiatives in response to local political pressure for improvements in water supply, and in each case the system inherited by the municipality was in extremely poor condition. In Tela, the system was in better physical condition due to a recent investment program; the transfer was promoted by SANAA, apparently in a crude attempt to discredit municipalization.

The first delegation was made in February 1993 to San Lorenzo, a port city of 18,000 people located in southern Honduras. The city had serious problems with water sources and coverage was estimated at only 55 percent of households, with very poor frequency of supply (once per week during some parts of the year). Physical losses were estimated at 60 percent of production. SANAA supported the delegation process with a system survey, an inventory of fixed assets, and staffing decisions.

At first, the municipality had problems dealing with the commercial administration and technical difficulties with the pumping system. Nevertheless, following the organization of a technical unit within the municipality's engineering department, the municipality assumed full responsibility for the system. The municipal administration replaced an important water main, opened new wells, and incorporated new *barrios* into the system. Coverage rose to 80 percent; physical losses were an estimated 30 percent; and service frequency improved to alternate days. Funds for these improvements came from a L 3.1 million loan from Germany's KFW and from the 4 percent of National Port Authority and customs revenues that is granted to port cities under *Decree 72–86*.

In Puerto Cortés, a north coast port city with a population of 50,000, the municipalization of water services was part of the winning platform of the Liberal Party in the 1993 mayoral elections. This followed protests (including closure of the main highway) when SANAA proved slow in repairing storm damage, which severely interrupted water services in 1993. In early 1994, SANAA approved the transfer. However, following the September 1994 appointment of Romero as general manager, SANAA reversed its policy. As a result, the negotiation took 16 months to complete and the transfer was delayed until April 1995. Puerto Cortés was required to cover L 1 million in severance pay of former SANAA employees, offset against the accounts receivable inherited from SANAA.

Following municipalization, a respected SANAA engineer was recruited as system manager and the World Bank and USAID provided sustained technical assistance, the latter through FUNDEMUN. Substantial improvements were achieved in production (up 40 percent) and service frequency (up from 12 to 20 hours a day). USAID provided a US$ 3 million loan (through the *Fondo Hondureño de Inversión Social*, FHIS) to build a new dam on the Río Tulian, further expanding productive capacity, and Puerto Cortés funded US$ 1.5 million of investment with its own funds (using the 4 percent of the National Port Aurthority and customs revenues that is payable to city governments where port facilities are located). The number of employees per thousand connections was reduced from 7.6 in April 1995 to 4.7 by mid-1996. The metering of industrial consumption rose from 102 functioning meters to 385, and in 1997 the municipality launched a program to establish 100 percent metering of residential consumption within two years. Illegal connections were halved, monthly billing rose from L 132,000 to L 520,000, and revenues as a share of billing increased from 61 percent to 103 percent, reflecting a successful effort to recoup overdue or unpaid accounts. On the basis of these successes, in 1997 Puerto Cortés secured Congressional approval for the definitive transfer of the system's ownership to the municipality.

In Tela, a north coast city of 35,000 inhabitants, SANAA invested L 6.4 million in water production, treatment, and distribution in the early 1990s, under the IDB's Four Cities project, raising coverage to 87 percent. However, the system still registered very large losses (60 percent), mainly attributable to the nonseparation of the old distribution system built by the Tela Railroad Company, and to nonexistent billing and collection.

In February 1996, SANAA unexpectedly and rapidly ceded administration to the municipality, which was not well prepared technically or administratively to assume it. The transfer was seen by many observers as a deliberate attempt to discredit the strategy of municipalization. The municipality recruited a relatively inexperienced manager who initially received technical assistance from FUNDEMUN on how to cut physical losses; FUNDEMUN recommended separating the Tela Railroad Company system and sectorializing the network[20]. However, a conflict arose when the tests for this work led to service cuts in the city. As a result, the FUNDEMUN contract was suspended and Tela began to depend on the SANAA regional office at El Progreso for support. These problems led to a meeting between the Ministry of Government, SANAA, AHMON, and the Municipality of Tela, where it was reportedly agreed that future municipalizations would be more carefully planned.

SANAA's Regionalization Strategy: The Case of La Ceiba

La Ceiba, a north coast city with 100,000 inhabitants and around 13,000 domestic connections, suffered problems similar to those of Puerto Cortés in 1993, when tropical storms damaged dams, storage tanks, and pipelines, severely disrupting services. Low rainfall in 1994 aggravated the crisis, when pumping from dry wells led to equipment damage. Thereafter, local pressure for municipalization began to grow. Alert to the danger of losing another major operation to municipal control, SANAA turned La Ceiba into a testing ground for the alternative strategy of regionalization.

In 1995, SANAA created a regional office in the city with autonomy in operations, including hiring, purchasing, and billing. All income generated by the La Ceiba system was to be retained locally to pay for the operation and maintenance of the system and to finance minor investments. The regional office also oversees rural water systems in the area of Atlántida, Colón, and Yoro, with the income generated by these systems remaining in their respective localities. However, the La Ceiba regional office has been characterized by managerial improvisation in the face of emergencies, and by early 1997 relations with SANAA headquarters in Tegucigalpa had not stabilized. SANAA still lacks a coherent operating model of regional decentralization.

---

[20] This refers to a process to separate the network into sectors that can be isolated from one another to control leakage.

SANAA has supported the La Ceiba initiative with a generous allocation of capital resources. Parallel to the creation of the regional office, SANAA obtained a Japanese grant of US$ 900,000 to install new wells, storage tanks, and pumping equipment to complement the gravity-run system. Although the investment program was clumsily managed and the funds spent considerable time on deposit awaiting implementation, the eventual result was a marked service improvement. The proportion of clients with 24-hour service rose from 6 percent in 1994 to 88 percent in 1996. Other performance indicators also registered marginal improvements: employees per thousand connections fell from 5.2 in 1994 to 4.2 in June 1996 and, in response to the incentive that income is now locally retained, monthly billing quadrupled to L 425,000 in mid 1996, up from L 111,000 in 1994. However, revenues rose by only 40 percent, barely ahead of inflation.

Meanwhile, the municipality of La Ceiba continued to receive technical assistance from USAID, through FUNDEMUN, to determine the technical and financial feasibility of muncipalization. The improvement in service under the SANAA initiative, however, has reduced local pressure for municipalization.

Lessons from the Municipalization Process

A definitive conclusion on the success of municipalization must await further implementation of the strategy and a review of performance in the medium and long run. But the experiences of San Lorenzo, Puerto Cortés, and Tela offer some important lessons on how to achieve success in the municipalization process.

First, the size of the municipality does not appear to be a decisive factor, within the range covered by these cases: in both San Lorenzo, the smallest of the three, and Puerto Cortés, the largest, the results are clearly positive. However, the administrative delegation of SANAA systems to the municipalities has been difficult to manage. It leads to a game in which each party seeks to unload responsibilities on the other and leaves open the possibility that SANAA might seek to cancel the arrangement once the principal problems have been resolved. The transfer of system ownership as contemplated in the proposed reform legislation, and already achieved in Puerto Cortés, is a much cleaner device.

Second, municipalization is most likely to succeed where there is strong local political support and where willingness to pay for improved services is high. Therefore, the priority in the decentralization program should be given to the cities where the problems are greatest and the potential for service improvement is highest. However, these conditions are most likely to exist when the system of production and distribution is in serious difficulty. This in turn implies that the availability of technical assistance and access to capital resources are likely to be important factors in the success of the transfer. In both San Lorenzo and Puerto Cortés, the interventions of bilateral and multilateral agencies proved important.

Third, managerial capacity is likely to be a key bottleneck in any form of a decentralization process in Honduras, where qualified professionals are scarce. Therefore, wherever feasible, municipalities should be encouraged to combine forces to exploit managerial and administrative economies of scale, and the pace of the reform process should be geared to the availability of the human and capital resources needed to make it a success, rather than to an externally imposed program of conditionalities.

This, in turn, implies that an adjustment operation is not an ideal vehicle for the reform project, since such operations require that irreversible change be demonstrated within a limited time frame. It is not easy to ensure irreversible change simply through framework legislation, and the implementation of sector reorganization may take longer than is normally permitted under an adjustment program. This sets up a tension between the need to design a program which is acceptable in terms of World Bank and IDB criteria for adjustment operations and the need to answer legitimate Honduran concerns about the risks of an overly precipitous process.

Fourth, in the absence of a properly defined national scheme for the allocation of technical assistance and capital resources, there has been a free for all in which the development agencies adopt one or more municipalities (as some aid agencies promote the adoption of a needy child). For example, USAID and the World Bank have supplied municipalized Puerto Cortés with technical assistance and capital resources, while JICA has supported SANAA's regionalization strategy through investments in La Ceiba. Some important municipalities have been able to take advantage of such programs, but the result is not necessarily conducive to a rational reorganization of the sector, especially since each agency uses the resources at its disposal to promote whatever model it happens to favor.

This experience highlights the need for a coherent national policy framework, tying the distribution of resources to an overall sector strategy. Generous injections of technical assistance and capital are likely to produce good results in service coverage and quality in the short run, regardless of the form of organization of service delivery, but these tell us little about the intrinsic virtues of the municipalization and regionalization options. The real test of both models is their ability to succeed when they are generalized over the long term, not just as demonstration projects with preferential access to technical and financial support.

Organization and Regulation of Service Provision: Key Issues for the Success of Reform

In the long run, the key indicators of success are those related to physical and financial efficiency rather than those related to a city's capacity to attract public investment funds. If decentralization were simply to reproduce at a local level the same systemic weaknesses that led to failure in the centralized model, the result might be a proliferation of mini-SANAA's with the familiar pattern of political, workforce, and user capture of system rents, stagnant coverage and poor service quality. In this sense, municipalization should not in itself be regarded as the central goal of sector reform.

Unfortunately, many supporters of the reform have seen it simply as part of the ongoing struggle to shift the balance of power between central government and the municipalities, and do not understand the importance of separating the functions of strategic planning, operation, and regulation for the reorganized sector to succeed. To have all of these functions under municipal control would simply reproduce in decentralized form the same systemic weaknesses that plague the existing centralized system. For this reason, there is a need to develop a working model for the municipal management of water services that protects the system from political, employee, or user capture of its rents, and provides the municipalities with technical assistance to manage the system efficiently. The following paragraphs detail the main aspects of such a model, as outlined in the latest version (1996) of the reform proposal.

System Organization

The proposed legislation provides that municipalities run their services either directly, through municipal departments, autonomous agencies or public corporations or indirectly, in the form of concessions, leases or management contracts with private agents or mixed capital companies jointly owned by municipalities and private investors (Article 33). The legislation also allows for intermunicipal associations in any of these forms (Article 35). However, it stipulates that indirect provision is the preferred form of service delivery that should normally be adopted unless there is no available agent or the cost of direct municipal service delivery is demonstrably lower (Article 37).

In this way, the legislation creates a strong presumption in favor of a clear organizational and financial separation of the water system from the rest of the municipality's operations. However, to turn this into a reality, it will be necessary to develop a model of independent provision that can be implemented in the major municipalities. To this end, during 1997, the IDB developed a pilot project in Puerto Cortés to establish a mixed-capital company, co-owned by the municipality and private investors, which would operate the water and sewerage system on a leasing arrangement, following the Spanish and French models.

Regulatory System

Regulation arrangements are central to the political viability of any plan for increased private sector participation. The lack of clarity on this issue was the main weakness of the proposal for a private management contract for Tegucigalpa.

Regulation should protect users from overcharging and also ensure that the expected return on the system's investment (the so-called quasi-rent) is not subject to capture by local politicians or system users, via pressure on the regulator to limit rates to unreasonably low levels. In the absence of such a mechanism, the fiscal costs of the publicly run systems will be high due to continued deficits, and it will be impossible to attract private capital to substitute for public resources and facilitate the expansion of coverage.

The 1996 draft legislation (summarized in Box 2.5) provides for a coherent national regulatory system. It contemplates the creation of a specialized three-person regulatory commission for water and sanitation services. Members of the *Comisión Nacional de Agua Potable y Alcantarillado Sanitario* (henceforth, the Commission) would be nominated for five years by the President of the Republic, with two members to be taken from slates submitted by the professional colleges of civil engineers and economists, respectively. To strengthen their independence from political interference and ensure regulatory continuity, the commissioners' five-year period of office would be different from that of the presidency (four years). The commissioners would themselves have different (overlapping) periods, rather than all being nominated at the same time. The Commission would be financed from the water rate charged to users by all system operators; its budget would be set by the national Congress.

The Commission would have the power to limit the maximum rate of any service provider to an efficiency level; the law would explicitly forbid the rate from including costs that result from inefficiency (Article 63). However, cross-subsidies would be permitted. Any rate change would require the Commission's approval and the operator would be required to supply the information necessary for its evaluation (Article 64). The definition of efficiency would be a cost plus or rate of return mechanism based on a model enterprise, similar to the Chilean model (Article 66). This is considered more appropriate for Honduras than a price cap due to macroeconomic uncertainty and the importance of guaranteeing a reasonable rate of return to private investors in the initial phase of private involvement.

The Commission would concentrate on the regulation of relatively large systems, delegating the regulatory function in rural areas to the municipalities. The Commission would also supervise compliance with contractual agreements among the government, municipalities, and private operators. In accordance with the principle of municipal autonomy, the municipalities would retain the freedom to set their own rates at levels below the recommended level. However, the rate regime of any municipality that takes loans from the central government to develop its water sector would be subject to regulation to ensure the financial viability of the loan.

Security of the Regulatory Environment

The regulatory provisions described above should provide a satisfactory basis for improved performance. However, they may not in themselves be sufficient to promote large-scale private investment in the sector. Potential investors are concerned not only with the content of the regulations, but also with the security of the regulatory environment. The letting of concessions to operate water services in the capital cities of Latin America has been constrained by the perception of high political risk, as illustrated most recently in Caracas.

Honduras has a poor international image for investment risk, due partly to macroeconomic factors (such as debt overhang) but also to a recent history of arbitrary action by the executive, legislative, and judicial authorities in matters involving transactions between the Honduran state and foreign companies (such as the privatization of state companies and the international letting of contracts for infrastructure development).

The reduction of this sort of risk depends on the overall process of political, administrative, and judicial modernization, which is still at an early stage. The design of a sectoral strategy in relation to the need for public investment resources should be based on reasonable assumptions about that process. In the short to medium term, the best prospects for private sector financial involvement in large-scale sunk investments are probably to be found in San Pedro Sula, where political risk may be perceived to be lower than in Tegucigalpa.

Conclusions and Recommendations

The Honduran water and sanitation sector's overall performance in recent years has been disappointing, and both the systems operated by the centralized *Servicio Autónomo Nacional de Agua y Alcantarillado* (SANAA) and those operated by municipal governments show similar weaknesses. The causes of poor performance are related to the existing organization of the sector, in a classic pattern of a low-level equilibrium. The roots of the problem lie, first, in the confusion between sector planning and resource allocation (which are strategic or political functions), on the one hand, and system operation (which should be isolated from political considerations), on the other.

This problem has two important manifestations. At a national level, SANAA both operates systems and plays a leading role in determining priorities for capital resources. As a result, the SANAA-operated systems (especially that of the capital city, Tegucigalpa) get more than their share of subsidized capital. More generally, the political control of the operating bodies (SANAA by the national government and municipal operators by the local authority) means that water utilities lack financial independence and are subject to the capture of system rents by users, politicians, and workers. This leads to undercharging, and results in inefficiencies in the scale of service provision (underexpansion, low coverage) and in the operation of existing systems (poor maintenance, low productivity, and generally feeble commercial systems). It also leads to a vicious circle of low credibility and low willingness to pay, because users—with reason—do not believe that revenues from the water rate will necessarily be used to improve services. The new evidence on willingness to pay presented in this study supports this conclusion.

The second factor contributing to this low-level equilibrium is the generalized failure of the regulatory function. No organization exists to define or defend the rights and interests of the actual and potential users of water and sewerage services. The regulation of water quality is ineffectual and the only form of economic regulation is that of the SANAA water rate, which is highly politicized and directly contributes to undercharging. Municipal systems are effectively unregulated.

Nontransparent subsidies make SANAA's financial balance sustainable, and the existing situation is an equilibrium in the classic sense of the term, in that it could continue indefinitely for as long as the political settlements that facilitate it are left in place. But there is no objective need for wholesale subsidies to the sector. Based on reasonable assumptions about improved performance, SANAA's systems could be self-financing within five years, and enormous potential welfare benefits would result from these systems breaking out of this low-level equilibrium.

The case for reform is therefore overwhelming, but the interests favoring the status quo are strong and well organized, so the political task of organizing reform is considerable. A stakeholder analysis of the failed Water and Sanitation Sector Structural Adjustment Credit, supported jointly by the World Bank and the IDB during 1994–96, highlights the problems of reform and illustrates the limited capacity of adjustment finance to secure change in the absence of a clear national policy decision.

However, the reform's failure was not simply one of political management. The reform proposal itself suffered from important weaknesses, which undermined its support. It made a central principle of municipalization, but failed to address the poor performance of many existing municipal systems and placed insufficient emphasis on the need to protect system operation from political interference. Most municipal governments in Honduras suffer from credibility problems similar to those of the central government, so a proposal that did not address these issues was bound to be unconvincing.

In addition, as a result of the municipalities' reluctance to be subjected to a national regulatory agency, the reform proposal did not adequately address the issue of regulation until it was too late. Early drafts of the legislation concentrated on linking municipalities' access to capital resources to good financial performance. The emphasis was on the use of incentives to avoid undercharging, but there was no regulatory provision to prevent overcharging. This led to a setback when the municipality of the capital city, Tegucigalpa, refused to take over its water system, which accounts for half of SANAA's operation, and in response, a plan to privatize the management of the metropolitan water system was hurriedly tacked on to the reform. In the absence of a clear regulatory guarantee for users, the reform's opponents had a field day with the prospect of a private operator levying exorbitant rates.

In the final draft of the reform proposal most of these issues are satisfactorily resolved. The law creates a presumption in favor of indirect forms of service provision in which the opportunities for political capture are minimized, and the regulatory arrangements are well conceived. The reform effort should now proceed on parallel tracks at the national and local levels. The approval of the framework law and creation of the national regulatory, planning, and technical assistance bodies should be complemented by the development at the municipal level of a workable model of indirect service provision. This could first be applied in existing municipal systems and could be extended to the SANAA systems once the law is passed.

References

AHMON. 1995. "Posición de los alcaldes en lo referente al plan de reformas al sector agua y saneamiento." Paper presented to the Seminario sobre Reforma al Sector Agua y Saneamiento en Honduras. Roatan, Honduras.

Ardila, S. 1993. *Guía para la utilización de modelos econométricos en aplicaciones del método de valorización contingente.* Inter-American Development Bank. Washington, DC.

Aquagest. 1995. "Informe diagnóstico del servicio de acueductos y alcantarillado en Tegucigalpa: Diagnosis de su operación y recomendaciones para mejorar su ejecucción y atraer al sector privado." Consultant report for the World Bank.

Badías, J. 1995. "Modelo conceptual de contrato de gestión en los servicios de agua y alcantarillado para la ciudad de Tegucigalpa." Consultant report for the CPME.

Chama, R. 1995. "Honduras—programa de reforma del sector agua y saneamiento—desarrollo del marco institucional y regulatorio." Consultant report for the World Bank.

CPME, UDAPE, World Bank. 1995. "Memoria del seminario sobre reforma al sector agua y saneamiento en Honduras."

Comisión para la Modernización del Estado (CPME). 1993. "Cuadernos de la descentralización: Categorización municipal." Unpublished document.

——— . 1996. "Documento de evaluación del proceso de reforma y modernización de los servicios de agua potable y saneamiento en Honduras." Unpublished document.

Crosby, B. 1992 (a). "Stakeholder Analysis: A Vital Tool for Strategic Managers". USAID Implementing Policy Change Project. Washington, DC.

_____. 1992 (b). "Management and the environment for implementation of policy change: Part one—political mapping." USAID Implementing Policy Change Project. Washington, DC.

_____. 1992 (c). "Management and the Environment for Implementation of Policy Change: Part Two: Policy Environment Mapping Techniques." USAID Implementing Policy Change Project. Washington, DC.

Ducci, J. and Alvarez, M. 1994. "Proyecto de reforma del sector agua potable y saneamiento Honduras. Preparación de la estrategia y el plan de acción para la reorganización institucional del sector." Consultant report for CPME.

Foster, V. 1996. "Modernización y reforma del sector de agua potable y saneamiento: Aspectos conceptuales". Oxford Economic Research Associates (OXERA). Paper presented at the Regional Conference on Reform and Modernization of Drinking Water and Sanitation Services for Mexico, Central America, Haiti, and the Dominican Republic. San Pedro Sula, Honduras.

IDB, World Bank, PAHO. 1994. "Honduras—estudio del sector de agua y saneamiento." Draft paper.

Irias, C. 1996. "DIMA—un ejemplo a considerar sobre la municipalización de los sistemas de agua potable y alcantarillados." Paper presented to the *Seminario sobre Reforma al Sector Agua y Saneamiento en Honduras*. Roatan, Honduras.

McConnell, K. 1995. "Issues in Estimating Benefits with Nonmarket Methods." Working paper Series 308. Office of the Chief Economist, Inter-American Development Bank.

Ochoa. 1995. "Honduras: Misión de evaluación de la inversión pública. Informe del sector de agua y saneamiento." Consultant report prepared for the World Bank.

Pan American Health Organization (PAHO), World Health Organization (WHO). 1993. "Situación actual del sector agua y saneamiento de Honduras: Cobertura." Tegucigalpa, Honduras.

Panting, D. 1995. "Acción de DIMA en el marco de la reforma sectorial." Paper presented to the *Seminario sobre Reforma al Sector Agua y Saneamiento en Honduras*. Roatan, Honduras.

Rendón Cano, J. 1995. "Análisis del marco legal administativo relacionado con el sector de abastecimiento de agua a poblaciones y saneamiento." Consultant report for CPME.

Rendón Cano, J. 1996. "Anteproyecto de ley para el sector agua potable y alcantarillado sanitario." Consultant report prepared for CPME.

Rousseau, M.P. (No date). "Regulación mediante contrato o a través de la competencia?" *In* C. Martinande. *La experiencia francesa de financiación privada de los equipamientos públicos.* DAEI. Paris.

SANAA. 1993. "Propuesta base para la delegación de la administración, operación y mantenimiento del sistema de agua potable de la ciudad de San Lorenzo a la municipalidad." Working Paper.

SANAA. 1995. "La transformación del sector agua potable y saneamiento: Bases para una propuesta nacional en el marco del combate a la pobreza." Document presented to the *Seminario sobre Reforma al Sector Agua y Saneamiento en Honduras*. Roatan, Honduras.

Sappington, D. 1994. "Principles of Regulatory Policy Design." Background paper for the *World Development Report*. World Bank. Washington, DC.

Savedoff, W. 1993. "Cost Benefit Analysis of Projects with Water Meters." Working Paper No. 104–94. Project Analysis Department, Project Advisory Office. Inter-American Development Bank.

Walker I. and Ordoñez, F. 1995. *Encuesta de usuarios de agua en Honduras.* ESA Consultores. Tegucigalpa, Honduras.

Walker I. and Soto, R. 1995. "Estimated Fiscal and Welfare Impacts of the Reform of the Water and Sanitation Sector in Honduras." Consultant report for the World Bank and IDB. ESA Consultores. Tegucigalpa, Honduras.

Walker, I., Velásquez, M., Ordoñez, F, and Rodríguez, F. 1997. "Regulation, Organization and Incentives: The Political Economy of Potable Water Services in Honduras" Working Paper No. R-314. Inter-American Development Bank. Washington, DC. http://www.iadb.org/oce/41.htm

World Bank. 1995. "Honduras—Reforming Public Investment and the Infrastructure Sectors." Report No. 14084.

Zambrano, D. 1996. "Evaluación del servicio de agua potable y procaine de inversions del alcantarillado sanitario de la Ceiba." Consultant report for FUNDEMUN.

CHAPTER 3

Reform Efforts and Low-Level Equilibrium in the Peruvian Water Sector

Gonzalo Tamayo, Roxana Barrantes,
Elena Conterno, and Alberto Bustamante[1]

Since 1990, the water and sanitation sector in Peru has changed from a highly centralized structure to one that assigns primary responsibility to municipalities. Reforms of the water and sanitation sector have been largely driven by political factors external to the sector, including the APRA government's effort to fragment power in its final days of office and the current government's interruption of the privatization of SEDAPAL prior to elections. This chapter analyzes these reforms and demonstrates the fragility of the sector's financial sources, which depend heavily upon payroll taxes, themselves the subjects of reform debates. It also compares the performance of three water companies— SEDAQOSQO, SEDAPAL, and SEDAPIURA—in the face of this changing political and economic context. The comparison demonstrates that SEDAPAL has improved its performance and does better on various efficiency measures than the municipal firms. This improved performance is attributed to the tutelage of external financing agencies that introduce a stakeholder with an interest in efficiency. By contrast, the municipal water companies are unable to break the vicious cycle of low

---

[1] Gonzalo Tamayo is chief of economic studies of Macroconsult, S.A; Roxana Barrantes is professor of economics at Pontificia Universidad Católica del Perú; Elena Conterno is a consultant for Macroconsult; and Alberto Bustamante is a partner at Estudio Yori-Bustamante.

tariffs, insufficient funds, inefficient operation, and political interference. However, SEDAPAL's current arrangement is unlikely to sustain its efficiency gains without continuing external involvement. A discussion of policy alternatives gives special attention to the potential role of the private sector and a new regulatory framework.

Since 1990, the potable water and sewerage system in Peru has been in transition from a centralized structure to a largely decentralized one in which the provincial municipalities are responsible for providing the service. The one exception is the most important market, Greater Lima (the capital of the country), which is under the central government. The transition has taken place under two successive governments with contrasting economic orientations. Part of the reform process involves the support provided by multilateral agencies: the World Bank, which has financed SEDAPAL, the company that supplies Greater Lima, and the Inter-American Development Bank, which has financed municipal water companies. In both cases, the multilateral institutions are expected to continue financing investment in the sector in coming years.

What has happened in the industry during the transition, and why has reform of the water sector proceeded more slowly than that of other areas of the economy? Answering these questions begins with an analysis of the characteristics of providing water services in comparison to other public utilities and a discussion of how the institutional features in Peru affect contractual relationships between economic actors. The industry had a long tradition of centralization but embarked on a reform process in 1990. Surprisingly, the process of municipalization of services was quite rapid but reform has been much slower. A cycle of expansion in investment began but its sustainability seems questionable given the main sources of financing. In evaluating the reform process, it is important to consider the current government's efforts to privatize the water sector and introduce economic pricing of water, and to compare the interrupted privatization process for the water sector with the more successful effort in other public infrastructure sectors. A comparison of the performance of three specific water companies—SEDAPAL, SEDAQOSQO, and SEDAPIURA—also reveals interesting results and contributes to conclusions and recommendations for improving the institutional arrangement of the country's water sector.

Analytical Framework

Water and Other Public Utilities

It is important to begin by recognizing how the water and sewerage sector shares common characteristics with other public utilities, but also differs in significant ways. The water, electric power, and telecommunications sectors share characteristics that affect the incentives for efficient supply: their technologies are based on specific investments; they display aspects of a natural monopoly as well as externalities of a network; and their products are used massively by consumers whose demand is inelastic (Guasch and Spiller 1994).

But just as they are similar in some ways, they are significantly different in others that also impact decisively on incentives: the dynamics of technological change, multiproduct production function, and vertical integration. For example, the dynamics of technological change make specific assets less important in telecommunications because services change, innovation takes place, and a wide range of services can be offered over the same network. That cannot happen in water, which is not subject to significant technological change: potable water is practically the same product with a minimum standard of quality to preserve human health. This quality standard is the only characteristic that can change over time. In telecommunications, a company can offer a number of services by utilizing economies of scope, but that cannot happen in water because the water distribution network can only distribute water. Likewise, electric power companies may be the next participants in the telecommunications business; by taking advantage of their cable networks, they can transmit telecommunications signals quite cheaply. Similarly, vertical integration is common in water distribution and wastewater collection systems due to the nature of the supply of the basic input; competition can take place only by comparing different districts. Table 3.1 sums up this analysis.

Specificity of assets is a considerably more important factor in the water industry than in other public utilities and hence the risks for private sector involvement are higher and transaction costs are greater. The World Bank demonstrates that in the water sector the specific assets are three or four times higher than in the other two sectors, measured in terms of the ratio of assets needed for every dollar of annual revenue (World Bank 1995). Demand is more inelastic than for the other utilities, leading companies to

Table 3.1 Comparing Public Utilities

	Type of Public Service		
Factor	Water	Electricity	Telecommunications
Technological change	Little or none	Limited	Important
Multiproduct production function	None	Possible	Important
Vertical integration	Possible	Possible, but less suitable	Many economies of scope to be exploited

apply high margins over marginal costs and encouraging governments to provide closer supervision than in other sectors. In many cases it leads governments to decide to supply the service directly through government companies. That is still the norm in Peru.

In the water industry, competition requires more information and demands a specific regulatory design to assure reasonable prices for consumers. These characteristics will have important consequences in the analysis to follow.

Contracting Problems in Peru

The framework proposed by Guasch and Spiller (1994) is helpful in examining contracting problems in the water industry and possible solutions to them through regulatory design for a given institutional endowment.

Institutional Endowment

Lack of credibility is a problem in Peru. The state is not regarded as a player that follows its own rules of the game, customary practices tend to raise transaction costs, and the state has little or no administrative ability. In contracting between the state and the private sector, there have been cases of expropriation at unfair prices, confiscation, and in some relatively recent periods, an environment quite unfavorable to private investment, especially from foreign investors. Since taking office in 1990, President Alberto Fujimori has sought to buy credibility by signing what are called "law contracts," in which the state places itself on the same level as the private investor with whom it signs a contract. This has been the short-term option as the government builds its own reputation and strengthens institutions such as the judiciary so they may play their assigned third-party role in guaranteeing contracts and legal stability. Legislative activity is shared between the executive and the legislature but in recent years the executive has become the main legislative body in the country. Efforts have been made to enhance the state's administrative capacity by creating bodies independent of the central government's budget and decision-making powers, in other words, bodies that are not very dependent on their respective ministry. For example, the agency regulating telecommunications falls under the presidency of the Council of Ministers, not the Ministry of Communications, and it is financed with a monitoring fee established as a percentage of the billing of operating companies. Few public institutions, however, have been given such treatment. This is the setting in which relationships between the various actors with an interest in the water industry operate. Obviously, efficiency in providing service requires significant transaction costs.

Contracting Problems

Between the government and companies: Governments tend to distort the investment decisions of companies because they have incentives to appropriate for themselves the quasirents generated by them. In Peru, three factors increase such incentives:

1) There are no procedures, either formal or informal, for regulatory decisions. Peru has a long tradition of direct public intervention but very little in the way of market regulation because broad state intervention in the economy was the norm in the past. Regulatory decision-making procedures are now in a process of definition, execution, and learning, and in some cases training of human capital is needed.

2) Regulatory power is centered in the administration of the executive branch. At present, the regulatory body of the water industry is the Superintendency of Water Services (SUNASS), which is under the vice-ministry of infrastructure of the Ministry of the Presidency. This is actually a ministry of public works. It is the main executor of tax expenditure, and hence is subject to strong political pressures.

3) The judiciary has neither the tradition nor the power to review the administrative decisions of the executive. The Court of Constitutional Guarantees has serious limitations arising from the demanding conditions for declaring laws and regulations issued by the executive unconstitutional.

Between companies and consumers. Even as the government has strong incentives to act opportunistically, the economic characteristics of water services also offer opportunities for water companies to exert power over the market. This is why regulatory design is so important, particularly for rate setting, performance criteria, and compliance monitoring. Currently, SUNASS supervises the setting of, and compliance with, rates and investment plans of water service providers (*Empresas Prestadoras de Servicios de Sanamiento*) with formulas specified in the law's regulations, but these can be modified or reversed by ministerial decisions.

Between the government and interest groups: The influence of various interest groups in government decisions distorts water rates to the benefit of some groups. This influence translates into cross-subsidies which can move in different directions: from low-income to high-income customers; from industrial to residential consumers. In Peru, it is common to charge users for presumed consumption levels because the installation of water meters is not very extensive. Subsidies mainly flow from industrial and commercial users toward residential consumers. Among residential consumers, subsidies flow from low-volume to high-volume consumers.

In short, Peru has a weak state that is in the process of building its reputation and credibility in order to motivate the private sector to become involved in long-term investments. However, the water industry faces distortions due to the weakness of the regulatory body and other matters involved in the reform process.

Process of Water Industry Reform

Until the 1990s, management of potable water and sewerage services was centralized, except for the smallest and most dispersed settlements. However, two fundamental but unrelated changes have taken place since 1990 in the organization of the potable water and sewerage sector in Peru. Each change was associated with different governments, those of Alan García Pérez and Alberto Fujimori, with contradictory economic policies. The first of these is decentralization involving the transfer of responsibility for providing service to provincial municipalities. The second is the market-oriented reform of this sector under a structural reform program that allows and encourages private participation in infrastructure investment and management of water companies through privatization.

Institutional Arrangements

Centralization: A Tradition

Peru's geography is such that the availability of water resources does not mesh well with the spatial distribution of the population. More than half of Peru's population (52 percent) lives along the coast, which accounts for 10.6 percent of the country's surface and is largely arid with precipitation levels below 150 mm a year.

Responsibility for water services was centralized in the Ministry of Public Works, except in some major cities, which had some degree of autonomy. After 1970, responsibility was shared between the Ministry of Housing for urban areas and the Ministry of Health for rural areas, through the Department of Basic Rural Water Services (DISABAR). Under the democratic government that took office in 1980, the National Service of Potable Water and Sewerage (SENAPA) was created.

The system was made up of a central body that assumed responsibility for the sectors by way of technical support, administration, financing, oversight, training, research, etc. Regional bodies in the form of subsidiary companies had administrative autonomy[2] while operating units directly under the central headquarters had limited autonomy for production, sales, and related service operations.[3] The SENAPA system and the three subsidiary companies covered 55 percent of the urban population. Alongside this centralized organization, potable water and sewerage services in approximately 200 urban locations, encompassing 20 percent of the total urban population, remained under the direct control of provincial and/or district mu-

---

[2] SEDAPAL, SEDAPAR, SEDAPAT, in Lima, Arequipa, and Trujillo, the largest cities in Peru.
[3] The system was made up of 11 subsidiary companies and 14 operating units.

nicipalities. The Ministry of Health continued to be responsible for providing services to rural areas. According to the 1981 census, 49 percent of houses
had access to the public water system and only 35 percent had access to
sewerage. As was to be expected, access to the public water system in urban
areas was higher, reaching 77 percent of houses, while coverage was only 2.5
percent in the rural areas.

While subsidiary companies had a certain degree of autonomy, their
development was still influenced by SENAPA, as the central body,[4] and the
Potable Water and Sewerage Rate Regulating Commission (CORTAPA),
which set rates. The central government handled investment requirements
and pricing policies. Water rates were set on an accounting basis to cover the
expenses of management, operation, maintenance, and depreciation of installations as well as the repayment of construction loans. Together with the
regulations in effect since 1979, potable water services were classified in five
categories[5] with a rate structure characterized by cross-subsidies favoring
the residential consumer at the expense of industry and business. Sewerage
rates were set as a fixed proportion of the bill for potable water that did not
distinguish between customers with and without access to the public system. For example, lower percentages were not applied to rural areas that
lacked such services.

The access of water companies to their resource—water—has been
regulated since 1969 by the General Law on Water (Decree Law 17752). According to that law, the country's water resources belong to the state and
cannot be privately owned or transferred. The law sets up a preferential order in water use, giving human consumption the highest priority. This criterion makes it impossible to grant rights on the basis of the value water
resources have for different sectors.

Water companies must obtain a water use license, but many of these
applications are still being processed. In addition, they must pay a fee, regarded as low, for the use of water. While legally this fee must reflect the
volume of water used, it is rarely charged on this basis.

There are major shortcomings in wastewater treatment and waste disposal. The result is environmental contamination, which is quite significant

---

[4] SENAPA was collecting 3 percent of the revenues of provider companies in order to create a
national investment fund.
[5] Residential, commercial, industrial, public, and provisional.

Table 3.2 Private Homes with Potable Water Supply

	1961	1972	1981	1993
Number of Homes[1]	1,962,290	2,686,471	3,257,124	4,427,517
Percent With	21.1	32.8	49.2	57.4
Percent Without	78.9	67.2	50.8	42.6

Note 1/ Homes with public provision of water, whether inside the home, building, or access to a public standpipe.

Table 3.3 Private Homes with Sewerage

	1961	1972	1981	1993
Number of Homes[1]	1,962,260	2,686,471	3,257,124	4,427,517
Percent With	45.0	27.3	35.0	40.0
Percent Without	55.0	72.7	65.0[2]	60.0[2]

Notes 1/ Homes with connections to the public network or with access to public connections.
      2/ Includes those with septic or other solutions.
Source: INEI

in some cases. Nationwide, the installed capacity for treating wastewater is insufficient or operates at below capacity.[6]

Census data illustrate the limited capacity of the centralized system to handle the needs of a larger, more urban population. In 1993, the share of housing units connected to the public potable water system (57.4 percent) was substantially higher than it was during the 1960s, but its rate of growth has been notably lower in recent years (Table 3.2). The situation is even worse for sewerage: 40 percent of dwellings surveyed in 1993 were connected to the public system, a rate lower than that existing in the 1960s (45 percent) (Table 3.3).

---

[6] For example, in Greater Lima, the largest market, over 20 cubic meters a second are emptied untreated into the ocean shoreline facing the city, thereby contributing to contamination of the coastal region. Despite the relative seriousness of raw sewage as a pollution source, the effective power of the responsible office of the Ministry of Health to monitor, enforce, and/or sanction is limited.

The data indicate that centralized organization for supplying the service had reached its limits. The state was accordingly forced to seek organizational options and the alternative chosen was municipalization.

Two Reforms: Municipalization and Privatization

Municipalization of Water Services

The 1979 constitution, promulgated as part of the transition from the military government of the 1970s to democracy, made the government responsible for dividing the country into 12 regions and providing for regional government elections. The process began in mid-1988 and was carried out hastily and incompletely. Even though most of the regions were established, only five regional governments actually began to function.

During the last six months of the García administration (January–June 1990), the *Alianza Popular Revolucionaria Americana* (APRA) party sought to reorganize and redefine the functions of the executive through legislative powers delegated by Congress (where it had majority control). These powers enabled it to issue laws seemingly connected to the regionalization process initiated in previous years. Through the Law on the Organization and Function of the Ministry of Housing, and Legislative Decree 601, issued in April 1990, SENAPA companies and operating units were transferred to provincial municipalities in already established regions. Since the region for Lima and Callao had never been set up, SEDAPAL was not brought into the process and it remained under the central government.

In accordance with the legal provisions of transfer issued in the first half of 1990, and with the government focused on a stabilization program intended to control major macroeconomic imbalances, the new government of President Fujimori quickly transferred the established companies to municipalities. This was the only step taken to transfer authority from the central to the local government in an administration that has faced ongoing conflict between both levels and has resisted demands for decentralization.

There are two possible reasons this transfer was completed. First, it is likely that the choice was made to transfer responsibility for the supply of a service with local characteristics to the politically most important local actors. At the same time, the government reduced its battle lines while it was in the midst of a severe stabilization process that entailed substantial hikes in prices of public goods and services (fuel, electricity), which contributed to a monthly inflation rate of nearly 400 percent. Secondly, while there has been political resistance to decentralization, failure to comply with the law issued by the previous government would have demanded that new laws be passed by the legislature, where the administration's party did not have a majority. Even if this were possible, it would have put further pressure on the stabilization program, which would have aggravated discontent in the provinces, where the party in power did not even have an organized presence.

Hence, in less than six months, 19 utilities (both companies and operating units) had been transferred to municipalities, and a somewhat slower process had begun for SENAPA operating units. Because the transfer was so quick, there was often no transition process and receiving entities were left unprepared to function in this new situation. Later, the transfer process became disconnected from the regionalization process due to clashes in 1990 and 1991 between the central and regional governments about control over assets, companies, and special projects. The problem was resolved by disbanding the regional assemblies that had been set up during the April 5, 1992, coup and creating transitory regional administration commissions (*Comisiones Transitorias de Administración Regional*) whose officials were appointed by the executive. The reform process was later expanded when SEDAPAL, the only water company under the central government, was brought into the process of privatizing government companies.

Reform: Promoting Private Investment in Water Services

The government calculates that over the next five years investment needs will total US$ 2.7 billion, a sum the public sector is unlikely to be able to finance. Therefore, private investment is indispensable for water service coverage to improve, and the need for private investment in water companies (most of them municipal) demands a context where market mechanisms are used intensively and private investment is encouraged.

In the past few years, a number of laws[7] aimed at reforming this sector have been passed, building on the municipalization passed by the previous

---

[7] Among the main ones are the Law on Private Investment in Public Utility Infrastructure (DL 758) and the Law on Private Investment in Water Services (DL 697), the Law on Water Services and its regulations, and the Law on the Superintendency of Water Services.

government. As a result of these laws, government agencies no longer have sole rights to operate in this sector, clearing the way for private investment through concession arrangements. In this sense, investment in water service will enjoy legal stability—a major plus given the state's low credibility. Reorganization of the sector continued between 1991 and 1994 with legal arrangements that made the following institutions the main participants in the industry:

The **Ministry of the Presidency** formulates government policy on the industry for urban and rural areas, and supervises, operates, and maintains the infrastructure of water services. It performs these functions through specialized institutions.

The **National Superintendency of Water Services (SUNASS)** controls service quality. It has power over rate setting and monitoring, coordinates between sectors, and issues the standards for carrying out and monitoring investment plans.

The **National Potable Water and Sewerage Program (PRONAP)**, an agency under the Ministry of the Presidency, evaluates improvement projects and guides strategic planning for expanding service coverage. It also carries out investment programs for improving and extending them. PRONAP was created to solicit and utilize foreign credit (like that received from the multilateral banks) to carry out the Basic Water Sector Support Program in order to make the water companies financially viable and reorganize the institutional arrangement of the sector.[8]

Service Provider Companies (*Empresas Prestadoras de Servicios*—EPS) are classified according to the number of connections they handle: the largest EPS (over 10,000 connections) will be set up as corporations and smaller EPS (under 10,000 connections but no less than 1,000) will be made limited liability companies. According to the General Law on Water Services, EPS receive the concession rights from municipalities. Thus, when there is a municipal EPS in a province, it acquires the operating rights and the provincial and dis-

---

[8] In September 1996, PRONAP's purpose was changed so that it would direct the operation of the Program of Support for Basic Water Services (PASSB) and the Waste Water Management Program for Greater Lima (PROMAR). Aspects of PASSB include aiding in the legal reorganization of this sector; making the water companies financially viable; creating a portfolio of projects for extending water services for Phase Two of the PASSB; and potentially taking charge of the water services that the government might entrust to it.

trict mayors decide the makeup of its board. The votes are distributed according to the number of existing connections. However, the composition of the EPS boards poses incentive problems. Mayors in high coverage districts have no incentive to carry out investment programs to expand to districts with low coverage because their relative power would be reduced.

The **National Fund for Housing** (*Fondo Nacional de Vivienda—* FONAVI) was created in 1979 to handle the housing needs of those paying into the fund and to finance construction of basic services (potable water, sewerage, electricity). After June 1992, changes were introduced allowing FONAVI funds to be handled by the Ministry of the Presidency with the idea that it would gradually deal with the housing needs of the poorest people. That was to be attained through financing water infrastructure, electrification of settlements, development of slum clearance projects, and so forth, in both urban and rural areas. Currently, financing for the fund comes from only the employer's portion of the contribution, which is equivalent to 9 percent of the firm's wage bill.[9] Resources have been directed primarily to financing public sector infrastructure and to EPSs. The water sector has received the largest share. Programs to rehabilitate water-related infrastructure represented 53 percent of total funding, 73 percent of which was spent in the provinces.

The **National Compensation and Social Development Fund** (*Fondo Nacional de Compensación y Desarrollo Social—*FONCODES) is a decentralized agency under the Ministry of the Presidency responsible for implementing part of the government's social policy with emphasis on areas of poverty and extreme poverty. The central government supplies most funds for FONCODES, although it also receives assistance from multilateral agencies such as the IDB and the World Bank for the water sector.

In tandem with these developments, in 1996 the legislative agenda included discussion of the new Water Law, which has, however, been set aside. The purpose of the bill was to establish legal norms for the use and conservation of water. If approved, this law would grant exclusive water use rights, thereby breaking the pattern of priorities established and managed by the

---

[9] As of January 1997, the tax rate was lowered to 7 percent. FONAVI coverage was also extended to self-employed workers and imposed on 14 pay periods (12 months and two bonuses). These changes went into effect in 1997. The net effect would be a slight increase in resources available to the government because it would increase both the number of payments affected and the number of contributors.

state since 1969.[10] The bill would make it possible to purchase water rights of many kinds: for consumption or other uses, and for permanent or intermittent use. These rights can be obtained by petition, provided water is available and a minimum supply is maintained for safeguarding the environment and the quality of life of cities and people. Initially, rights would be allocated on the basis of volumes utilized by the current users who benefited under the law. Once this allocation has been made, those who have title to rights may freely dispose of them or buy new ones at prices set by the market. Thus, a water company facing growing demand may buy water rights from other holders, without necessarily having to deal with the political problem of asking the state to change water allocations. Rights to new surface water may also be obtained without placing them on public auction or recording them in the registry of water rights. To search for underground water, the company must first carry out exploration and then request the Water Authority to issue the right. In this case, those holding water rights must pay a fee proportional to the volume of water used, to safeguard the operation and maintenance of the system.

This reform constitutes a very important change in the way the water sector is organized in Peru. Its three most important features are the promotion of private investment in infrastructure, the linking of long-term marginal costs to water rate reform, and the creation of a specialized regulatory body, SUNASS. SUNASS was the major contribution of the General Law on Water Services, but it was created with serious weaknesses because it is under the Ministry of the Presidency. Furthermore, it functions both as a regulatory body and as a participant in investment programs by controlling approval and oversight. The participation of SUNASS in designing and approving investment plans (master plans envisioned in legislation) and the involvement of agencies under the Ministry of the Presidency (PRONAP) create a duplication of functions relating to the EPSs, which impacts negatively on the organization and efficiency of the sector. Moreover, the Ministry of the Presidency, through aid programs carried out by FONCODES, performs work that falls within the scope of the EPSs, without the necessary coordination. Furthermore, FONAVI grants credit directly to people in poor neighborhoods for

---

[10] This has to do with changes made in the 1993 Constitution that relate to the granting of concessions for natural resources. It supplies a constitutional basis for granting rights of exploitation and consumption to the concessionaire.

water-related investments, connecting users to the existing distribution networks in the EPSs, sometimes without the safeguards necessary to assure the systems remain technically and economically sustainable.

Changes in the way water is priced start with the natural resource itself. The creation of a water market will impact water companies significantly in terms of their access to this basic input. Since EPSs are not currently charged for water, and water rights cannot be traded, the opportunity cost of water is not incorporated in the final price to consumers. However, with the reform, the key input, potable water, will have an explicit price, and as a production cost, will be incorporated into the rate to the final user; that is not what happens now.

Second, this explicit price will affect investment decisions by creating incentives to increase the ratio of water billed to water treated by reducing water loss. Third, by clarifying property rights and water use rights, it is hoped there will be greater investment in projects to develop new sources. Fourth, while the bill does not explicitly mention watercourses as dumping grounds, it does contain specific legal language prohibiting any change in the quality of surface and underground waters to the detriment of human health, flora and fauna, as well as damage to third parties. In addition, in the case of nonconsumption rights, substitution of lower quality water or changes in normal runoff conditions require compensation to those affected along with applying sanctions, if called for.

An overall analysis of the various institutions involved in the water sector shows that even in 1996, functions, authorities, and responsibilities continued to overlap. Clearly, there is a need for greater order in the sector, especially in encouraging investment, financing, and oversight. Moreover, by postponing the debate on the new water law and other measures to be spelled out in the following pages, the government shows that it does not intend to move forward in reforming the sector.

Industry Performance

Collapse of Centralization

Under the populist program of the administration of Alan García Pérez from 1985 to 1990, water rates were frozen while inflation was accelerating; hence, water rates fell continually in real terms. In some companies, rates fell by

Figure 3.1
Investment in Water Sector
(Current US$ per 1,000 connections)

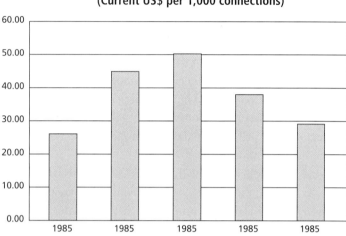

Source: PRONAP

more than 50 percent in real terms. During this period, service quality declined (with falling pressure and rationing, especially in Lima and Cuzco),
maintenance expenditures dropped, and investment fell to the point where
the ability of companies to serve new users was compromised (Figure 3.1).

Policies to cut financial losses contributed to low investment levels
and a growing share of labor costs in expenditures.[11] Between 1985 and 1990,
investment was no more than US$ 80 on average for every 1,000 connec-
tions, and fell to US$18.50 in the final year.[12] Given Peru's moratorium on
the foreign debt and its international financial isolation, investment was limited to domestic resources, which became increasingly scarce as the economic crisis deepened. Government investment in water services in 1989–
90 fell by more than 60 percent from the levels of 1985–88. Hence, the major

---

[11] In some companies for which information is available (SEDAPAL, SEDAQOSQO, and
SEDAPIURA), expenditures on employees were over 50 percent of total expenditures. (Editor's
Note: This is compared to an average of 30 percent to 40 percent in Argentina and only 20
percent in the United States—despite higher wages. See Chapter 1).
[12] In some particular companies, annual investment was less than US$ 5 for every 1,000
connections.

Table 3.4 Water and Sewerage Services by Type of Service

Services	National	
	1981	1993
Type of Water Supply		
Number of Homes	3,257,124	4,427,517
Public Network[1]	49.2%	57.4%
Private Provision[2]	19.5%	16.8%
Other[3]	31.4%	25.9%
	100.0%	100.0%
Type of Sewerage Services		
Number of Homes	3,257,124	4,427,517
Public Network[4]	35.0%	40.0%
Private Service[5]	9.1%	20.5%
Other[6]	0.0%	1.7%
Without Service	55.9%	37.8%
	100.0%	100.0%

Notes:

1/ Supplied by public network, whether inside the home or outside (e.g., public standpipe).

2/ Supplied by well, truck, cistern, etc.

3/ Supplied from rivers, streams, irrigation, etc.

4/ Public sewerage network connection whether inside or outside the home (e.g., shared toilet facilities).

5/ Septic systems.

6/ Direct discharge into streams or canals.

Source: INEI—Censos Nacionales 1981, 1993.

investment plans for supplying water to Lima, advocated by studies made since the early 1980s, were postponed.

Survey statistics (Table 3.4) show that the public system did not expand enough to satisfy demand from consumers, who increasingly turned to private solutions, particularly for wastewater disposal. These private solutions doubled between 1981 and 1993 and a substantial disparity between urban and rural areas remained. About 7 percent of urban dwellings continued to receive water from traditional sources (e.g., rivers) in 1993. In the rural area, the figure rose to 67 percent of dwellings. The disparity is also evident in the population without sewerage service: 21 percent of dwellings in urban areas and 75 percent in rural areas.[13]

Paradoxically, the government that so politicized potable water and sewerage rates in a highly centralized administration created a decentralized structure by transferring companies to local government. The explanation for this apparent anomaly is political.

Facing imminent electoral defeat in the presidential election, APRA sought an additional political base at the local level to increase its bargaining power with the incoming administration, which was expected to have only a minority in congress and was not strongly organized at the national level.[14] Thus, APRA aimed to transfer decision making and control from the central body to the most important local political actors, where APRA traditionally had a representative force due to its nationwide organizing capability. The same step was not taken with regard to other public utilities like electricity or telecommunications for two reasons.

First, the legislation on municipalities included responsibility for sewerage services, while authority for other economic activities was divided between regional governments and the central government. Second, as the analytical framework shows, the local nature of sewerage services differentiates

---

[13] In some companies, particularly SEDAPAL, it was apparent that expansion was higher among commercial and industrial customers. This reflected the relatively greater incentives for serving them compared to residential clients, namely higher rates, higher average consumption, and lower monitoring costs.

[14] As a result of the heightened economic crisis after 1987, people became increasingly discontented with the party in power, to the point that APRA's national share of the vote fell to 15 percent in the 1989 municipal elections. In the 1990 election campaign no candidate was expected to win the presidency without a second round of voting which would entail negotiating and forming alliances. The results of the first round showed that, as anticipated, the winner did not have an absolute majority and, that no political group had a majority in the legislature. Since the APRA candidate came in third in the national vote, he was eliminated from the second round. APRA's margin for negotiation was the result of its representation in congress with 16 senators of a total of 60, and 53 deputies of a total of 180. In both cases, APRA's representatives outnumbered those of the political organization of Alberto Fujimori, who was in second place and would eventually be elected president. The upshot was that the party leaving power gained greater relative importance in view of the apparent need of the new head of state to negotiate with other political groups.

it from other public services, which are structured as systems with nation-wide coverage. Hence, while at first glance the transfer may look like a political process coming from the outside, actually the aim was to transfer decision-making power on further development of the service to the local level, where the decisions of directly involved actors become more important.

Recovery of Investment

Since 1991, investment in water service in Peru has recovered rapidly from the low levels of the previous government to 0.5 percent of GDP between 1994 and 1995,[15] even though the private sector is not directly involved in providing the service (Table 3.5).

Investment has recovered in recent years for two reasons. First, as relations with foreign creditors and multilateral agencies have improved, funds from the IDB and the World Bank have become available for rural projects through FONCODES and for work undertaken by SEDAPAL and PRONAP to help the municipal companies. Secondly, FONAVI has become a new and significant source of investment funds. On average, FONAVI financed around 50 percent of all investment in the sector, mainly through loans granted to organized neighborhood groups and in some cases by directly financing investment by water companies.

Once the former are connected to the public water or sewerage system, responsibility for recovering the loan passes to municipal companies through extra charges on the bill for service.

The previous section offered a breakdown of the composition of FONAVI resources, defined as a variable percentage of wage costs. Hence, the most significant source of financing in the sector is in the form of an earmarked tax, although current legislation does not classify it as such.

FONAVI has been able to assume this role as a major investor because of its special status under current legislation, which regards the payroll "contribution" as revenue belonging to FONAVI. Therefore, these funds do not enter into the accounts of the public treasury and since they are not part of the fiscal budget, they do not require prior approval from Congress for program spending and are not subject to congressional review. Moreover, un-

---

[15] If GDP is corrected for suspected overestimation, the figure rises to around 0.7 percent.

Table 3.5 Water Sector Investments by Institutions: 1985–1995 (Current US$ Millions)

Institutions	1985	1986	1987	1988	1989	1990	1991	1992	1993	1994	1995
I. Central Government	2	6	7	3	3	1	1	13	30	26	50
II. Regional/Local Governments	14	22	12	10	5	5	5	9	24	24	10
FONAVI Credits	0	0	0	0	0	0	0	8	18	16	2
III. Water Companies	13	24	42	34	30	16	42	61	84	80	65
IV. Consumer Investment Financed by FONAVI	0	0	0	0	0	0	0	24	105	160	110
V. Other	0	0	0	1	1	1	1	1	2	2	3
Total	29	52	61	48	39	23	49	109	245	292	238
Total FONAVI Financing	0	0	0	0	0	0	0	33	123	176	112
Share of FONAVI	0%	0%	0%	0%	0%	0%	0%	30%	50%	60%	47%

Source: PRONAP

like other government funds, they can be used with broad discretion. FONAVI very quickly adapts to demands for greater spending when the economic and political cycle calls upon it, as was the case during the 1994 presidential campaign.

Nevertheless, it is questionable whether these resources will remain available over the medium term since they come from a percentage charge on employee payrolls paid by employers.[16] FONAVI effectively operates as a tax on hiring labor in the formal sector, and constitutes a constraint on formal employment and an incentive to informal employment. For this reason, FONAVI's revenue may be affected by the debate regarding Peru's loss of competitiveness at a time when the exchange rate is appreciating, or on the FONAVI contribution's character as a nonlegislated labor tax. Hence, from the standpoint of economic analysis, it is difficult to justify the existence of FONAVI. However, the greater emphasis given it in recent years has led to a response that is "optimal" for the context of political and economic decisions about managing water industry activities.[17] Whether it can be sustained as the main funding source for maintaining investment levels in this sector is open to question.

FONAVI is used to resolve conflicts over redistribution. FONAVI funds serve a number of actors: consumers, who enter the public system with financing they receive through the institution; building contractors (although not as much as they hoped for);[18] municipal companies that have access to funding;[19] and the government, which reaps substantial political returns in low-income sectors. The main ones who suffer are formal companies that bear the burden of payment, although they transfer it to workers. But workers do not necessarily recognize that excessive labor costs (primarily FONAVI) contribute to the serious unemployment problem in Peru. The importance of financing for the water industry through wage-related charges must be understood in two interrelated ways:

---

[16] In previous years, both employer and employee contributed.

[17] FONAVI—funded projects are usually presented to the beneficiaries through ads or billboards, as having been provided by the Ministry of the Presidency. This leads people to think the government is directly financing such projects.

[18] Funds are allocated through small-scale loans distributed nationally.

[19] Nevertheless, the company must collect on the loans, thereby transferring the problem of delinquency.

First, from the traditional centralized institutional arrangement, the government has always been heavily involved in providing the service and financing its expansion, and water rates have been set without reference to economic criteria. Moreover, not long ago the high degree of politicization in water rates led to the collapse of the centralized system, which was blamed in the 1990s for the low pace of water service expansion and for the complete halt of investment in sewerage. Since its creation as a payroll charge, FONAVI was expected to finance the expansion of service to low-income populations. It reached its greatest growth, relative importance, and discretionary power as a consequence of the changes implemented in 1992. If it has a rationale for existing, it is as an alternative to financing expansion by raising taxes or water rates, which would probably have been more costly in political terms. Its extensive use in recent years reflects this experience.

Second, given the government's incentives and its budgetary constraints in the next few years, FONAVI's administrative advantages give the government a greater degree of discretionary power in using these public funds. This money is especially vulnerable to political cycles when the government can capitalize on the political returns from investments made with those resources. Such advantages explain in part why the government has sought to increase the number of contributors while the private sector logically seeks to avoid paying.

This discretionary power in the use of public resources makes it possible to continue subsidizing the supply of water services by increasing investment, which acts as a brake on real reform and on private sector involvement in providing service by resolving problems superficially. FONAVI investments helped to halt privatization of the country's most important water company and the one most attractive to the private sector by resolving short-term water shortages. Moreover, the continuation of that wage-benefit expense weakens the country's competitiveness, and jeopardizes the sustainability of expanded investment in the sector. Yet FONAVI funds have made it possible to extend coverage by increasing investment and production without much impact on real water rates.

Relative Performance in the Short Run

In the short period of municipal experience in potable water and sewerage services, SEDAPAL (as a company under the central government) has per-

Table 3.6 Principle Characteristics of Three Water Companies: 1995

Firms	Water Connections (Thousands)	Covered Population (Thousands)	Production (1,000m3)	Total Assets (US$1,000)	Net Revenues (US$1,000)
SEDAPAL	791	6,563	663,664	835,387	151,992
SEDAPIURA	130	613	60,030*	33,446	18,616
SULLANA Office	29	170	14,503*	—	—
SEDAQOSQO	29	250	15,888	18,847*	4,076*

Figures for 1994

Sources: SEDAPAL, SEDAPIURA, SEDAQOSQO.

formed qualitatively better than a sampling of municipal companies, which have been influenced politically by their mayors. When seen on the national level, however, the results are uneven. One explanation is that SEDAPAL has made agreements with the World Bank as part of the privatization process. These agreements provided incentives to improve management, thus confirming the importance of having a third party involved in contractual processes that affect performance. Still, the agreements alone would have been insufficient to deal with issues related to water services for Greater Lima. For this, the support of top political and economic officials, especially the involvement of President Fujimori, was needed.

The performance of the three water companies, which differ in size and geographic location, makes it possible to identify certain common features in their short-term behavior, as well as significant differences. SEDAPAL supplies Greater Lima and is controlled by the central government. Management of SULLANA, which is part of SEDAPIURA (the second largest municipal company in the country in terms of number of customers) is relatively comparable in market size to SEDAQOSQO, which is a municipally owned company and, unlike the other two, is located in the mountain highlands (Table 3.6).

The following features are critical to understanding the relative performance of the different companies.

Figure 3.2
Real Water Rates: SEDAPAL, SEDAQOSQO and SEDAPIURA—Sullana
(Constant 1995 US$ per m3)

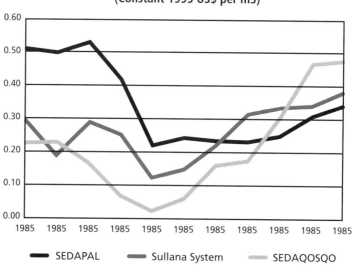

━━ SEDAPAL   ━━ Sullana System   ━━ SEDAQOSQO

Source: SEDAPAL, SEDAPIURA, SEDAQOSQO.

Water Rates. Water rates were quickly adjusted after 1990 as part of policies
aimed at restoring the financial stability of government companies and the
central government (Figure 3.2). At first, some municipal companies imposed readjustments that were larger than SEDAPAL.[20] That may have been
necessary to compensate for the loss of working capital because they lagged
behind the major adjustment in government prices in August 1990. However, in recent years it has become more apparent that rates are politicized at
the local level,[21] although far less than they were in the preceding five-year
period.

---

[20] By 1995, the average SEDAPAL rate had rebounded 53 percent from the low reached in
1989, although it was still below that of 1985.

[21] Experiences in Piura show that as municipal elections drew near, mayors were sensitive to
pressure from the people and overturned water rate adjustments in response to popular opposition. Indeed in Sullana, the mayor took the side of the people in poor neighborhoods
over the rate increase set by the company. In Urubamba, in the province of Cuzco, the mayor
opposed meter installation during the election campaign and supported the idea that water
ought to be free.

Table 3.7 Relative Water Rates by Consumer Type: 1985–1995

Firms	1985–1987	1988–1990	1991–1992	1993–1995
SEDAPAL				
Commercial/Residential	2.1	2.8	4.4	3.7
Industrial/Residential	2.7	2.8	4.4	3.7
SEDAPIURA—Sistema Sullana				
Commercial/Residential	2.0	2.2	3.2	3.9
Industrial/Residential	2.8	2.6	2.1	2.5
SEDAQOSQO				
Commercial/Residential	1.6	1.5	2.5	3.0
Industrial/Residential	2.4	2.3	3.8	5.3

Sources: SEDAPAL, SEDAPIURA, SEDAQOSQO.

Table 3.8 Water Company Investments: 1985–1995
(Constant 1995 US$ per 1,000 connections)

Year	National	SEDAPAL	SEDAPIURA	SEDAQOSQO
1985	68.9	48.6	106.9	2.6
1986	104.2	32.3	75.2	0.3
1987	135.2	21.0	39.0	n.d.
1988	101.2	18.9	18.5	n.d.
1989	48.6	29.1	3.2	0.0
1990	18.5	43.3	17.1	1.6
1991	36.1	25.4	3.5	14.6
1992	82.7	24.7	40.2	102.5
1993	185.2	16.1	20.7	70.9
1994	229.2	13.8	43.6	177.1
1995	n.d.	20.7	n.d.	n.d.

Sources: SEDAPAL, SEDAPIURA, SEDAQOSQO:

The rise in the average rate for municipal companies was attained by increasing cross-subsidies from industrial and commercial to residential consumers between 1990 and 1995 (Table 3.7). This strategy reflects the incentives generated by limited metering, easy monitoring of costs of high consumption customers, and the importance of consumers as potential voters.

Table 3.9 Billing and Water Losses: 1985–1995
(As share of volume produced)

Years	SEDAPAL		SULLANA		SEDAQOSQO	
	Billing	Water Losses	Billing	Water Losses	Billing	Water Losses
1985–1987	48.5%	51.5%	62.0%	38.0%	50.6%	49.4%
1988–1990	57.1%	42.9%	60.9%	39.1%	60.8%	39.2%
1991–1992	65.7%	34.3%	47.4%	52.6%	64.9%	35.1%
1993–1995	61.9%	38.1%	44.9%	55.1%	50.8%	49.2%

Sources: SEDAPIURA, SEDAQOSQO.

Investment. National investment in water services has recovered, reaching US$ 229 per thousand connections in 1994, which represents a more than 1,000 percent rise over the low 1990 level (Table 3.8). Nevertheless, the investment pattern across companies is uneven and depends primarily on the availability of external funding, whether in the form of government-backed foreign borrowing or funds from other government bodies. Here, the degree of leadership exercised by mayors seems to have been important.

As a result of this rebound in investment, a new expansion phase is underway, particularly in the case of SEDAPAL. A similar drive to expand coverage is evident in the Cuzco and Piura companies.

Production: Companies raised production during the 1990–1995 period. However, the combination of limited metering, the absence of effective micro- and macrometering, and the extensive practice of charging by "assumed" monthly consumption, led to a paradox—while municipal companies increased production over 15 percent and increased water rates, billing declined by 10 percent to 20 percent indicating higher water losses (Table 3.9)

Management: Excessive staffing has been a key contributor to inefficiency yet staff reduction policies have operated differently in these three cases. SEDAPAL rapidly cut back its staffing to 2.1 workers for every thousand connections in 1995, which is near the level considered acceptable for companies of its size (Table 3.10). The municipal companies, by contrast, have been timid about

Table 3.10 Employees per 1,000 Connections: 1985–1995

Year	SEDAPAL	SEDAPIURA	Sullana System	SEDAQOSQO
1985	6.4	10.9	5.6	n.d.
1986	6.4	n.d.	n.d.	n.d.
1987	6.3	n.d.	n.d.	n.d.
1988	6.2	n.d.	n.d.	n.d.
1989	5.7	9.3	5.5	6.9
1990	5.3	8.9	n.d.	7.2
1991	4.7	7.1	n.d.	8.1
1992	3.5	6.7	n.d.	7.2
1993	2.6	6.5	3.7	7.5
1994	2.5	7.5	3.7	6.7
1995	2.1	n.d.	4.4	5.7

Sources: SEDAPAL, SEDAPIURA, SEDAQOSQO.

trimming excess staff. In 1995, Cuzco still had around 5.7 workers per thousand connections (although it cut the payroll burden to around 28 percent of current expenditures); for Sullana, the figure was around 4 and at SEDAPIURA it was around 7. Despite these high staffing levels, the municipal water companies do not necessarily have the people with the qualifications and skills they require. In some cases, there is a high turnover rate among top management due to politicization at the local level. In other cases, low salaries and inadequate pay scales make it impossible to attract qualified professionals.

The poor financial results of the municipal companies indicate that rate increases, greater production, and more connections have not led to improved efficiency and profitability. Some of this poor performance is due to physical water losses, but a large share is due to commercial losses. In some cases, delinquency has risen dramatically. In contrast, SEDAPAL has reduced delinquency substantially, from 30 percent in 1990 to around 10 percent at the close of 1995, in accordance with what had been agreed upon with the World Bank (Table 3.11). Even with rate adjustments below those in some municipal companies, commercial and financial results for SEDAPAL were generally superior.

Five years after transfer to municipal authority, major organizational and institutional weaknesses are apparent in some of the municipal compa-

Table 3.11 Financial Indicators by Water Company: 1985–1995

Ratios	1985–1987	1988–1990	1991–1992	1993–1994
SEDAPAL				
Collection Ratio	76	97	94	75
Liquidity: Acid Test	1.53	0.32	0.72	0.78
Current Liquidity	1.69	0.35	0.8	0.86
Cash Ratio	0.49	0.03	0.07	0.18
Return on Sales	−0.29	−2.22	−0.22	0.17
Return on Equity	−0.02	−0.1	−0.04	0.06
SEDAPIURA				
Collection Ratio	87	80	102	172
Liquidity: Acid Test	0.85	1.62	1.51	1.6
Current Liquidity	0.98	1.92	1.8	2.31
Cash Ratio	0.35	0.44	0.49	0.06
Return on Sales	−0.08	−0.2	0.08	−0.03
Return on Equity	−0.06	−0.08	0.04	−0.03
SEDAQOSQO				
Collection Ratio	116	173	89	128
Liquidity: Acid Test	3.37	2.58	2.31	3.35
Current Liquidity	4.34	2.81	2.57	4.31
Cash Ratio	0.89	0.24	0.71	1.55
Return on Sales	0.14	−0.32	0.24	0.16
Return on Equity	0.04	−0.02	0.11	0.06

Note: Years are not exact and depend upon availability of data. For details, see Tamayo, et al., 1997, Table 3.11.

METHODOLOGY

Collection Rate = 360* (Commercial Accounts Receivable / Total Operational Income)

Liquidity: Acid Test = (Total Current Assets—Inventoriers—Prepaid Expenses) / Total Current Liabilties

Current Liquidity = Total Current Assets / Total Current Liabilities

Cash Ratio = (Cash in Bank + Marketable Securities) / Current Liabilities

Return on Equity = Net Earnings of Fiscal Year / Total Assets

Return on Sales = Net Rate of Return of Fiscal Year / Total Net Sales

Creditworthiness = Total Liability / Total Assets

Sources: SEDAPAL, SEDAPIURA, SEDAQOSQO.

nies. These weaknesses are a legacy from the previous administration that have not been resolved. In most cases, the companies do not have up-to-date systems for registering customers or for connecting the billing and collection systems. They suffer from poor maintenance of meters and neglect of micrometering, and they are unable to attract qualified personnel. In this sense, there is a danger that the municipal companies will fall back into a low-level equilibrium in which local level political constraints prevail over expanding service.

While it has been impossible to control for the effects of variables such as scale of operation, staff notifications, or political support by the central government, it is clear that since the institutional changes of 1990—and specifically since 1993—SEDEPAL's institutional performance has improved significantly over that of selected municipal companies. This superb performance, however, can be largely attributed to the agreements and conditions accepted by the company as it prepared for privatization. One condition was to include SEDAPAL in the process of privatizing government companies that was part of the opening to private investment in infrastructure. Also, the government had to invite specialized companies to participate in the process as a demonstration of its political will to introduce changes in the supply of public services in Greater Lima. Built into the agreement, as a necessary condition, was the design of a privatization strategy linked to a World Bank loan to upgrade infrastructure in order to make SEDAPAL more attractive to the private sector. Thus, the loan negotiations established incentives for the company and the government together to adjust prices, rationalize staffing, and improve trade policy. However, the commitments signed by the company would not have been sufficient by themselves to assure improved company efficiency had there not been a political commitment on the part of the country's highest officials. By late 1994, SEDAPAL had met most of the requirements set by the World Bank, and approval was given to the US\$ 300 million loan operation for the privatization program and the beginning of a major program for upgrading infrastructure in Greater Lima.

It is likely that if SEDAPAL had not been included in the privatization program sponsored by the World Bank, less progress would have been made. And, since the company's charges were not institutionalized, it is reasonable to expect that once the World Bank's involvement in the company concludes, the efficiency gains may be lost. Experience with the water industry suggests there is a danger the company will be politicized in the future, lowering the profitability of the resources invested.

Privatization Interrupted by Politics

Since 1990, Peru has undergone a structural reform program designed to reestablish macroeconomic equilibrium and make the economy more efficient. As part of that program, the state was to withdraw from directly conducting economic activities that could be performed by the private sector—including water service.

The involvement of the private sector in potable water and sewerage began in 1991, when SEDAPAL was brought into the privatization program being applied by the new government and private investors could legally request municipalities to grant them concessions for such services. In accordance with the privatization strategy, a special committee was charged with administering the process at SEDEPAL. In mid-1993, with guidance from the World Bank, consulting studies were carried out, leading to the recommendation that the best alternative for the company would be a long-term concession to private operators. The main reasons for this choice relate to the deteriorated condition of SEDAPAL's infrastructure, the consequence of inadequate investment in years past, that would require a large infusion of new capital managed efficiently. This strategy was politically risky because the large investment requirements, high sunk costs, and exposure to risk meant that private investors would need to choose very high water rates.

A bidding process was initiated among specialized operators. To compete, companies had to have a minimum billing of US$ 180 million and a net worth of over US$ 750 million; they also had to be responsible for serving urban regions of at least four million inhabitants. The manner chosen was prior negotiation of a contract with selected operators (at that time three consortia headed by Lyonnaise des Eaux, Compagnie Generales des Eaux, and Canal de Isabel II). Obligations and responsibilities were defined for a 30-year concession, in which asset ownership remained with SEDAPAL as the concession-granting entity. The contract set goals of service quality and a "price cap" mechanism for regulating rates, with five-year horizons for revising it. The operator was to be selected by public auction, and the bidder offering the lowest rate would be the winner.

The privatization arrangement, prepared under World Bank guidance, envisioned prior signing of a US$ 300 million loan agreement, which was part of a US$ 600 million infrastructure rehabilitation strategy, jointly financed by the company itself, the OECF in Japan, and FONAVI (which had close to a 20 percent share in the project). The program, designed by SEDEPAL and the World Bank, envisioned a five-year period for significantly upgrading potable water and sewerage systems in Greater Lima, and expanding service to low-income areas through greater use of micrometering in high consumption areas, as well as tapping into new water sources.

The World Bank conditioned approval of the loan on improved efficiency in SEDAPAL. The conditions included the following measures:

1) Rationalization of staffing. By the end of 1995, there had to be 2.5 workers per 1,000 connections, and the figure had to drop to 2.0 by the year 2000.

2) Rate increases. Water rates had to rise to meet long-term marginal costs, and were to be regulated by SUNASS.

3) Improved management. During the transition to privatization, the company had to meet certain targets, including greater liquidity and reassessment of assets.

4) Service coverage would increase so that 90 percent of the population would have access to service by the year 2005.

These conditions were linked to preparing the company for privatization. Disbursement of the loan was not made conditional on actually carrying out the auction, but instead on meeting the management goals. Should the privatization be successful, the funds were to be transferred to the winning consortium with the added possibility of a second loan.

Prequalification of bidders and the defining of the concession contract with interested operators was planned for 1994, and the transfer was to be completed six months prior to the general elections scheduled for the first half of 1995. That entailed a significant wager against the electoral calendar since it opened the possibility that during the contest for power, the populace could be convinced to resist the transfer of the company. The auction was, in fact, delayed; and in the months following the reelection of President Fujimori by a wide majority, the government gradually lost interest in carrying out the privatization.

Presumably, privatization of SEDAPAL has been postponed indefinitely since it was not mentioned in the Letter of Intent signed by Peru with the International Monetary Fund setting the policy goals for 1996 through 1998. Subsequent government announcements have confirmed that the government has decided to keep the company in the government domain. Meanwhile, SEDAPAL is executing the investment program to which it is bound by agreement with the World Bank, and the results are expected around 1999—the eve of another election in the year 2000. SEDAPAL's fate will therefore continue to be tied to the political cycle, especially since a legal change has allowed Fujimori to be reelected again should he choose to run.

While the Ministry of the Economy and Finance was an active defender and promoter of the privatization process[22], important economic officials have become less supportive. Given the characteristics of the transfer mechanism envisioned for this company, their behavior may reflect the lack of incentives for insisting on the reform. Contrary to other privatizations, the sale of SEDAPAL would not have generated fresh resources to build up international reserves. Similarly, it does not provide funds that can be registered as short-term earnings resulting from a concession to the private sector, as is common with other privatizations.

All this suggests that politics is to blame for the postponement of SEDAPAL's privatization[23], and the same thing is expected to happen around the year 2000. Simply put, the expansion of service carries too heavy an electoral burden. Moreover, the public behavior of key government officials and their efforts to seek financing to increase investment in water services suggest that politically speaking, it is preferable to maintain government investment in this sector. That impression is reinforced by the lack of clarity about restarting the privatization process.[24] The decision to keep the company within the public domain is made easier because, according to the agree-

---

[22] The explanation is that resources from privatization would have financed the buildup of international reserves at a time of growing deficits in the balance of payments current account.

[23] It also delayed other privatizations, particularly in the oil industry, around which there was much discussion even after the election was over. In this case, however, the privatization process has resumed once again.

[24] No replacement has yet been found for the president of the privatization team who resigned two years ago. Informally it has been reported that candidates willing to speed up the process encountered opposition in the government.

ment with the World Bank, the agreed upon loan[25]cannot be suspended on the basis of that decision. In fact, the loan continues to make funds available for financing much of the planned rehabilitation program.[26]

Finally, this indefinite postponement has a significant demonstration effect on the treatment of private investment in municipal water services companies. Even though there is private sector interest in this sector, the government will have a hard time encouraging the transfer of municipal companies to the private sector when market size makes it more attractive for the main international operators to be involved in supplying Greater Lima. Moreover, given the country's weak institutional endowment and the process of improving credibility, private investment at the municipal level requires guarantees in the areas of taxes and exchange rates, for example, which are the responsibility of the central, not local, government.

Institutional Endowment and Limits to Private Participation

To better understand the process of promoting private sector participation in the water sector, it must be analyzed relative to other public utilities.[27] In the early 1990s, laws were passed eliminating the state monopoly in such activities, allowing private sector participation and seeking to promote competition. At the same time, regulatory frameworks and specialized bodies to oversee activities with natural monopoly features were established.

In the case of telephone service, due to poor performance indicators when the restructuring process began, a scheme was chosen that defined different market segments associated with different market structures. For basic phone and long distance service, a five-year monopoly was set up to take advantage of economies of scale since there were very few lines (2.9 phones per 100 inhabitants in 1994). In implementing this arrangement, stock packages and control over the two state companies were sold to a

---

[25] This is probably the only area where the government has departed substantially from the structural reform objectives encouraged by multilateral agencies.

[26] The World Bank did not anticipate the possibility that the government might move away from privatizing SEDAPAL because it overestimated the government's commitment to reforming this sector and its ability to influence it.

[27] For a discussion of the main features of the legislation governing reform of the water industry as part of the public utility modernization process, see Tamayo et al. (1997).

Table 3.12 Main Characteristics of Water Section Companies: EPSs (As of May 1996)

Companies[1]	Department	Annual Potable Water Production (In thous. of m3)	Water Losses%	Connections[2] Potable Water	Sewerage	Coverage[2] Potable Water	Sewerage	Macrometering Meters[2]
1 SEDAPAL	Lima	663,664	36	806,884		75		20
2 SEDAPAR	Arequipa	38,920	44	132,071	112,149	84	64*	77
3 SEDAPIURA	Piura	68,568	55	130,329	92,170	81	61	10
4 SEDALIB	La Libertad		30	117,456	80,771	80	72*	81
5 EMAPAL	Lambayeque	35,009	28	88,791	70,851	80	65	24
6 SEDACHIMBOTE	Ancash	23,433	52	48,151	40,659	72	70	5
7 EMAPA (Tacna)	Tacna	11,781		39,424	35,633	89	84	39
8 SEDALORETO	Loreto	3,626	47	39,417	24,700	67	49	36
9 EMAPICA S.A.	Ica		45	30,988	20,800	80	70*	0
10 SEDAQOSQO	Cuzco	14,289	43	29,294	16,475	55	43*	77
11 EMAPA SAN MARTÍN	San Martín	12,794	40	22,741	14,127	74	55	43
12 SEMAPACH S.A.	Ica	10,771		22,610	10,110	75	32	n.d.
13 EMAPATUMBES	Tumbes	9,076	48	21,930	6,903	71	25	26
14 EMAPA (Ayacucho)	Ayacucho	13,284	60	19,951	11,751	73	48	20
15 SEDAHUANUCO	Huánuco	15,023	57	17,993	8,875	58	28	56
16 SEDAJULIACA	Puno	4,305	45	16,984	15,263	52	51	23
17 EMSA PUNO S.A.	Puno	5,777	51	16,720	11,912	72	52	45
18 EMAPA CAÑETE S.A.	Lima	9,377	54	14,471	11,734	62	47*	43
19 SEMDACAJ S.A.	Cajamarca	5,948	25	14,406	12,124	70	55	72
20 EPS SELVA CENTRAL S.A.	Junin—Cerro de Pasco			13,889				
21 SEMAPA BARRANCA	Lima		52	13,726				0
22 EMAPA HUACHO	Lima		49	12,947				0
23 EMAPACOP	Pucallpa		35	12,635				0
24 EMAPISCO S.A.	Ica	4,673	50	12,246	9,610	80	66	2
25 EMAPASA (Huaraz)	Ancash		54	11,807	9,750	69	65*	65

Table 3.12 (continued)

Companies[1]	Department	Annual Potable Water Production (In thous. of m3)	Water Losses%	Connections[2]		Coverage[2]		Macro-metering
				Potable Water	Sewerage	Potable Water	Sewerage	Meters[2]
26 SEDAILO	Moquegua	3,971	45	8,548		64	57	86
27 EMAPA HUARAL	Lima		50	7,728				14
28 ESAMO	Moquegua	4,082	37	7,300		63	60	36
29 EMPSSAPAL S.A.	Cuzco			5,550				
30 EMAPA MOYOBAMBA	Amazonas	2,470	34	5,101		92	74	59
31 EMAPAVIGNA S.A.	Ica		25	4,162				3
32 EMAPA UTCUBAMBA	Amazonas	2,177		4,067		97	70	3
33 EMAQ S.A.	Cuzco			3,836				
34 SEMAPA HUANCAVELICA	Huancavelica		55	3,352				14
35 EMAPAT S.A.	Madre de Dios			3,325				n.d.
36 EMUSAP AMAZONAS S.A.	Amazonas	2,319	70	2,867	3,663	86	80	65
37 EMAPA BAGUA	Amazonas			2,500				
38 EMAPA YUNGUYO	Puno			2,056				
39 EMAPA JAEN—BELLAVISTA	Cajamarca	2,851	76	1,500		15	15	13
40 EMAPA PASCO S.A.	Cerro de Pasco	7,422	25	355		70	0	
41 EMUSAP ABANCAY	Abancay				0	60	0*	35
42 SEDAM Huancayo	Junín		25		27,606	83	58*	
NATIONAL AVERAGE			45	—	—	72	52	33

Notes:
1/ Recognized by SUNASS from February 22, 1995, to May 5, 1996.
2/ Information from SUNASS, except for those with asterisk (*). * Information from PRONAP.
Sources: SUNASS, PRONAP.

TABLE 3.13 Main Characteristics of Water Sector Companies: EPSs
(As of May 1996)

Companies[1]	Department	Population Served	Continuity of Service	Rate Level (S/.per m3)	Rate Level (US$ Per m3)[4, 5]	Net Earnings/ Net Worth
1 SEDAPAL	Lima	5,164,058	14		0.34	0.03
2 SEDAPAR	Arequipa	653,512	24	0.94*	0.39*	0.10
3 SEDAPIURA	Piura	635,962	18	1.42	0.59	
4 SEDALIB	La Libertad					0.09
5 EMAPAL	Lambayeque	523,153	8	1.21	0.50	−0.04
6 SEDACHIMBOTE	Ancash	240,755	8	0.93	0.39	0.39
7 EMAPA (Tacna)	Tacna	201,032	14	0.82	0.34	0.04
8 SEDALORET	Loreto	236,502	9	0.7	0.29	0.07
9 EMAPICA S.A.	Ica					0.01
10 SEDAQOSQO	Cuzco			1.6*	0.66*	0.06
11 PA SAN MARTÍN	San Martín	113,548	17	0.91	0.38	0.02
12 MAPACH S.A.	Ica	113,050	12	0.86	0.36	
13 APATUMBES	Tumbes	109,650	6	0.51	0.21	-0.37
14 APA (Ayacucho)	Ayacucho	90,445	10	0.7	0.29	
15 DAHUANUCO	Huánuco	110,945	23	0.74	0.31	0.02
16 DAJULIACA	Puno	84,920	12	0.37	0.15	−0.02
17 SA PUNO S.A.	Puno	83,600	10	0.94	0.39	−0.14
18 APA CAÑETE S.A.	Lima	72,355	22	1	0.41	0.11
19 MDACAJ S.A.	Cajamarca	72,031	24	0.89	0.37	0.20
20 S SELVA CENTRAL S.A.	Junin— Cerro de Pasco					
21 MAPA BARRANCA	Lima			0.275*	0.11*	0.12
22 APA HUACHO	Lima					
23 APACOP	Pucallpa			0.84*	0.35*	−0.08
24 APISCO S.A.	Ica	73,176	5	0.8	0.33	0.04
25 APASA (Huaraz)	Ancash					0.05
26 DAILO	Moquegua	39,049	8	1.97	0.82	0.03

TABLE 3.13 (continued)

Companies[1]	Department	Population Served	Continuity of Service	Rate Level (S/.per m3)	Rate Level (US$ Per m3)[4, 5]	Net Earnings/ Net Worth
27 APA HUARAL	Lima					0.03
28 AMO	Moquegua	32,850	10	0.71	0.29	
29 PSSAPAL[3] S.A.	Cuzco					
30 APA MOYOBAMBA	Amazonas	23,975	23	2.71	1.12	0.00
31 APAVIGNA S.A.	Ica			0.44		
32 APA UTCUBAMBA	Amazonas	20,335	18	1.05	0.44	
33 AQ S.A.	Cuzco					
34 MAPA HUANCAVELICA	Huancavelica					0.01
35 APAT S.A.	Madre de Dios					0.20
36 USAP AMAZONAS S.A.	Amazonas	14,500	18	1.09	0.45	−0.19
37 APA BAGUA	Amazonas					
38 APA YUNGUYO	Puno					
39 APA JAEN— BELLAVISTA	Cajamarca	9,000	24	0.6	0.25	
40 APA PASCO S.A.	Cerrode Pasco	31,820	5	2.75	1.14	0.01
41 USAP[2] ABANCAY				0.79*	0.33*	0.01
42 AM Huancayo[2]						
NATIONAL AVERAGE			14		0.43	0.00

Notes:

1/ Recognized by SUNASS from February 22, 1995, to May 9, 1996.

2/ Not recognized by SUNASS

3/ In process of receiving connections from other locations.

4/ As of May 1996 (1 US$ = S/. 2.41)

5/ Information from SUNASS, except that marked with asterisk (*) Information from PRONAP.

Sources: SUNASS, PRONAP.

suitably qualified operator. Likewise, the two companies could merge in order to take advantage of possible economies of a diversified supply of services. Before stock was sold, the regulatory body was established and the main regulations—such as the rate rebalancing program to eliminate cross-subsidies—were published. The existing duopoly was retained for analog cell phone service, and remaining services were allowed to develop under competition.

With regard to electric power, Peru followed the pattern widely adopted around the world (England and Chile are the best known cases) to separate the three activities of generation, transmission, and distribution, and establish different market structures for each activity. Since there is a natural monopoly associated with distribution, this activity is under a single concessionaire per area, except in Lima where the city has been divided into two. Thus far, distribution in the largest market, Greater Lima, has been privatized through the sale of majority stock packages in companies as well as in one small city. Power generation is open to free competition. The relatively larger generator plants (hydroelectric for the most part) are still being privatized, but progress has been made in the transfer of generators under 100 MW[28]. The transmission networks are another natural monopoly, but they are still in state hands.

With regard to water services, the legislation establishes that, with the exception of Greater Lima, provincial municipalities are to provide service, thereby retaining the local character of service provision. During the past few years, however, the central government has been investing more in this sector, even in the municipalities and usually without much coordination with municipal companies, in an effort to extend coverage in marginal areas as part of the government's poverty relief strategy. Successive statements by high-level officials, including the president, indicate the government's intention to maintain state investment in this sector.

Existing laws encourage the formation of municipal companies that hold a concession right once they have been set up and legally recognized.[29] Shareholders, as well as district and provincial mayors, are evidently unwill-

---

[28] One reason why this process is slow is the uncertainty caused by the lack of a law on granting real rights over water; such a law is still being discussed in the legislature.

[29] In 1995, 61 percent of rulings issued by SUNASS were for the purpose of granting such recognition.

ing to release their control over the companies in exchange for long-term
private sector involvement in the industry and high levels of independence
and responsibility.[30] Indeed, water rate policy has been politicized, especially during election periods, and consequently the ability to generate surpluses to finance investment in the companies has been limited. Hence, a
major portion of the companies' capital spending continues to come from
central government transfers to municipalities, FONAVI loans, and in some
companies, government-backed foreign loans. The financial situation of the
municipal companies does not allow them to finance major infrastructure
works. Furthermore, under decentralization it has been found that the delinquent customers of some municipal companies include some of their own
shareholders (municipalities) since there are no proper incentives at the local level to keep the system going.

Yet another factor is that ownership of the companies is spread among
provincial and district municipalities whose share of stock is proportional
to existing connections and who appoint the members of the board. As already noted, this power structure offers conflicting incentives to mayors:
those representing districts with low coverage struggle to get resources to
expand it, while those representing districts with high coverage struggle to
prevent expansion. A potential private investor would have to negotiate with
a good number of actors, who by their nature may have opposing political
interests, thereby raising the costs of consolidating private participation.

Current legislation for the utilities sectors reflects incompatibilities
between functions granted in different legislation for SUNASS, PRONAP,
the Ministry of Health, and other entities. In part, these incompatibilities
reflect a lack of coordination between the aims of the government and multilateral agencies in the area of reform. In terms of its role as regulator,
SUNASS' functions are to formulate technical standards, monitor companies, and approve the guidelines of the master plans of the companies to
control investment. One of its assigned functions, that of regulating and
promoting the industry, has been superimposed on those of PRONAP. Because the legislation encourages the formation of municipal companies, given
the current lack of human capital and institutional and organizational limi-

---

[30] Information derived through interviews with mayors, deputy mayors, and high-level officials
of the SEDAPIURA and SEDAQOSQO companies and the Sullana operating management.

tations, legally SUNASS must seek to make up for the planning and technical deficiencies of the municipal companies by acting as an external agent.
Such restrictions would not necessarily be present if there were private participation in the industry, because if SUNASS were to retain its functions, it
would interfere with the technical decisions of specialized operators. Instead,
contracts would have to be made between the competent authority and the
private investor.

Moreover, while the regulatory framework had already been established
in other public utilities, in the area of water services, clear registries on property rights over its basic input are still unavailable.[31] In part, this is due to
the lack of a water law establishing property rights that can be transferred in
a market. This represents an additional risk for a potential private investor,
especially in coastal areas, where the availability of water is extremely sea-
sonal, and there are strong political pressures not to apply a price mechanism that reflects the relative scarcity of the resources.

Conclusions

Peru continues to lag seriously behind many countries in coverage of potable water and sewerage. The modest progress of the past 15 years is largely
attributable to the use of FONAVI funds (collected as a payroll tax) which to
some extent cushioned the sharp decline of state investment in the late 1980s.

The water sector in Peru has been undergoing a reform process, which
is the legacy of successive governments with diametrically opposed economic
orientations. The first was populist. It municipalized services, but the
politicization and misuse of water rates between 1985 and 1990, under a
centralized structure, reduced investment and compromised service quality.
The second government had a free-market orientation and focused on correcting the macroeconomic imbalances it inherited from its predecessor. It
originally sought to privatize the sector, in keeping with the market orientation of legislation. However, the government backed off from this policy
when the political benefits of directing investments and controlling water
rates became apparent.

The reform of the water sector begun in 1991 aimed to liberalize the
sector, eliminate the state monopoly, and attract private investment as part of

---

[31] Currently, SUNASS has focused on registering the original rights of the companies.

the long-term structural reform program applied to the Peruvian economy. Laws were also issued to consolidate decentralization of the industry, encourage the establishment of municipal companies, create a regulatory body, introduce rate setting on the basis of long-term marginal costs, and include SEDEPAL (which supplies the largest market, Greater Lima) in the program for privatizing government companies. Nevertheless, reform of water utilities has progressed at a substantially slower pace than that of other public utilities with a natural monopoly, and is in danger of failing for the following reasons:

1) In practice, current legislation limits private participation: by encouraging the formation of municipal companies with boards composed of representatives of the provincial and district mayors, transaction costs for private sector participation—as envisioned in the legislation—have increased substantially. Mayors are likewise resistant to having companies transferred to private operators, in part because the municipalities themselves are indebted to the companies. Moreover, the tendency has been to break up existing systems at the prerogative of provincial municipalities, even when technical criteria recommend keeping them together.

Given the institutional characteristics of the country and the specific nature of assets in water services, attracting the private sector requires the central government to guarantee such issues as the scope of their powers and long-term investments. These guarantees could be achieved by signing "law-contracts" between the state and private investors, as envisioned in the legislation, but since municipal companies are not authorized to sign them, the central government would have to be involved. Because local water supply is a natural monopoly, it requires effective regulation to encourage efficiency in investment, while protecting consumers from the abuse of market power. In addition, given the poor reputation of the judicial power as a means for resolving conflicts, arbitration mechanisms that have been employed successfully in other privatization processes in the country should be used. Furthermore, the regulatory framework must be completed by passing the Water Law, which will make it possible to apply property rights to this resource and improve the efficiency of its allocation.

2) The powers granted to the regulatory body, SUNASS, reinforce the municipal orientation of existing legislation because it is responsible for providing the municipal companies with technical support and investment.

That structure is inappropriate vis-à-vis a potential private investor who would be subject not only to the normal regulation of water rates, coverage goals, and service quality, but to interference in its investment programs. Likewise, giving the regulated entities of the Ministry of the Presidency the tasks of planning, investment, regulation, and functional authority (and to some extent economic authority to finance the investment of municipal companies) is an institutional arrangement that limits the regulatory agency's independence.

3) The political cycle of the 1995 presidential election delayed the privatization of SEDAPAL. The fact that the political decisions to resume its privatization have not been made indicates a gap between the government's political possibilities and effective reform of the sector. It also sends contradictory signals to municipal companies about encouraging private investment in the sector, while maintaining efforts to obtain financing so the public sector may further expand coverage. Multilateral agencies apparently overestimated the commitment of the government to reform or their degree of influence over the governments. In the case of SEDAPAL, the possibility that the government might resist reform was not considered a risk of the World Bank's privatization arrangement. That has not halted the disbursements or execution of the investment programs (the results of which will be apparent prior to elections in the year 2000), since there were no explicit agreements on penalties to be applied should the government fail to carry out the privatization. Given the country's institutional characteristics and the previous politicization of the sector, a prompt return to the privatization of SEDAPAL is required in order to sustain the benefits of current investments and consolidate the efficiency gains already achieved.

4) An expansive phase of state investment in water services is now underway thanks to borrowing from international agencies, and primarily to funds raised through payroll-related contributions. It would be preferable to raise water rates to expand investment in the sector, but political choices have led the country to rely on those other sources instead. The reliance upon a payroll tax, however, cannot be a long-term solution for financing water sector investment because it distorts the labor market, making Peru less competitive even as the exchange rate appreciates. Nevertheless, the payroll tax remains attractive because its administrative features

(revenues from within a government agency) exempt it from some budgetary control, thereby granting the government greater discretion in the use of such resources, even for political ends. Consequently, the government has incentives to maintain this source of revenue, given that workers are unaware of the tax's impact on employment and the private sector is not organized to oppose this.

5) SEDAPAL's efficiency improvements, which stemmed from commitments reached with the World Bank, far overshadowed the inferior performance of the municipal companies. Its relatively better performance demonstrates the short-term benefits of having a third party participate in the reform process since it introduces accountability to encourage change in the sector. SEDAPAL also benefited from the advantages of serving a larger market, enjoying a stronger business tradition, more qualified staff, and, especially, support from key political officials.

Economic inefficiency is increasing among a sample of municipal companies despite water rate hikes that exceed those of SEDAPAL. Among municipal water companies, cross-subsidies favoring residential consumers are increasing, and progress in cutting losses, excess staffing, and delinquency is limited. The consequences of a hasty municipalization of services are thus coming to light. The present situation is characterized by institutional weakness, a limited planning horizon (three-year municipal periods) and serious contracting problems between the owner of the company (the municipality) and existing and potential customers. In this context, there is a danger that the "low-level equilibrium" prevailing in the industry in previous years will be recreated in the municipalities, and that new funds expected from multilateral agencies to support the decentralized systems will be at risk.

Given the trends in the country's fiscal accounts and the experience in managing state companies, private investment in the potable water and sewerage market in Peru must be actively promoted to expand service coverage under conditions of equity and efficiency. Private sector involvement linked to a strong regulatory body has two advantages over the organizational forms examined in this document. First, there is no need for outside agents to assure that efficiency goals are met. Second, it is the private sector that can efficiently mobilize the capital needed for providing service. And it is returns on such capital that the regulatory body and a stable macroeconomic and institutional environment are charged with assuring. Given the previous institutional background of the country and the industry, deepening the reform process is the only guarantee that the infrastructure erected with new funds from multilateral agencies and the government itself will not subsequently deteriorate.

References

Asociación Saniplan—AMSA Consultores. 1994. *Mejoramiento institucional y operativo*—Empresa Sedapiura. Diagnostic report. Lima, Peru: Ministerio de la Presidencia-PRONAP.

Banco Central de Reserva (BCR). 1990. *Evolución de precios de productos y servicios bajo control y regulación: 1985–1989.* Lima, Perú: BCR.

————. Annual Reports, various years.

————. Memorias, various years.

————. Weekly Notes, various editions.

Consorcio "HAGROI". 1994a. *Mejoramiento institucional y operativo—Empresa Sedaqosco.* Diagnostic report. Lima, Peru: Ministerio de la Presidencia-PRONAP.

————. 1994b. *Mejoramiento institucional y operativo—Empresa Sedaqosco.* Final Report. Lima, Perú: Ministerio de la Presidencia-PRONAP.

Cotillo, Pedro. 1985. *Diagnostico integral de la empresa de servicio de agua potable.* Thesis. Piura:Perú.

Demsetz, Harold. 1968. "Why Regulate Utilities." *Journal of Law and Economics.* 11(41):55–65.

Guasch, Luis and Spiller, Pablo. 1994. *Regulation and Private Sector Development in Latin America.*

Laffont, Jean Jacques and Tirole, Jean. 1994. *A Theory of Incentives in Procurement and Regulation*. Cambridge, Massachusetts: MIT Press.

Instituto Nacional de Estadistica y Informática (INEI). 1981, 1993. National census of population and housing. Lima, Perú: INEI.

————. 1993a. Perfil socio-demográfico del departamento de Cuzco.

————. 1993b. Perfil socio-demográfico del departamento de Lima.

————. 1993c. Perfil socio-demográfico del departamento de Piura.

————. 1993d. Perfil socio-demográfico de la Provincia Constitucional del Callao.

————. 1995a. Perú: Estadísticas del Medio Ambiente 1995. Dirección Nacional de Estadísticas Básicas. Lima: Perú. INEI.

Instituto Nacional de Recursos Naturales (INRENA) y Dirección General de Aguas y Suelos (DGAS). 1995. *Estudio del recurso hídrico por los diferentes sectores productivos en el Perú*. Lima: Perú. INRENA.

Ministerio de Salud. 1984. *Contaminación de aguas en la costa de Lima Metropolitana*. Dirección General del Medio Ambiente y Dirección de Protección del Medio Ambiente. Lima, Perú: Ministerio de Salud.

OIST. 1994. *Actualización de estudios de fuentes de agua para Lima*. Report on Sedapal. OIST. Lima, Peru.

Ringskog, Klas. 1995. *Como responder al desafío de la infraestructura en América Latina y el Caribe*. Washington, DC: World Bank.

Superintendencia Nacional de Servicios de Saneamiento (SUNASS). 1995. *Compendio de normas sobre saneamiento*. Lima, Peru.

————. Ley General de Servicios de Saneamiento. Exposición de Motivos.

Tamayo, G., Barrantes, R., Conterno, C., and Bustamante, A. 1997. "Retos de Economía Política en Agua Potable: El Proceso de Reforma en Perú." Working Paper R-311. Washington, DC.: Inter-American Development Bank.

Tokman, Victor and Martinez, Daniel. 1996. *Costo laboral manufacturero: Incidencia sobre la competitividad y la protección de los trabajadores.* Lima, Peru: Oficina Internacional del Trabajo.

Ugaz, Federico. 1994. "Tarifas y costos del agua en el Sistema Chira—Piura". In Informativo. Suplemento 74. Piura, Perú: CIPCA.

Villafuerte, Iris and Rojas, Carmen. 1994. *Contaminación del Río Rímac por la descarga de residuos sólidos.* Lima, Peru: ESMELL.

World Bank. *World Development Report 1994: Infrastructure for Development.* Washington, DC: World Bank.

————. 1994. Staff Appraisal Report. *Peru: Lima Water Rehabilitation and Management Project.* Document of the World Bank. Washington, DC.

CHAPTER 4

Governance and Regulation: Decentralization in Mexico's Water Sector

Teofilo Ozuna, Jr. and Irma Adriana Gómez[1]

Mexico's public water companies have been undergoing a gradual process of decentralization. Perhaps more than any other country, the water sector in Mexico was highly centralized in the federal government. Since the 1980s, the states have assumed much of the responsibility and a variety of arrangements have been developed. In some states, the centralized system has been recreated at the state level, with regulatory and operational responsibilities combined in a state water company. In other cases, regulatory and operational functions have been separated. In still others, municipalities have assumed regulatory and operational responsibilities. An econometric evaluation of more than 200 water companies shows that there are few economies of scale in Mexico's water sector, that firms are generally quite inefficient, and that the existence of a modern water law has little impact on efficiency. Most importantly, it shows that municipal firms operate more efficiently than state-level authorities, whether or not they have separated regulatory and operational functions. This suggests that the low-level equilibrium experienced at the federal level may be broken by linking service provision, and decisions over investment and water rates, to authorities that are more closely related to the service area in question.

---

[1] Teofilo Ozuna, Jr. is professor of agricultural economics at Texas A&M University; Irma Gómez is assistant professor of economics at the Instituto Tecnológico y de Estudios Superiores de Monterrey.

By the end of the 1980s, the provision of potable water, sewerage, and wastewater treatment services in Mexico had come to the forefront as a major social problem. In 1990, some 16.7 million people lacked potable water and 28.8 million had no sewerage services. Moreover, an analysis by the Comisión Nacional del Agua (1995) of data available for 1990 revealed that the provision of potable water and sewerage services is biased towards larger and richer cities. Additionally, of the 250 cubic meters per second provided to the population in 1990, 160 cubic meters per second returned to the environment as wastewater and of this total only 10 percent was treated.

At the same time, the majority of the water utilities operating in Mexico had severe financial, technical, organizational, and institutional problems. Most water utilities were seriously deteriorated due to the lack of funds to carry out maintenance programs and to expand their services. The lack of financing was a result of very low water and sewerage rates and poor revenue collection systems. The result was a "low-level equilibrium" in which the services provided by water utilities were of poor quality and, as a consequence, water users refused to pay more for poor water services.

Responding to the challenge, the Mexican federal government undertook three major policy initiatives: (1) expansion of the existing potable water and sewerage infrastructure; (2) implementation of measures aimed at improving water use efficiency; and (3) reduction of water pollution. The fundamental principles underlying this new water policy focus were:

- using integrated planning to make good use of scarce water;
- strengthening the regulatory capacity of the central water authority;
- introducing market mechanisms, such as water pricing and incentives, to induce the efficient use of water and to control pollution;
- strengthening institutional coordination at all government levels;
- effective decentralization of tasks and responsibilities;
- modernization of federal and state water laws; and
- participation of water users in decisions relating to water use and pollution.

Additionally, in 1990 the Programa Nacional de Agua Potable, Alcantarillado y Saneamiento came into being to respond to increased potable water, sewerage service, and wastewater treatment needs (Comisión Nacional del Agua 1994).

This chapter examines how institutional changes in Mexico's potable water sector influence public and private investment, incentives, efficient water use, and administrative capacities in the sector. Given the institutional structure of Mexico's water utilities, it formulates and tests hypotheses relating to institutional changes that have occurred in the sector and to the regulation, organization, and efficiency of the sector. Finally, it offers policy recommendations aimed at improving the services provided by this sector.

Two main points emerge from analyzing the decentralization process of Mexico's water sector. First, over the past eight decades, and in particular the last two, Mexico has moved toward the separation of regulation and operation in its state and municipal water utilities and in some cases even toward privatization. Thus, it is illuminating to compare the performance of water utilities operating under different organizational structures (i.e., directly administered—combined regulatory and operational functions—at the state level, autonomous—separated regulatory and operational functions—at the state level, directly administered at the municipal level, and autonomous at the municipal level). Some of the lessons that can be learned from this comparison relate to how the organizational structure of the water utilities influences their efficiency and to the role played by the state in bringing about institutional changes designed to promote efficiency in the sector.[2]

Second, Mexico's federal government is currently promoting the updating of the potable water and sewerage laws of each Mexican state. Here too, it would be revealing to compare the performance of water utilities with different organizational structures under different legislative regimes. From this comparison one may infer how water legislation influences the efficiency of the sector.

It should be noted that over the last five years, Mexico's federal government has encouraged the privatization of its public water utilities through its water utility concession model. To date, four water utilities have been privatized or partially privatized[3]. Although it would be instructive to examine and compare the performance of privatized water utilities to that of public water utilities, or to explore the incentive structure of water utility concession contracts, no data was available for the privatized water utilities.

---

[2] In Mexico, the separation of regulatory and operational functions is called *decentralización* independent of any change from state to municipal levels.

[3] Editor's note: The slow pace of privatization of Mexico's water sector stands in sharp contrast to telecommunications and other sectors.

Institutional Reform

Until 1946, the administration of Mexico's potable water and sewerage sector was highly centralized at the federal level. However, in 1947, the Mexican government created the Secretaría de Recursos Hidráulicos, under which the Juntas Federales de Agua Potable y Alcantarillado (Potable Water and Sanitation Federal Boards) were created. These Federal Boards were Mexico's first attempt to decentralize the administration of this sector (Palma 1996). Additionally, in 1956 the "Ley de Cooperación Para la Dotación de Agua Potable a los Municipios" water law was enacted, which enabled the creation of the Sistemas de Administracion Directa (Direct Administration Systems) and the Comités Municipales de Agua Potable (Potable Water Municipal Committees). These administrative systems as well as the Federal Boards gave this sector a certain degree of decentralization and stimulated the participation of the citizenry in the decision-making process (Sahab 1993).

In 1976, the administration of the sector was assigned to the Secretaría de Asentamientos Humanos y Obras Públicas (Human Settlement and Pubic Works Secretary) and, in 1980, this *Secretaría* relinquished the operation of the water utilities to the state governments. The states, in turn, reserved a regulatory role for themselves and established various administrative schemes. The schemes ranged from the establishment of independent statewide or municipal water utilities to deconcentration and fiduciary administrative schemes. Because of the diversity of schemes, water rate increases could be approved by either the state government, the governor, or by local councils. Additionally, in 1983, new reforms and additions to Article 115 of Mexico's constitution established that potable water and sewerage services were the responsibility of the municipalities. However, the states ignored these reforms and opted (during most of the 1980s) to create autonomous state water utilities instead of decentralized municipal water utilities (Palma 1996).

During the 1980s, the autonomous state water utilities ran into difficulties. First, they were not generating enough revenue for water supply expansions or maintenance requirements. Second, the utilities were being decapitalized as scant water utility revenues were being devoted to other state government uses. In many cases, the decapitalization of the water utilities led to a demand for subsidies not only for maintenance and additional infrastructure but also for the mere operation of the water utility itself. Political factors also tended to weaken the authority of water utilities, especially with respect to the setting of rates (Navarrete 1996). Furthermore, state laws also hampered the autonomy and administrative options water utilities had at their disposal.

Consequently, in 1989, the federal government created the Comisión Nacional de Agua (National Water Commission). The commission was charged, among other things, with the task of defining policies and strategies aimed at re-enforcing the technical, administrative, and financial autonomy of state and municipal water utilities. The commission's major effort with respect to the potable water and sewerage sector has been the creation of the *Programa Nacional de Agua Potable, Alcantarillado, Saneamiento y Consolidación de Organismos Operadores* (National Potable Water, Drainage, Sewerage and Water Utility Consolidation Program). This program was designed to respond to a series of deficiencies encountered in the potable water and sewerage sector. Two of its basic objectives are to further the decentralization of Mexico's water utilities at the municipal level and to assure the adequacy of state water legislative efforts (Palma 1996).

Since 1992, Mexico's National Water Commission has also been promoting modern legislative recommendations throughout the nation. The National Water Commission has developed a "model state water law," which is based on the water law enacted by the state of Sonora. To date, only four states have adopted this model state water law and another seven have adopted some modified version of it. The law is aimed at promoting the autonomy of water utilities, the ability to suspend water services, and private sector participation, among other things.

In summary, two underlying themes can be gleaned from this overview of the institutional reforms that have occurred in Mexico's potable water and sewerage sector. The first theme indicates that Mexico has strongly encouraged the separation of the regulatory and operational functions of its water utilities. At first, Mexico promoted this separation at the state level, but now promotes it at the municipal level. Mexico believed that by making the water utilities autonomous it would make the water utilities more efficient since they had to respond to local concerns and were more in touch with water users. The second theme indicates that since 1992, Mexico's National Water Commission has been promoting its "model state water law." The rationale behind the promotion of this model law is that adapting it will also promote efficiency within the potable water and sewerage sector.

Table 4.1 Level of Coverage of Potable Water and Sewerage Services: 1990–1994

Year	Total Population (Millions)	Population Served (Millions)	Level of Coverage (percent)
Potable Water			
1989	80.7	63.1	78.2
1990	82.5	65.8	79.8
1991	84.1	67.8	80.6
1992	85.7	71.3	83.2
1993	87.3	73.7	84.4
1994	88.9	75.5	84.9
Sewerage			
1990	82.5	53.7	65.1
1991	84.1	55.4	65.9
1992	85.7	58.5	68.3
1993	87.3	60.8	69.6
1994	88.9	62.6	70.4

Source: Comisión Nacional del Agua, 1995.

However, a shortcoming inherent to this model law is that it still maintains a centralized administrative scheme and, in some cases, requires that water rates be set by congress. This might prevent the gains in efficiency that are its goal.

Current Status of the Sector

Coverage

Over the last two decades, the provision of potable water in Mexico has expanded enormously. Until the beginning of the 1980s, the level of potable water coverage was low. According to Noriega (1990), the percentage of the population with access to potable water services was 50 percent in 1980. By the end of the 1980s, the level of coverage had increased to 78.2 percent and by 1994 to almost 85 percent (see Table 4.1).

Although this increase in the provision of potable water was substantial, Table 4.2 indicates that there are still serious problems in the sector.

Table 4.2 Level of Coverage of Potable Water and Sewerage Services by Size of Locality: 1994

Size of Locality (Population)	Total Population (Millions)	Population Served (Millions)	Level of Coverage (percent)
Potable Water			
1–99	2.2	0.8	38.0
100–499	7.9	3.8	48.1
500–2,499	14.6	9.6	65.8
2,500–4,999	5.3	4.1	77.8
5,000–49,999	14.6	12.9	88.4
50,000–79,990	2.5	2.2	89.7
80,000 or more	41.8	39.6	94.7
Total	88.9	75.5	84.9
Sewerage			
1–99	2.2	0.6	25.8
100–499	7.9	2.1	26.1
500–2,499	14.6	5.3	36.1
2,500–4,999	5.3	2.7	51.5
5,000–49,999	14.6	11.1	76.0
50,000–79,990	2.5	2.1	83.8
80,000 or more	41.8	38.8	92.8
Total	88.9	62.6	70.4

Source: Comisión Nacional del Agua, 1995.

Table 4.2 contains a breakdown for 1994 of the level of potable water services by size of locality. The table shows that there are still great potable water needs in localities with populations of less than 2,500 inhabitants. These localities represent about 28 percent of the population of Mexico. In localities with less than 99 inhabitants, the level of potable water coverage is 38 percent; in localities with 100 to 499 inhabitants, the level of coverage is 48.1 percent and; in localities with 500 to 2,500 inhabitants, the level is 65.8 percent. This contrasts sharply with the level of potable water coverage found in localities with more than 2,500 inhabitants. The larger localities have coverage levels that range from 77.8 percent to 94.7 percent.

An examination of the data relating to sewerage services reveals that the level of coverage has also increased in the past five years. Table 4.1 shows that the level of coverage of sewerage services increased from 65 percent in 1990 to 70 percent in 1994. Compared to potable water, the coverage level of sewerage services has lagged. Table 4.2 also indicates that the localities with populations of less than 5,000 have severe problems with the level of coverage of sewerage services as well.

Water Treatment

Mexico's wastewater treatment capacity is very low. For example, in 1994, installed capacity was only 42,788 liters/second to treat the 160,000 liters/second of wastewater that was generated in that year. This implies that in 1994, only about 27 percent of the wastewater that was generated was adequately treated. Furthermore, for this same year, 196 wastewater treatment plants with a capacity to treat 4,090 liters/second were out of operation. As of 1994, the following states still had severe wastewater treatment problems: Baja California Sur (treats 28 percent), Chihuahua (treats 7 percent), Hidalgo (treats 1 percent), Mexico City (treats 54 percent), Michoacan (treats 8 percent), Oaxaca (treats 0 percent), San Luis Potosi (treats 28 percent), Veracruz (treats 44 percent), and Zacatecas (treats 46 percent).

Private investment in the wastewater treatment sector has become very evident recently. For example, between the last months of 1992 and December of 1994, 32 plants with a combined wastewater treatment capacity of 23,344 liters/second and a total investment figure of $179.3 million were put up for bid.[4] These wastewater treatment plants will be operated under private participation schemes of finance, construction, and operation. In these schemes, the investor will finance, construct, and operate the wastewater treatment system and the water utility will pay for this service based on a price per cubic meter turned over to the system. The private investor will not be involved in charging the users.

Rate Structure, Water Losses, and Revenue Collection

Water rates in Mexico vary substantially across water utilities. In 1993, the domestic water rate ranged from $0.05 per cubic meter in the state of Tabasco

---

[4] In this study all U.S. dollar figures are in 1995 dollars.

Table 4.3 Ranges of Water Losses for a Sample of Localities Throughout Mexico: 1993–1994

Unaccounted Water (percent)	Number of Localities 1993	Number of Localities 1994
20–30	4	11
31–40	11	18
41–50	18	21
51–60	28	23
60–70	8	10
> 70	2	3

Source: Comisión Nacional del Agua: 1994, 1995.

to $4.16 per cubic meter in the state of Zacatecas. At the same time, the commercial and industrial rates ranged from $0.17 per cubic meter in the state of Sonora to $7.22 per cubic meter in the state of Tlaxcala. In 1994, the ranges were ($0.10–$9.80), ($0.15–$7.33), and ($0.16–$3.18) for the domestic, commercial, and industrial sectors.

During 1994, water rates were modified in 24 states. Most states increased their water rates by about 10 percent. However, some cities increased their rates substantially more. For example, Aguascalientes increased its rates by more than 100 percent, La Paz by 40 percent, and Pachuca by 30 percent in the commercial and industrial sectors (Comisión Nacional del Agua 1995). Overall the majority of the rates in Mexico are insufficient to cover the costs incurred by the water utilities.

Water losses as a percentage of total production are defined as the share of the volume of water produced by the water utility that is not billed. Water losses represent a serious problem in Mexico. Applying this measure to 71 localities throughout Mexico in 1993 and 86 localities in 1994 yields an average measure of water losses of 48 percent and 43 percent, respectively. This implies that in Mexico at least 45 percent of the water is unaccounted for or lost. Table 4.3 provides an overview of the distribution of water losses for the localities examined in 1993 and 1994. The largest number of localities lost between 51 percent and 60 percent of the water that entered the distribution system.

Table 4.4 Investment Profile for Cities with Populations of More than 80,000: 1994

Item	Credit	Fiscal Funds	Private Investment
Potable Water	100%	0	0
Drainage	0	100%	0
Wastewater Treatment			
Primary	100%	0	0
Secondary	0	0	100%

Source: Comisión Nacional del Agua: 1994, 1995.

Note: Credit also contains funds generated from the water utility itself and Fiscal Funds are 50 percent federal and 50 percent state.

The total amount of revenue collected during 1993 by the 730 water utilities that provide information to Mexico's National Water Commission amounted to $1,556 million. In 1994, this amount increased to $1,634 million. A comparison of the revenue collected for 1993 and 1994 reveals that not all states increased their revenues in 1994. For example, the states of Guerrero, Morelos, Sonora, Veracruz, and Oaxaca registered declines of 44 percent, 67 percent, 41 percent, 34 percent, and 44 percent, respectively. There is still much to do with respect to revenue collection in Mexico.

Investment

Financial resources for the potable water, sewerage, and wastewater treatment sectors of Mexico come from a wide range of sources including: (1) federal government, (2) state governments, (3) international banks, (4) social groups, (5) private sector, and (6) water utilities themselves. To guarantee a more effective use of the scarce funds in this sector, the government of Mexico has developed an investment profile that specifies how investments in the sector will be undertaken. The investment profile for 1994 for cities with a population of more than 80,000 is presented in Table 4.4. Compared to previous years, this investment profile allocates 100 percent of these funds to the drainage sectors and none to the potable water sector. Notice also that the secondary wastewater treatment investment is 100 percent from the pri-

Table 4.5 Investment in Potable Water, Sewerage, and Wastewater Treatment: 1994
(Millions of dollars)

Area	Federal	State/Local	Credit	Private	TOTAL
Mexico City	143				143
Monterrey	82		19	20	121
Guadalajara	12		4	11	27
Other Cities	106	86	88	9	289
Rural Areas	111	50			161
TOTAL	454	136	111	40	741

Source: Comisión Nacional del Agua: 1994, 1995.

Note: Private also contains funds generated from the water utility itself.

vate sector. This indicates that public funds are going to drainage and primary wastewater treatment and that secondary wastewater treatment investment will be forthcoming only to the degree that the private sector can be attracted to it. This implies that Mexico wants (1) the potable water sector to pay for itself, (2) the private sector to invest in secondary wastewater treatment and to recover its investment by charging potable water, and (3) a pure fiscal transfer for drainage.

The amount of investment that has occurred in the potable water, sewerage, and wastewater treatment sectors in 1993 was $1,090 million and in 1994, $741 million. As can be observed, investment in this sector decreased by 26 percent in 1994 as compared to 1993 (Comisión Nacional del Agua 1995). Table 4.5 presents a breakdown of the 1994 investment level. Of the total amount invested in this sector, 36 percent went to the three biggest cities, 39 percent to all the other urban cities, and only 22 percent to rural areas. Additionally, there is no private investment in rural areas. Also, credit and private funds make up only 15 percent of the funds invested in this sector (Comisión Nacional del Agua 1995).

Since 1993, the private sector has jointly participated with the Mexican government at all three levels in financing and administering some water utilities. This participation has been made possible because of the implementation of a new financial framework that has well established and transparent rules (Comisión Nacional del Agua 1995). This new financial framework has given private investors more security with respect to their investments. Additionally, Mexico's recently modified National Water Law promotes the participation of private citizens in the potable water, sewerage, and wastewater treatment sector through various arrangements as outlined below.

Econometric Analysis

A review of the institutional, regulatory, and organizational changes that have occurred in the potable water sector indicates that Mexico is promoting (1) the separation of the regulatory and operational functions of its water utilities, (2) the municipal management of water utilities, and (3) the adoption of a model state water law aimed at improving the efficiency of the potable water sector. Additionally, the overview of the sector's current status indicates that Mexico needs to provide more potable water services to localities with populations of less than 5,000 inhabitants, treat more of its wastewater, improve its rate structure, and attract more private sector participation in Mexico's water sector.

This suggests several hypotheses that need to be addressed or tested. First, does autonomy (in terms of separating regulatory and operational functions) increase water utility efficiency? Second, does greater autonomy in state systems have a greater impact on performance for large systems than for small systems? Third, do autonomous municipal systems have a greater impact on performance for large systems than for small systems? Fourth, are water utilities that set their own rates more efficient than those whose rates are set by congress? Fifth, does the adoption of the National Water Commission's model state water law promote efficiency?

These questions and hypotheses can be addressed with an econometric model.

Model Specification

Following the studies of Atkinson and Halvorsen (1984), Bhattacharyya, Parker, and Raffiee (1994), and Koh, Berg, and Kenny (1996), this model uses an actual variable cost function that exhibits the regular characteristics of the neoclassical variable cost function. It is assumed that the water utilities produce water (Q) using labor (L), energy (E), and a quasifixed capital stock (K). To account for the influence of institutional factors, input shadow prices (P_i^*, $i = L,E$) are assumed to differ from observed market prices (P_i). As in Atkinson and Halvorsen (1984) and Koh, Berg, and Kenny (1996), shadow prices are related to observed market prices through a proportionality factor that is input specific and depends on institutional factors (i.e., $P_i^* = k_i P_i$).

Following Atkinson and Halvorsen (1984), it is assumed that water utilities choose inputs so as to minimize the shadow variable costs, $\Sigma_i (k_i P_i) X_i$, of the chosen level of output. P and X represent the observed input market prices and quantities. The water utility's shadow variable cost function is defined as $VC^S \equiv VC^S (kP, K, Q)$ where kP is a vector of input specific shadow prices that depend on institutional factors and K and Q are as defined above. Actual input demand functions can be derived from the shadow variable cost function by applying Shephard's Lemma, $\partial VC^S / \partial (k_i P_i) = X_i$. Thus, the water utility's actual variable cost function can be written as $VC^A = \Sigma_i P_i X_i = \Sigma_i P_i [\partial VC^S / \partial (k_i P_i)]$. By specifying an appropriate functional form for the shadow variable cost function, a parametric expression for the water utility's actual variable costs can be derived.

To simplify notation, define M_i^S as the shadow variable cost share of input i, that is

$$M_i^S \equiv \frac{k_i P_i X_i}{VC^S}. \qquad [1]$$

From [1] it is found that

$$X_i = M_i^S (VC^S)(k_i P_i)^{-1}$$

which, when substituted in the actual variable cost function yields

$$VC^A = (VC^S) \sum_i k_i^{-1} M_i^S.$$

Taking logarithms it is found that

$$\ln(VC^A) = \ln(VC^S) + \ln \sum_i k_i^{-1} M_i^S. \qquad [2]$$

For purposes of estimation, the logarithmic shadow variable cost function, $\ln(VC^S)$, is specified as a translog function

$$\ln(VC^S) = \alpha_0 + \alpha_K \ln(K) + \alpha_Q \ln(Q) + \sum_i \alpha_i \ln(k_i P_i) +$$

$$\frac{1}{2} \sum_i \sum_j \beta_{ij} \ln(k_i P_i) \ln(k_j P_j) + \frac{1}{2} \beta_{KK} [\ln(Q)]^2 +$$

$$\sum_i \beta_{ik} \ln(k_i P_i) \ln(K) + \frac{1}{2} \beta_{QQ} [\ln(Q)]^2 + \qquad [3]$$

$$\sum_i \beta_{iQ} \ln(k_i P_i) \ln(Q)$$

where $(\beta_{ij} = \beta_{ji})$. Linear homogeneity of the shadow variable cost function in shadow prices implies the following relationships among the parameters

$$\alpha_L + \alpha_E = 1,$$
$$\beta_{LL} + \beta_{EL} = 0,$$
$$\beta_{LE} + \beta_{EE} = 0,$$
$$\beta_{LK} + \beta_{EK} = 0, \text{ and}$$
$$\beta_{LQ} + \beta_{EQ} = 0.$$

Logarithmic differentiation of equation [3] yields parametric expressions for the shadow variable cost shares specified in equation [1],

$$\frac{\partial \ln(VC^S)}{\partial \ln(k_i P_i)} = \frac{k_i P_i}{VC^S} \frac{\partial(VC^S)}{\partial(k_i P_i)} = \frac{k_i P_i X_i}{VC^S}$$

$$= M_i^S = \alpha_i + \sum_j \beta_{ij} \ln(k_i p_j) + \beta_{iK} \ln(K) + \beta_{iQ} \ln(Q) \quad i, j = L, E \ [4]$$

Substituting in equation [2] for $\ln(VC^S)$ from equation [3] and for M_i^S from equation [4] yields the actual variable cost function

$$\ln(VC^A) = \alpha_0 + \sum_i \alpha_i \ln(k_i P_i) + \alpha_K \ln(K) + \alpha_Q \ln(Q) +$$

$$\frac{1}{2} \sum_i \sum_i \beta_{ij} \ln(k_i P_i) \ln(k_j P_j) + \frac{1}{2} \beta_{KK} [\ln(Q)]^2 +$$

$$\sum_i \beta_{iK} \ln(k_i P_i) \ln(K) + \frac{1}{2} \beta_{QQ} [\ln(Q)]^2 + \qquad [5]$$

$$\sum_i \beta_{iQ} \ln(k_i P_i) \ln(Q) +$$

$$\ln \left\{ \sum_i k_i^{-1} \left[\alpha_i + \sum_j \beta_{ij} \ln(k_i p_i) + \beta_{iK} \ln(K) + \beta_{iQ} \ln(Q) \right] \right\}$$

If in equation [5], $k_i = k_j$ for all i, j, the water utility's actual variable cost function, [5], reduces to its shadow variable cost function, [3], which in turn is equivalent under these conditions to the neoclassical variable cost function.

The actual variable cost share of input i ($i = L, E$) is defined as

$$M_i^A \equiv \frac{P_i X_i}{VC^A}. \qquad [6]$$

Substituting for X_i and VC^A yields

$$M_i^A = \frac{M_i^S k_i^{-1}}{\sum_i M_i^S k_i^{-1}}.$$

and substituting for M_i^S from equation [4] results in

$$M_i^A = \frac{\left[\alpha_i + \sum_j \beta_{ij} \ln(k_j p_j) + \beta_{iK} \ln(K) + \beta_{iQ} \ln Q \right] k_i^{-1}}{\sum_i \left[\alpha_i + \sum_j \beta_{ij} \ln(k_j p_j) + \beta_{iK} \ln(K) + \beta_{iQ} \ln Q \right] k_i^{-1}} \quad i, j = L, E. \quad [7]$$

After imposing symmetry and homogeneity restrictions on the actual variable cost equation [5], it will be jointly estimated along with the actual cost share equation [7]. Since the sum of the actual variable cost shares is equal to one, the energy cost share equation is dropped during the estimation process.

To address the questions raised at the beginning of this section, the translog actual variable cost function intercept (α_0) and the linear terms in output (α_Q) and in shadow prices (α_i, $i = L,E$) are expanded as

$$\alpha_0 = a_0 + b_0 Z_1 + c_0 Z_2 + d_0 Z_3 + e_0 Z_4 + f_0 Z_5$$
$$\alpha_Q = a_Q + b_Q Z_1 + c_Q Z_2 + d_Q Z_3 + e_Q Z_4 + f_Q Z_5 \qquad [8]$$
$$\alpha_i = a_i + b_i Z_1 + c_i Z_2 + d_i Z_3 + e_i Z_4 + f_i Z_5$$

where

$$Z_1 = \begin{cases} 1 & \text{if water utility is managed by the municipality} \\ 0 & \text{if water utility is managed by the state} \end{cases}$$

$$Z_2 = \begin{cases} 1 & \text{if water utility is directly administerd} \\ 0 & \text{if water utility is autonomous} \end{cases}$$

$$Z_3 = \text{percentage of connections with continuous service}$$

$$Z_4 = \begin{cases} 1 & \text{if the state adopted the model law} \\ 0 & \text{otherwise} \end{cases}$$

$$Z_5 = \begin{cases} 1 & \text{if water utility is located in a water abundant area} \\ 0 & \text{otherwise} \end{cases}$$

It is through these Z variables that the hypotheses or questions posed at the beginning of this section can be tested. For example, the sign of the coefficient associated with variable Z_1 could show whether water utilities managed by municipalities are more efficient (have lower variable cost) than water utilities managed by states and whether this is also true at higher output levels (Q) and lower input costs (P_i). If the coefficient is negative it will imply that municipal water utilities are more efficient than state water utilities. Likewise, if the sign of the coefficient associated with variable Z_2 is negative it will indicate that directly administered water utilities with combined regulatory and operational functions are more efficient than autonomous water utilities that separate these functions. The sign of the coefficients on Z_1 and Z_2 could be examined jointly to rank (in terms of efficiency) the various types of water utilities (i.e., directly administered at the state level, autonomous at the state level, directly administered at the municipal level, and autonomous at the municipal level).

The variable Z_3 was introduced because it is expected that water utilities with a greater percentage of connections with continuous service will have higher variable costs than those with a lower percentage of connections with continuous service. It is expected that the sign of the coefficient associated with Z_3 will be positive.

The variable Z_4 was included in the model to determine whether the adoption of the National Water Commission's model state water law influences the performance of water utilities. It is expected that water utilities located in states that have adopted the model law, will have lower variable costs since the law promotes the efficient use of water. Therefore, it is expected that the sign of the coefficient associated with this variable should be negative.

Variable Z_5 was included to examine whether water scarcity influences the variable cost of the water utilities. It is expected that the sign of the coefficient of this variable will be negative, implying that variable costs are lower for water utilities located in water abundant areas. This is so because water utilities located in water scarce areas will have to transport water from water abundant areas, which will lead to increased costs.

To complete the model, factors of proportionality were specified as $k_i = \gamma_i + \omega_i Z_1$. This specification implies that differences in price efficiency between municipal and state managed water utilities are reflected in the k_i coefficient. Since the actual variable cost function and the actual share equations are homogenous of degree zero in the k_i's, one normalization is incorporated on the k_i (Diewert 1974). Thus, k_E is normalized to one by setting γ_E equal to one and ω_E equal to zero.

Data

The data for this study were obtained from the Unidad de Programas Rurales y Participación Social branch of Mexico's National Water Commission. The data are from 1995 and represent a sample of 146 water utilities throughout Mexico, excluding Mexico City. The data come from the questionnaire that the water utilities fill out and submit to the National Water Commission. The questionnaire is divided into five sections: (1) general information, (2) the operational system, (3) the commercial system, (4) the administrative system, and (5) the financial system.

Due to missing data, the initial sample of 146 water utilities decreased to 115 water utilities. Using these data, the following variables were constructed. Total output (Q) was calculated as the total quantity of water produced and delivered in millions of liters per year. The output price was computed as total revenue divided by billed water in millions of liters. Variable cost was constructed as the sum of observed total expenditures on labor and energy. Observed labor costs per worker were obtained by dividing total annual costs of labor by the number of employees and is expressed in thousands of dollars per year. It was not possible to obtain observed energy cost per kilowatt since the questionnaire did not contain any information on the amount of energy the water utility consumed per year. To circumvent this problem, the price of energy per kilowatt for 1995 for each state was obtained from the annual statistics published by INEGI and this price was assigned to each water utility based on the state it was located in.

The capital stock was estimated, following Moroney and Trapani (1981), as the residual of revenue less variable cost divided by the opportunity cost of capital. The rate of cost of capital was obtained from Banobras and includes an average depreciation rate. The monetary data is expressed in 1995 U.S. dollars, the exchange rate used to convert 1995 pesos to dollars was 6.6 pesos/U.S. dollar.

The Z variables were obtained as follows. Variables Z_1 and Z_2 were obtained from data in the Unidad de Programas Rurales y Participación Social of the National Water Commission. Variables Z_3 and Z_4 were coded from the information contained in the water utility questionnaires. Variable Z_5 was obtained from information contained in the Ley Federal de Derechos en Materia de Agua (Comisión Nacional del Agua).

Estimation and Results

The econometric model, which consists of equations [5], [7] and [8], was estimated using an iterative nonlinear seemingly unrelated regression, which in convergence approximates maximum likelihood estimation. To facilitate the interpretation and estimation process the variable cost, output quantity, and input price data were divided by their respective mean values. The model was first estimated as specified in equation [5], [7], and [8] but the results were not reasonable. Many of the estimated values were insignificant or had the wrong sign. The model was subsequently estimated after deleting some of the Z variables that were insignificant. The parameter estimates and associated t-statistics are presented in Table 4.6. The overall R-squared value for the model was 0.82. The estimated model was checked for concavity, monotonicity, and nonnegative conditions and it was found that the conditions were all satisfactorily met.

It is interesting to note that the variable (Z_4) which indicates whether the state where the water utility is located has adopted the model law being advanced by the National Water Commission was insignificant, and subsequently was excluded from the final model. This implies that the adoption of the National Water Commission's model state law does not influence the performance (in terms of lower variable cost) of water utilities, at least not for the utilities included in the data. This could be the case because few water utilities in the sample data were located in states that had adopted the law or because the existence of the law, by itself, has no impact on water utility efficiency.

Another point to note is that the variable (Z_5) which indicates whether the water utility is located in a water abundant area or not, had the appropriate sign (negative) but was insignificant, and therefore was excluded from the final model. This implies that water abundance does not influence the variable cost function of water utilities.

As can be observed in Table 4.6, the intercept in the variable cost function was specified as being dependent on the municipal/state dummy variable, autonomous/directly administered variable, and on the percentage of connections with continuous service. Of these variables, only the municipal/state dummy variable is significant, with a negative coefficient. Holding all else constant, this implies that water utilities managed at the municipal level are relatively more efficient than water utilities managed at the state level. The insignificance of the autonomous/directly administered dummy variable implies that neither type of organizational structure (autonomous or directly administered) statistically influence the relative efficiency of water utilities. These results indicate that if Mexico wants more efficient water

Table 4.6 Generalized Variable Cost Function Estimates

	Municipal/ State	Autonomous/ Dir. Administered	% Connections With Cont. Serv.
Intercept			
α_0 a_0 -0.299 (-0.64)	b_0 -0.390* (-2.54)	c_0 0.102 (1.07)	d_0 0.072 (0.43)
Shadow Price Coefficients			
α_L a_L 0.439* (2.02)	b_L -0.177* (-1.69)	c_L 0.037 (1.25)	d_L 0.151* (2.88)
α_E a_E 0.561* (2.59)	b_E -0.124* (-1.69)	c_E 0.015 (1.25)	d_E 0.097* (2.88)
β_{LL} -0.126* (-7.31)			
β_{LE} 0.126* (7.31)			
β_{EE} -0.126* (-7.31)			
Shadow/Market Price Ratios			
k_L γ_L 0.881* (3.81)	ω_L -0.322 (-1.35)		
k_E γ_E 1.000	ω_E 0.000		
Output Coefficients			
α_Q a_Q 1.145 (1.36)	b_Q 0.204* (2.42)	c_Q -0.078 (-0.85)	d_Q 0.112 (0.72)
β_{QQ} -0.034 (-0.04)			
β_{LQ} 0.196 (1.03)			
β_{EQ} -0.196 (-1.03)			
β_{KQ} 0.006 (0.40)			
Capital Coefficients			
α_K a_K -0.002 (-0.12)	b_K 0.001 (0.73)	c_K 0.001 (0.30)	d_K -0.001 (-0.19)
β_{KK} 0.003 (0.47)			
β_{LK} 0.008 (1.65)*			
β_{EK} -0.008 (-1.65)*			

Notes: t-statistics in parenthesis; $\alpha_E = 1 - \alpha_L$; $\beta_{LE} = -\beta_{LL}$; $\beta_{EK} = -\beta_{LK}$; $\beta_{EQ} = -\beta_{LQ}$; $\beta_{EE} = \beta_{LL}$
* Significant at 5 percent level (one-tailed test)

utilities, it needs to focus more on managing water utilities at the municipal level rather than focusing on the separation of regulatory and operational functions.

Of the estimated coefficients associated with the linear terms in output, only b_Q is significant. The positive and significant b_Q coefficient implies that as output increases, water utilities that are managed by municipalities become relatively less efficient. Note also that the negative b_0 coefficient and the positive b_Q imply that water utilities managed by municipalities are more efficient than water utilities managed by the state at low output levels and are less efficient at high output levels. Alternatively, there is no evidence that the effect of output differs if the water utility is autonomous or not since the coefficients c_0 and c_Q are not significant.

As expected, the estimated values of α_L and α_E are positive. Six of the base coefficients (a_L, b_L, d_L and a_E, b_E, d_E) are significant. There are no differences between autonomous and directly administered water utilities in the effect of shadow prices on cost: the coefficients c_L are not significant. Alternatively, the negative b_L and b_E coefficients indicate that labor and energy prices have a lower impact on costs for municipally managed water utilities than state managed water utilities.

As noted above, the shadow price/market price ratio for energy (k_E) has been normalized to one. However, the shadow price/market price ratio for labor is allowed to vary with the municipal/state dummy variable. As can be observed in Table 4.6, there is no evidence that constraints imposed by a water utility's regulatory environment at the municipal or state level distorts their factor prices: the coefficient ω_L is insignificant. Furthermore, with the normalization of $k_E = 1$ imposed, the restriction for relative price efficiency with respect to all inputs becomes $k_L = 1$. This restriction was not rejected at the .05 level, indicating that the water utilities do minimize costs subject to market prices (i.e., they are relatively price efficient). This implies that shadow prices are not statistically distinguishable from market prices.

Conclusions

How do organizational structures and legislative regimes, under which Mexico's water utilities operate, influence the efficiency of the potable water and sewerage service sector? Overall, it was found that the institutional endowment of the sector significantly influences Mexico's potable water and sewerage sector specifically as follows:

- The adoption of the National Water Commission's model state law does not influence the performance of the potable water and sewerage sector.
- Water utilities managed at the municipal level are relatively more efficient (have lower variable costs) than water utilities managed at the state level.
- The separation of a water utilities' regulatory and operational functions does not influence its relative efficiency.
- At low output levels, water utilities managed at the municipal level are more efficient than water utilities managed at the state level, but the reverse occurs at high output levels.
- There is no evidence that constraints imposed by the regulatory environment in which a water utility operates distorts their factor prices.
- Mexico's water utilities are relatively price efficient.
- The location of water utilities in a water abundant area does not influence the variable cost function of water utilities.

References

Atkinson, S. E. and Halvorsen, R. 1984. "Parametric Efficiency Tests, Economies of Scale, and Input Demand in U.S. Electric Power Generations." *International Economic Review*, 25(October): 647-62.

Bhattacharyya, A., Parker, E., and Raffiee, K. 1994. "An Examination of the Effect of Ownership on the Relative Efficiency of Public and Private Water Utilities," Land Economics, 70:197–209.

Comisión Nacional del Agua 1990. "Programa Nacional de Agua Potable, Alcantarillado y Saneamiento." SARH, Mexico.

_____. 1991. "Programa Nacional de Aprovechamiento del Agua," 1991–1994. SARH, Mexico.

_____. 1991. "Programa Agua Limpia." SARH, Mexico.

_____. 1992. "Ley de Agua Nacionales." SARH, Mexico.

_____. 1993. "Situación Actual del Subsector Agua Potable, Alcantarillado y Saneamiento a Diciembre de 1992." SARH, Mexico.

_____. 1994. "Situación Actual del Subsector Agua Potable, Alcantarillado y Sancamicnto a Diciembre de 1993." SARII, Mexico.

_____. 1994. "Ley Federal de Derechos en Materia de Agua." SARH, Mexico.

Diewert, W.E. 1974. "Applications of Duality Theory." *In:* M. D. Intriligator and D. A. Kendrick, editors. *Frontiers of Quantitative Economics*. Vol. 2,. Amsterdam: North Holland.

Farías, U. 1993. Derecho Mexicano de Aguas Nacionales. Porrúa, Mexico.

Koh, D.S., Berg, S.V., and Kenny, L.W. 1996. "A Comparison of Costs in Privately Owned and Publicly Owned Electric Utilities: The Role of Scale." *Land Economics*, 72(1): 56–65.

Moroney, J.R. and Trapani, J.M. 1981. "Alternative Models of Substitution and Technical Change in Natural Resource Industries." In: E. R. Berndt and B. C. Field, editors. *Modelling and Measuring Natural Resource Substitution.* Cambridge, MA: The MIT Press.

Navarrete, A. F. Martinez. 1996. "Los Problemas del Agua en México y Algunas Lecciones del Caso Argentino." *Federalismo y Desarrollo*, 9(54): 25–31.

Palma, V. Alcantara. 1996. "Marco Legal Actual de los Servicios de Agua Potable, Alcantaillado y Saneamineto a Nivel Local." *Federalismo y Desarrollo*, 9(54): 55–66.

Sahab, E. H. 1993. "Aspectos Relevantes en La Evolución Institucional de la Autoridad del Agua en México dentro del Sector Agua Potable, Alcantarillado y Saneamiento." In: Memoria Técnica, 1a Reunión Internacional Sobre Economía del Agua y Medio Ambiente. Mexico City, Mexico.

Noriega, V. S. 1990. *El agua en el desarrollo regional de México.* Mexico City, Mexico.

CHAPTER 5

Governance and Regulation in Chile: Fragmentation of the Public Water Sector

Felipe Morandé and Juan E. Doña[1]

Chile's water and sanitation services have changed from a centralized public sector activity to a more decentralized one with a highly developed regulatory framework and the beginnings of private sector involvement in various forms. Private sector involvement in the provision of water services has been slower than in other sectors such as telephones and electricity because consumers were relatively content with the performance of public firms and private investors were less interested. In reviewing the current debates, consumers have been relatively absent from the discussion, and there has been low resistance from employees. Part of the reason that consumers have accepted substantial increases in water rates is due to the introduction of a demand subsidy that is effectively targeted to poorer households. Most of the debate over the proper regulation of the water sector has been affected by perceived problems with privatization initiatives in other sectors.

The water industry in Chile has developed substantially over the past 30 years, so much so that by 1995, in urban areas coverage of potable water was 98 percent and of sewerage, 89 percent. From the 1970s to the present, cov-

---

[1] Felipe Morandé is director of studies of the Central Bank of Chile and Adjunct Professor at the Instituto Latinoaméricano de Doctrina y Estudios Sociales (ILADES), Georgetown University; Juan E. Doña is associate researcher at ILADES, Georgetown University.

erage of potable water and sewerage has expanded significantly, a rate system has been applied by enabling operation and investment to be self-financing from fees collected from customers, and service in urban areas is now provided by companies regulated by an independent body.

Despite these organizational and institutional changes, there is no evidence that the adjustments have decisively affected performance in the sector. Performance over time has been generally adequate; it has had the necessary financing and teams of professional people and technicians have operated with substantial continuity. After reviewing accomplishments and remaining problems, it appears that in urban areas development has reached a point where government ownership is an obstacle to improving service quality (rationing, low pressure) and to widely extending treatment of waste water. Meanwhile, rural areas still lack institutional development.

Even though the level of institutional development in Chile enables it to attract private investment in public utilities, ownership of water and sewerage companies has remained primarily in government hands, unlike other sectors, such as electric power, telephone service, and intercity roadways, which have been privatized. The relative lag in involving private investment relates to the fact that this sector was less developed in terms of regulations and organization when the Chilean economy began to be liberalized (1973) and did not lack critical investments. Currently, there is a discussion underway in the country about the conditions needed to privatize water and sewerage companies. The primary parties involved are business sectors interested in investing in this area and political actors who want to avoid the shortcomings acknowledged in earlier privatization processes. Workers have not objected to privatization because they have been offered the incentive of a preferential purchase option, while consumers have been practically absent from the discussion.

When the development of the potable water industry is compared to that of electric power and telecommunications, two main issues come into focus. First, the effect of institutional and organizational changes on the performance of water services become clearer as they are examined over time. Secondly, insights are gleaned into why water services are provided primarily by government-owned companies while other public utility services have been privatized.

Characteristics of Production

The water industry provides a very large and essential public service that requires major investments in piping systems and other specialized installations. It is also a natural monopoly with both significant positive externalities, primarily in the realm of health, and negative ones, which affect the environment in the disposal of sewerage.

Like other public utilities such as electric power or telephone service, it is a natural monopoly. However, in water and sewerage services there may be a greater gap between the way it is valued in society (including externalities) and the willingness of low-income users to pay. On this basis, preferential support may be justified.

Water and sewerage services display a number of characteristics and conditioning factors. To begin with, these services can be divided into four distinct but interrelated segments:
- Production of potable water
- Distribution of potable water
- Collection of wastewater (also called "sewerage")
- Disposal of wastewater, treated or untreated

These four segments are interrelated because they offer potential economies of scope, and especially because the simplest way to enforce payment of each of the various processes is to cut off the supply of potable water.

The spatial density of the areas served determines the technical characteristics of the solutions needed and the cost of investment and operation per beneficiary. In Chile, there are three types of service:
1) Urban: settlements of over 3,500 inhabitants;
2) Concentrated rural: over 150 and up to 3,000 inhabitants, and at least 15 dwellings per kilometer of street or road; and
3) Dispersed rural.

Urban and concentrated rural services require collective solutions, whereas solutions for dispersed rural areas must be individual (wells, canals). Historically, a specific institutional arrangement and organizational system has been applied to each category.

The relative scarcity of water resources affects costs and investments for potable water production. In Chile, water is very scarce in the north, major restrictions exist in the central region, while the south has a great deal of water.

The distance from coastal areas affects the costs of disposing sewerage in a nonpolluting way. When the distances are shorter, costs are lower because sewage can be discharged into the ocean.

Performance

From a social standpoint, the performance of an activity is generally viewed relative to an optimum defined by net benefits. In the case of water and sewerage services, social demand is considered to be inelastic, due to the significant positive externalities associated with them. The primary determinant of social performance is the sum total of benefits to society. The efficiency of costs and investment is of secondary importance, primarily for its indirect effect as a constraint on the system's ability to generate benefits due to possible budgetary restrictions. That is, a system generating greater benefits with cost inefficiency would as a rule perform better than one providing fewer benefits at an efficient cost. Of course, a system with excessive costs would likely have fewer resources to increase benefits than an efficient one.

The benefits of water and sewerage services depend on two primary factors: coverage, and service quality, which is measured in terms of water quality, reliability of supply, and the pollutant level in effluents.

In turn, the benefits produced by each process are prioritized in the same order usually followed in expanding service coverage:

- Production and distribution of potable water, which produces major positive externalities in health, and for which users are quite willing to pay.
- Discharge of sewerage, which likewise brings about positive externalities in health and private benefits for users.
- Sewerage treatment, which only generates positive externalities (it avoids negative externalities from pollution) but does not generate direct private benefits for users.

Institutional Structure

Because water and sewerage services are a natural monopoly and have significant positive externalities, market mechanisms do not assure adequate resource allocation.

There are two main options for correcting the imperfections of the market and they are not mutually exclusive:

1) Direct management by the state through agencies of the central or local government, with varying degrees of autonomy.

2) Regulation and oversight of the conditions under which the service is provided and of rate levels for users.

In general, the absence of formal regulations goes along with direct management by the state, while supply by private actors tends to occur where an explicit regulation and oversight system is in place.

The institutional framework for this industry is determined by the kind of organization—public or private—that provides the service and the regulations to which it is subjected. This, in turn, defines both the resources available for carrying out the activity, and the controls and incentives for assuring that benefits are maximized and that costs and investment are efficient. Which institutional arrangement is chosen depends on the country's institutional endowment and on the political and economic conditions set by interest groups.

The institutional and organizational changes in water services will be examined in historic terms for urban areas. Water services in rural areas are not discussed but may be found in Morandé and Doña (1997).

Coverage and Quality of Service

Trends in coverage and the increase in connections, by type of service and population served, and the relationship between total urban potable water connections and coverage, are presented in Figures 5.1 and 5.2. Potable water services in Chile have always had wider coverage than sewerage services, but the gap has steadily narrowed. Potable water service was available to less than half the urban population in the early 1960s, but now reaches almost 100 percent. Sewerage services were provided to about 20 percent of the urban population in the early 1960s, but now reaches almost 90 percent. But the expansion of service has not always been smooth. Figure 5.2 shows that coverage increased in fits and starts, with large bursts of activity in 1975, the late 1980s, and again in 1993 and 1994.

Little information is available on service quality. In 1992, an analysis of the quality of monitored services (90 percent of the total) identified the following problems:

Figure 5.1
Urban Water Sector Coverage, 1963—1995,
(% Population)

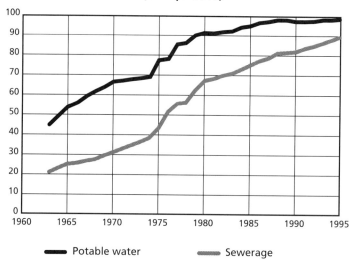

Potable water   Sewerage

Figure 5.2
Increase in Physical Connections
(Thousands per year)

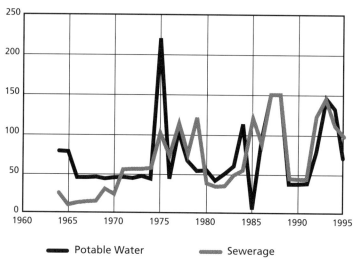

Potable Water   Sewerage

Sources: SENDOS. Organización Nacional del Sub-sector de Obras Sanitarias, 1986.
SENDOS. Organización Nacional del Sub-sector de Obras Sanitarias, 1988.
SISS. Depto. de Normalización y Control. Coberturas 1990–95.

- 8.3 percent of the total of services monitored had bacteriological problems.
- 6.3 percent had chlorine waste.
- 26.7 percent did not comply with chemical quality standards.
- 40.7 percent experienced turbidity.

At the end of 1995, water supply was restricted in 22 urban locations, with actual delivery varying between four and 22 hours a day. The affected population represents approximately 4.3 percent of the total urban population, but accounts for 18 percent of the population of the affected regions (northern zone). In Region One, served by the public company ESSAT, (340,000 urban inhabitants), everyone suffers from restrictions, with delivery between 10 and 12 hours a day.

Investment and Operating Costs

Overall investment in this industry and the total invested by the Ministry of Public Works are depicted in Figure 5.3 (no background information is available on urban investment or in terms of separate processes).

Figure 5.3
Ministry of Public Works (MOP) Investment in Water Services
(Real 1995 US$ millions)

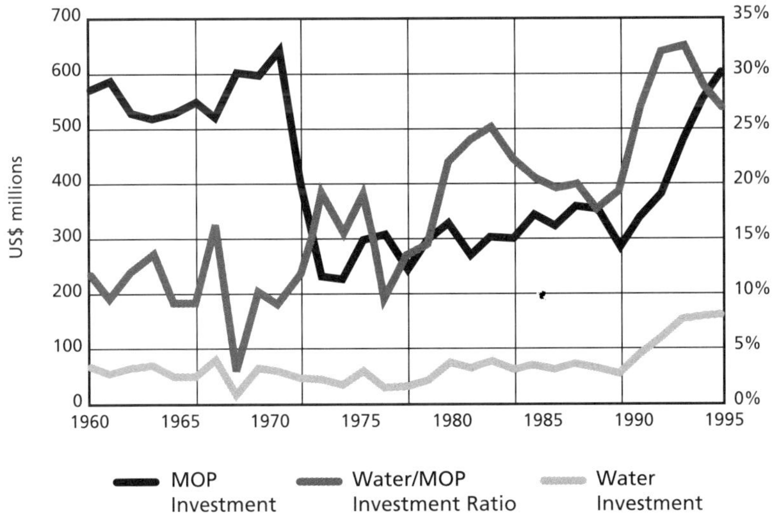

Source : SISS. 1990-1993 Annual Report.

Table 5.1 Operating Costs
(Real 1995 U.S. Dollars)

	Costs (millions)	Connections (thousands)	Cost per connection
1990	203	1.533	132
1991	233	1.751	133
1992	221	1.828	121
1993	215	1.909	112
1994	202	2.018	100
1995	199	2.100	95

According to existing estimates, around US$ 850 million must be invested in potable water and sewerage collection (excluding treatment) during the 1996–2000 period.[2] Similarly, an investment of around US$ 2.2 billion in sewerage treatment is needed,[3] much of which should be made in the short to medium term in order to meet the goal of increasing coverage of waste water treatment to 52 percent by the year 2000. Assuming that half the investment in water treatment must be made between 1996 and 2000, total average investment in water and sewerage services would have to be US$ 390 million a year over the next five years—more than double the investment made in 1995.

Due to organizational changes made in this industry, historical information on operating costs prior to 1990 is unavailable. Trends in the labor force provide the best reference point, but are inconsistent. In 1960, the Bureau of Water Works (DOS) work force totaled 3,800 employees, rising to 13,500 in 1973 (compared with roughly a doubling in the number of new potable water connections in that same period), and then falling to 7,000 in 1975, then 4,600 in 1977, and around 3,000 in 1979.

Cost cutting in the water and sewerage sector took place after the military government took power in late 1973 as part of an overall policy to streamline the public sector. From 1974 to 1978, Chile's government enterprises

---

[2] Information presented by the Superintendent of Water and Sewerage Services to the Combined Commissions of the Economy and Public Works of the Senate, 1995–96.
[3] Superintendencia de Servicios Sanitarios, Memoria 1995, p. 12

were pared dramatically to compensate for the soaring costs and excessive hiring that occurred between 1970 and 1973.

Between 1990 and 1995, the trend in operating costs for companies on which complete information exists (representing 77 percent of total urban connections in the country) has been quite good (see Table 5.1).

Organization and Legal Framework

The first projects to deliver potable water can be traced back to the colonial period in Santiago, and to the last century in some of the main cities: Valparaiso, Concepción, and Iquique ("Tarapacá Water Works"). The first sewerage evacuation services were developed in Santiago in the late 19th century. The state dominated the development of the sector and carried out its activities through numerous agencies that operated alongside one another.

A first step toward coordinating government activity in this sector was taken in 1953. The Bureau of Water Works (DOS) was created under the Ministry of Public Works (MOP), which merged the MOP Department of Hydraulics with the Bureau of Potable Water and Sewerage of the Ministry of the Interior. The purpose of the DOS was to study, plan, build, repair, maintain, sell, improve, and administer potable water, sewerage, and drainage services performed with government funds.

Until it closed in mid-1977, the DOS operated alongside other state agencies including the Division of Water and Sewerage Services (Ministry of Housing and Urban Planning), the Potable Water Company of Santiago, (Municipality of Santiago), the Municipal Sewerage Company of Valparaiso and Viña del Mar (Municipality of Valparaiso), the Office of Rural Sanitation (Ministry of Health), the Office of Sanitary Engineering of the Agrarian Reform Corporation (Ministry of Agriculture), and others.

Because it was part of the central government, the DOS had no assets of its own (its revenues were considered state revenues and hence could not be used) and it had no administrative or financial independence. Except for the DOS, water sector activities were performed by agencies whose main function was not in the potable water sector, and there were no entities to coordinate goals and activities.

Private potable water companies were created and operated during this time primarily to make real estate developments feasible (Lo Castillo

Potable Water Company and Santo Domingo Potable Water Company), rather than to provide the service as a profitable activity in and of itself. Those companies were not subject to formal regulation. At first their rates were set freely; later they were set by the Ministry of the Economy, Development, and Reconstruction at its own discretion with no pre-established rules. In practice, a number of smaller companies were unable to finance themselves with the rates set for them; they folded and were absorbed by the government system.

The overall vision until 1973 was that potable water service was a social good. As such, it should be provided by the state and financed with national funds for both investment purposes and the greater portion of operating expenses.

The National Service of Water and Sewerage Works (SENDOS) was created by public law in 1977 as an autonomous state institute with its own legal standing and assets apart from those of the Treasury (central government). SENDOS combined all government activity in the potable water supply and sewerage industry, operating directly in 11 of the country's 13 regions. It also had sole regulatory jurisdiction over the two autonomous companies operating in the other regions—the Water and Sewerage Works Company (EMOS) in Santiago, and the Water and Sewerage Works Company in Valparaiso (ESVAL)—which were free to manage their own revenues.

SENDOS was geographically decentralized, with a national office and 11 regional offices, and related to the national government through the Ministry of Public Works (MOP). It was responsible for all water and sewerage services, urban and rural, concentrated and dispersed. Water quality had to meet the standards set by the Ministry of Health, as established in the Health Code since 1916. The agency operated independently and established the standards and development plans for the service, applying rates that were set periodically by the Ministry of the Economy, Development, and Reconstruction based on the accounting costs of the service. Financial management was handled centrally by the national office.

Beginning in 1975, the focus and approach of the water sector changed. From its traditional focus as a public utility financed primarily by the national government, it became an industry that actively sought to finance its own services with the rates charged to its customers. With this change in focus, the sector began to rationalize costs. Changing the legal framework from agencies providing services to autonomous bodies with their own assets was intended to serve the new focus. Meanwhile, private companies in urban areas were supervised by SENDOS and their rates continued to be set by the Ministry of the Economy, Development, and Reconstruction with no predefined procedure.

In late 1989 and early 1990, there were 13 state-owned corporations (under private law) set up to absorb the urban water services of EMOS, ESVAL, and the 11 regional SENDOS offices. The companies that succeeded SENDOS were entrusted with the assets and complete operation of the services the agency was providing, including responsibility for making needed investments.

Until 1990, there were no explicit regulations for water and sewerage services. Starting that year, the system began to operate according to explicit regulations based on a set of laws issued between 1988 and 1990 that set the conditions for

- requesting, granting, and utilizing a water and sewerage concession (DFL No. 382 MOP, 1989);
- setting rates (DFL No.70, 1988);
- creating the regulatory body (Superintendency of Water and Sewerage Services) and defining its powers and responsibilities (Law No. 18,902, 1990);
- directly subsidizing demand for low-income users (law No. 18,778; 1989); and
- transforming the 11 SENDOS regional headquarters, EMOS and ESVAL into corporations, owned initially by the central government (law No. 18,777, 1989 and No. 18,885, 1990).

During this period, the regulatory body (see Box 5.1) was separated from management, and management was handled by companies established under private law but owned primarily by the government. At the same time, a rate-setting procedure was introduced to enable efficient companies to finance their operating costs and obtain a market return on the replacement value of their investment.

The new legislation envisioned concessions issued by the regulatory body for an indefinite time period, transferable, and differentiated into potable water production, potable water distribution, waste water collection, and waste water disposal and treatment. Concessions are granted for specific locations, and service is obligatory within a restricted geographical area, which was originally limited to populations being served and "zones included in expansion plans already underway."

Box 5.1 Regulatory and Oversight Body

The urban sector is regulated by the Superintendency of Water and Sewerage Services (SISS), an operationally decentralized service with its own legal identity and assets, under the supervision of the President of the Republic through the Ministry of Public Works (Article No. 18,902)

By law, the superintendency's main functions are as follows:

• Granting concessions
• Calculating rate formulas
• Studying, proposing, and monitoring technical standards
• Applying sanctions

In the event of a conflict between the regulator and the concessionaire, the law establishes an arbitration mechanism through a commission of three experts: one appointed by the regulator, a second by the concessionaire, and the third by the regulator based on a list previously agreed upon with the concessionaire. The rulings of the expert commission may be appealed through the ordinary court system.

The regulator oversees compliance with water quality standards (which are set by the Ministry of Health) and the service in general. It also sets goals for extending coverage within the concession area, should it be incomplete. In the event of noncompliance, the law establishes a system of sanctions ranging from fines to terminating the concession.

Information on the results of supervision is not publicly available. Through indirect sources it is known that the regulatory agency has issued many fines for failing to comply with water quality standards, but firms have not been fined for inadequate service.

There is no obligation to extend coverage to populations without service in the region where the company is operating or to new developments beyond the limits of the concession approved. Nevertheless, the concessionaire is obliged to connect all requests in its concession area, but not to finance piping systems in new developments, which are the responsibility of the developer. A total of 317 urban locations have potable water and they are served by 303 systems.

According to the law, the companies providing service when the General Law on Water Services was issued automatically acquired the concessions in the locations they were serving at that time but they had to formalize their concessions according to the terms established in the regulations. The original deadline for delivering the background information necessary

---

Box 5.2 Related Institutional Framework: Legislation on Water

---

Current legislation in Chile declares that all waters are in the public domain. However, it also requires them to be used through the right of utilization, which is a right that is real, perpetual, tradable, not subject to use conditions, and protected by the constitutional guarantees on property rights.

The law does not establish any preference among water uses, so much so that it does not sanction nonuse of a right. Likewise, it expressly rules out the possibility of establishing rights on spills, seepage, or any other kind of loss of users upstream, even when in practice waters with such origins have been used continually since the beginning of irrigation in the country. That has made it possible to significantly cut transaction costs, which can constitute a major impediment to the functioning of a water market.

The system in effect in Chile with unconditionally negotiable water rights has coincided with a significant increase in irrigation efficiency, which is calculated to have risen from 22 percent to 26 percent in the 1975–92 period.[3]

An important constraint in Chilean law is minimal regulation and control over underground water. This source is especially relevant for potable water because it normally allows for savings in the treatment of surface water and cushions water cycles. However, granting rights without considering the replenishment of water tables and the inability of officials to intervene promptly in cases where overexploitation is evident raises questions about the long-term sustainability of underground sources.

Given the low incidence of potable water within the use of water resources (5 percent), and the high value it represents for users, the tradable rights system allows for a fluid transfer from agriculture to potable water in a nonconflictive system where the only variable involved is price. Accordingly, a water service provider may obtain its primary resource independently, without depending on discretionary decisions by officials, thereby reducing uncertainty and rooting responsibility for supply solely in the company.

---

[3] M. Rosegrant and R. Gazmuri: "Chilean Water " pág. 35–36.

---

for formalization was January 31, 1991; June 30 of the following year was the deadline for delivering development plans. Those deadlines were subsequently extended. By the end of 1995, concessions had been approved for only six locations, and of a total of 304 development plans to be presented by the companies, only 126 (41 percent) had been approved, leaving 178 remaining.

In the past 20 years, the professional and technical personnel of the water industry has remained basically the same (taking into account normal turnover), despite the various organizational and institutional changes. In other words, the rules and agencies under which people work have changed, but the individuals have not. It appears that many of the professionals and technicians now working in high and midlevel administrative positions in the water companies, the Superintendency of Water Services, and the Department of Water Programs of the MOP (rural sector), came originally from SENDOS and to a lesser extent from the DOS.

Financing and Rates

Information on rates, revenues, and operating costs in the pre-1990 period (when the companies operating under private law were created) is scarce because information was lost when the organizational structure changed. (SENDOS ended before the successor companies and the regulatory agency came into existence.) Information available for the pre-1977 (pre-SENDOS) period is even less reliable: baselines are not clearly specified and information is inconsistent due to the variety of organizations providing service.

It is estimated that in 1968, revenues from rates accounted for only 16 percent of the total DOS budget. That conforms to the traditional model in which water services are provided by the government and financed with public funds. Political changes during the Salvador Allende administration (1970–73) led to a further decline in revenues from user charges. By 1973, they represented 3 percent of the total budget of the sector, leaving the government to finance 94 percent (the balance came from other revenues).

The focus changed after 1976, when user charges were gradually hiked, with the goal of reaching self-financing. The rate increase was applied by an authoritarian government, thereby limiting the opposition of interest groups and reducing the need to seek agreements or compensatory measures. Nevertheless, the design of the rate framework explicitly envisioned cross-subsidies to prevent potable water from becoming too expensive for low-income sectors. The rate increase went hand in hand with improvements in the collection system and a campaign to achieve full micrometering across cities. By 1982, coverage was already 90 percent and reached 100 percent by the end of the decade. By charging customers more and cutting costs, SENDOS was able to finance its operating costs with its own revenues by

**Table 5.2 Average Water Rates for a Sample of State Enterprises
(US$/m³, constant currency)**

	Dec. '89	Dec. '90	Dec. '91	Dec. '92	Dec. '93	Dec. '94	Dec. '95
Northern Zone (Desert) ESSAN	0.45	0.50	0.74	0.78	0.80	1.29	1.29
Center North (Semidesert) ESVAL	0.33	0.39	0.41	0.44	0.49	0.57	0.72
Central Zone EMOS	0.22	0.27	0.28	0.30	0.34	0.34	0.39
Center South ESSBIO	0.21	0.29	0.32	0.37	0.38	0.41	0.46
Southern Zone ESMAG	0.33	0.36	0.45	0.52	0.53	0.63	0.68

Sources: SISS. Memoria 1990–93 and 1995.

1979, but not its investment costs, which for the most part continued to be financed by the national government out of public funds.

In 1990, a rate-setting system went into effect. This system aimed to set rates at a level that would cover the operating costs of an efficient company and with a market-level profit rate measured as a return to the replacement value of its assets (see Box 5.3). The rate increases derived from the new method of calculation were applied gradually through 1995 when they were completed in companies with the highest rates (primarily in the northern part of the country, which has to deal with water scarcity). Trends in the average rates of the various companies are shown in Table 5.2.

The final stage of the rate increase took place entirely under the democratic government inaugurated in 1990, and eliminated cross-subsidies at the same time. It is believed that the rate increase was accepted by users and ultimately feasible thanks to direct subsidies for potable water consumption for low-income groups (see summary of subsidy in Box 5.4).

According to the law, the rate must assure that an efficient company will have market profitability above the replacement value of required investment. That value was set at 9.6 percent in the first rate setting and at 9.16 percent in the second (1995–96) for all companies in the sector.

Box 5.3 Rate Regulation in Effect since 1990

The current rate system is intended to simulate competitive market price conditions. Rates are set for financing an efficient company ("model" company) and to generate a market return on its replacement value. The rate of return is set on the basis of the Capital Asset Pricing Model (CAPM). CAPM assumes that the returns demanded by the market are the return for a "certain" investment, plus a reward for risk, which is inversely proportional to the covariance between returns on an activity and the average return on the market. The rate structure on various types of collection is set by the marginal cost ratio and then the level is adjusted to generate self-financing of the model company during the rate-setting period (see description in Morandé and Doña 1997). Rates are set for five-year periods and envision an indexation mechanism.

The "model company" method consists of defining the organization and designing the most efficient investments and installations required for meeting anticipated demand. The investments and installations are then assessed at the real cost of carrying them out. Designing "model companies" in the water services sector is relatively simple because all phases of the service are regulated; as a rule there are no "multiproduct" investments aimed at unregulated markets; the main component of cost is return and wear and tear on fixed assets; inputs have broad competitive markets; and technology does not change abruptly.

The "model company" system has the advantage that it does not require assessment of the efficiency level of the expenditures and investments of real companies, which inevitably display suboptimal levels due to wear and tear of facilities in addition to the limitations that management may display. Hence, the "real company" method reduces the needs for information on the part of the regulator, especially in the critical area of the inefficiencies that could be overcome at low cost and that may generate excessive profit for the regulated company if it makes improvements after rates have been set. Within the method, the value of the real company with its inefficiencies is defined implicitly, and the regulated entity has every incentive to make its operation more efficient.

As a rule, the law seeks to assure that a for-profit company with no financing restrictions may obtain market profitability on its efficient investments. At the same time, it expects users to pay rates that cover all investment and operating costs for receiving water services.

Nevertheless, the actual return depends on the degree of efficiency attained by the real company. Return on assets of the companies between 1988 and 1996 (estimate for SENDOS regional offices for 1988 and 1989) and of water losses (water produced but not billed) has varied (see Table 5.3).

Box 5.4 Subsidizing Demand

In 1989, a system of directly subsidizing low-income users was set up for pay-ing potable water and sewerage discharge bills. The subsidy is administered by the municipalities, which enroll and select those applicants who meet the con-ditions for receiving it and inform the particular water company, which then bills beneficiaries, separating the amount the user must pay from the part to be paid directly by the municipality.

After two modifications, the subsidy may now represent from 25 per-cent to 85 percent of the total bill, depending on the area and family income level. The general criterion is that the cost of potable water and sewerage services may not be over 5 percent of monthly family income. Awarding the subsidy and setting the category is carried out in accordance with the CASEN Survey, conducted nationwide by the Ministry of National Planning, which defines indicators making it possible to calculate family incomes and hence the eligibility of each subsidy applicant by applying parameters that are indi-rect and hard to falsify.

In 1995, budgeting was provided for a maximum of 452,297 subsidies; 438,253 were allocated, and 388,234 were actually billed (86 percent of what was budgeted). The subsidy benefited 17.6 percent of residential customers and cost the government US$ 23 million, or 5.2 percent of total billing of wa-ter companies (see breakdown in Morandé and Doña 1997).

Subsidizing demand in the application of a rate structure is important in enabling this activity to become self-financing in the long run and has gradu-ally eliminated cross-subsidies. The process has allowed real rates to double between 1989 and 1995, without arousing great opposition from customers. The system of directly subsidizing demand, focused on low-income users, has meant that payments did not rise for low-income users as a result of the rate increase, but in some cases even fell.

As is evident, the profitability of state enterprises is on average less than that of the main private companies and the levels of water losses are very high. (EMOS and ESSCO are the exception with total losses of 21.3 percent and 21.6 percent respectively for 1995. They also reduced water losses the most between 1990 and 1995.)

In 1995 state-owned water companies had net earnings of approxi-mately US$ 107 million, which together with depreciation meant that funds of around US$ 177 million (before payment of dividends) were generated internally. That sum equals less than half of investment requirements, as-suming that an average of US$ 390 million a year is required between 1996

Table 5.3 Profitability of Water Losses: 1988–1995

	Net profitability on total assets		Water losses		
			State companies		
	State companies	Others	Total	Leaving out EMOS y ESSCO	Others
1988	−1.4%	−1.0%			
1989	−1.6%	13.1%			
1990	−1.1%	3.9%	35.2%	41.0%	
1991	−0.2%	1.6%			
1992	0.9%	4.0%			
1993	3.4%	6.5%			
1994	5.1%	7.2%			
1995	5.9%	10.0%	31.1%	39.8%	17.0%

Box 5.5 Water Losses

Water losses in production and distribution take two forms:
1. Physical losses: water produced that is physically lost in transfer and distribution and does not reach customers. Controlling it entails costs and investments that can be high. By some estimates, the level of physical water losses that would be economically efficient
2. Water delivered to customers that is not billed, due to metering mistakes, stealing, tampering with meters, and so forth. In this instance, the cost necessary for prevention is for monitoring, and as a rule offers a high private return.

and 2000. Hence, in order to carry out the required programs, the state-owned water companies would need major amounts of financing either through borrowing or through capital contributions.

In order to provide a market return on needed investments, current legislation assures that the companies can go to the capital market both for loans and for capitalization should they need investments exceeding their own resources. In the case of state enterprises, however, their own borrowing and the capital contributions from the Treasury must be authorized by the government's annual budget law.

In general, the state's capital contributions to its own companies for major investments compete with social projects without recovering costs, even if the project generates a positive long-term net value and therefore does not entail net costs for the state. Thus, contrary to the provisions in the law, government companies are not assured financing for their major investments, even when they are needed for service and should be profitable for their provider, since the decision to allow borrowing or capital contributions is made by political officials outside the industry.

Institutional Structure and Performance

Table 5.4 summarizes the development over time of the main features of the provision and coverage of urban water services.

A Snapshot of the Urban Water Sector

There are several main conclusions that can be drawn from the relationship between institutional structure, organization, incentives, and performance on the basis of the development of urban water services over time in Chile.

Coverage has been increasing steadily to the point where it has reached 98 percent of the urban population for potable water and 89 percent for sewerage, under a variety of organizational and legal arrangements. The overall trend is satisfactory and does not appear to be related to the changing institutional arrangements.

The quality of potable water service in terms of continuity of delivery and the bacteriological, chemical, and other quality factors of the water is now presenting problems that reflect underinvestment. Sewerage treatment is minimal (14 percent in 1995) and is centered primarily on cheaper solutions, namely undersea emissions. No institutional arrangement seems to have provided an appropriate solution to the problem thus far.

In theory, current legislation makes it possible to make the necessary investments and finance them over time by charging customers. However, the amount of investment entailed goes beyond the cash surpluses generated by the companies, meaning additional funds would be required, either through borrowing or capital contributions. Since the state is the largest

Table 5.4 Summary of Institutional Changes over Time and Performance Indicators for Urban Water Services

	1950	1955	1960	1965	1970	1975	1980	1985	1990	1995
Coverage										
Potable water				53.5%	66.5%	77.4%	91.4%	95.2%	97.4%	98.6%
Sewerage				25.4%	31.1%	43.5%	67.4%	75.1%	81.8%	89.2%
Treatment									8.0%	14.0%
Average connections (thous./year)										
Potable water					45	80	64	53	107	78
Sewerage					20	65	83	58	111	85
Average Investment amount (US$ million/year)										
Investment per connection (US$/connection)				58	54	40	64	64	136	
Operating costs (US$ million)					869	404	234	547	364	703
Operating costs (US$/ new connection)								75	115	199
Staffing			3.800		13.500 (1973)	7.000	3.000 (1979)		95	
Organization	Various state institutions and bodies not independent, uncoordinated.					SENDOS (1977), decentralized autonomous state agency with its own assets. Combines state water activity.			State-owned companies under private law. Private companies (8%)	
Law	No regulations established by law. The Ministry of the Economy sets rates, without any predefined procedure, in accordance with policies toward the sector.								Since 1990, regulations set by law, applied by an independent regulatory and supervisory agency.	
Financing										
Operating	State: over 80%					State 94%	Self-financing by fees since 1979			Billing
Minor investments							State/self-generated funds			Company surpluses
Major investments							State			Capital contribution or borrowing
Profitability										
State agencies					(1.1%)	5.94%				
Private companies					3.9%	9.99%				
Losses										
State companies									35.2%	31.1%
State comp. except EMOS y ESSCO									41.0%	39.8%
Private companies										17.0%

owner of the companies, both capital contributions and borrowing are limited by budgetary constraints on the Treasury. According to the law, the regulatory body has the power to oblige companies to make needed investments and to sanction failure to provide service with fines and even loss of the concession. However, the regulatory body has demanded only limited investment in waste water treatment and has not applied sanctions for significant service failures. (For example, there are major urban areas that get water for less than half the day and the company responsible has not been fined.) It is thought that the main reason why the regulatory body is lax is that it is also a government agency. Thus, for government water companies, regulator and regulated are not really separated.

Investment in this sector remained relatively steady until 1990, even though during the 1975–90 period public investment in Chile fell significantly. This relatively steady investment stream during an overall public financing drought reflects in part a policy choice given the impact of this sector on the health of the population. It also reflects the 1975 change in the policy of charging for services, which allowed for self-financing of operating costs by 1979.

In turn, increased investment since 1990 was made possible by incorporating a market return on investment into water rates. This was established by law and was applied gradually in the 1990–95 period to soften the significant cost increase that it entailed for customers. It should be noted that when the new companies were set up they were endowed with initial resources in the form of loans to make the various investments pending at that time.

Over time, investment per connection has fluctuated significantly but erratically, with no clear link to changes in institutional relationships. Based on the information available, it cannot be concluded that the increase in unit costs of investment means less efficiency, since investments in various processes or in different kinds of customers for the same process vary widely. On the contrary, the legal framework and type of organization applied starting in 1990 ought to create incentives to lower investment costs, yet investment per connection has practically doubled from the 1985–90 average.

The greatest changes in operating costs occurred in 1970–73 when staffing tripled and in 1974–77 when staffing was cut to one-third. In both instances, the explanation is a general policy affecting the water industry as well as all other activities performed by the government.[4] In the first case, the policy of a socialist government was to create jobs; in the second case, the policy was to make government services decisively more efficient, applied without any counterbalances by an authoritarian government. Both experiences are regarded as unique and quite unlikely to be repeated or applied under other circumstances.

Application of the new organizational and legal framework starting in 1990, which was intended to provide incentives for lower costs, has been accompanied by a rise in absolute operating costs and unit costs (measured on total connections of potable water and sewerage). Whether or not this is due to changes in efficiency cannot be determined on the basis of available information, because it may also reflect changes in service quality or the extension of service to areas and sectors where unit costs are higher.

Based on the available information, for the past 30 years urban areas had adequate financing, at first almost entirely from the government and later from charges to customers generating a market return on the replacement value of assets for an efficient company. That is, no clear relationship between availability of funds and the institutional arrangement and incentives can be established. However, while institutional changes may not have affected the availability of financing in the industry, the change from general government funds to self-financing of costs and investments through water rates provides a measure of long-term financial security. Public financing is a discretionary source that is uncertain over time while self-financing allows companies to go to capital markets to cover their needs for additional funding.

Raising water rates high enough to make the sector fully self-financing did not encounter major opposition from customers, probably because the effect was cushioned by granting direct subsidies to demand, thereby reducing its impact on low-income sectors. It was also applied at a time when real incomes were rising throughout the country.[5] Application of those

---

[4] However, concentrating functions in a single agency (SENDOS) in 1977 may have made it possible to intensify cost cutting by eliminating overlapping operations. In any case, its relative impact on correcting for politically motivated overstaffing is unclear.

[5] Nevertheless, it can be argued that the high levels of underinvoicing noted in service could reflect a way in which customers manifest their opposition to the cost represented in rates. However, the fact that there are at least two state enterprises (EMOS and ESSCO) whose losses reflect low underbilling (total losses of 26 percent, most of which comes from physical losses, while underbilling is less than 10 percent), would indicate that levels of under-invoicing are more a reflection of the management of the companies than a coordinated stance by customers.

direct subsidies entails costs to the state of approximately 5.2 percent of total billing of the companies (1995), and benefits 17 percent of customers, under the general criterion that spending on water should be limited to no more than 5 percent of family income. It is believed that any relevant option of subsidizing supply with an equivalent protection for low-income strata would cost significantly more.

The legislation in effect since 1990 allows service to be provided by companies under private law for profit. The regulatory framework sets rates and determines the conditions for providing service by simulating competitive conditions in order to generate incentives and controls. The goal is for customers to receive efficient service at the lowest cost and for companies to obtain a market return so they can access the financing needed for all required investment. Nevertheless, it is believed that the incentives have not operated effectively for state enterprises. Thus, the fact that water losses go beyond levels of economic efficiency in most state enterprises is a sign that these enterprises tend to respond insufficiently to financial incentives, inasmuch as reducing underbilling is probably the most profitable action the companies can take. (That is not the case for cutting physical water losses, which might require heavy investment.) Similarly, government companies do not optimize their financial structure: they have a very low debt level— less than that allowed by the characteristics of their activity—even though they could make use of credits at rates lower than the return they obtain on their assets. The explanation for such nonoptimizing behavior would seem to lie in the fact that attaining limited efficiency is sufficient for financing operating costs and lesser investments. Financing major investments goes far beyond the ability of even the most efficient companies to generate surpluses and therefore depends on capital contributions or authorization to borrow, which plainly entail a decision that is political rather than financial.

Government ownership of companies providing water services is thought to have the following main effects:

- They are not adequately responsive to economic incentives, which are the main tool envisioned in current legislation for assuring efficient performance.
- They inhibit the action of the regulatory body, leaving customers of government-owned companies without protection for the quality of service they receive even though the rates they pay are high enough to finance a service that meets all standards of quantity and quality.

- The financial restrictions faced by government companies in making even profitable investments has limited the development of sewerage treatment systems, which require heavy investments.

In Chile, the development of the current institutional and legislative framework has been eased by the existence of complementary legislation:

- Direct subsidy to demand, which made it easier to introduce self-financing rates.
- Water rights that are tradable between sectors, thereby making companies no longer dependent on officials for obtaining a supply of their crucial input.

According to sources, the professional and technical staff in this sector has remained relatively stable throughout the various changes in agencies and their regulatory framework. Their performance is said to have more to do with their professional ability than with the incentives that may have been introduced or withdrawn with institutional changes. It may be that the sector's satisfactory development over time has depended largely on the continuity of the trained professional and technical employees, rather than on agency and rule changes.

Privatizing Public Utility Services

Conditions in Chile are particularly favorable for the involvement of private investors in state-regulated sectors because the political structure tends to create legislative stability, and the country has an independent judiciary, assuring compliance with both legal and contractual arrangements (see Box 5.6).

Background

In mass consumption public utility services that are natural monopolies and require discrete large investments, such as water services, the government has normally been actively involved as supplier, regulator, or a combination of both. Among such service sectors are electric power, telephone, road and port infrastructure, railways, irrigation, and so forth.

During this century, government policy in Chile toward public services has gone through three clearly differentiated phases. Until 1925–30, development was at the initiative of private individuals, and the government was not involved (with the exception of the railways). Around 1925,

Box 5.6 Summary of the Institutional Political Framework

In the Chilean political system, the executive, legislative, and judicial powers are separated, each of them being constituted independently. The executive power is exercised by the president, who is elected through a direct vote for a six-year term with right to a second term. The legislative branch is made up of two chambers, with elections every four years at times other than presidential elections; one chamber is completely replaced and the other partially. The judicial branch is headed by the Supreme Court, whose judges are appointed for life by the president from among three names proposed by the Court. The judicial power generally operates with independence, and there are many precedents of rulings against the national government.

The Chilean legal system follows the tradition of codified laws, with strict adherence to the letter of the law, leaving a relatively narrow margin for interpretation by judges, which reduces uncertainty. The Political Constitution is the basis of the legal code and contains strong protection for property rights. Changes in the Constitution require highly demanding special quorums. Laws issued must be consistent with constitutional provisions, and in the event of conflict, the Constitutional Court, an independent body whose composition comes from a consensus of the different branches of government, resolves it.

The political party structure in the country has traditionally been spread among no fewer than five parties, each having voting and representation of between 8 and 10 percent. Historically, the various parties have lined up and established alliances in terms of three main positions: right, center, and left. The current electoral system encourages lining up along two lines, creating conditions for maintaining a relative parity of representation by both within wide voting ranges.

Major changes in the law must be constitutional and are constrained by the existence of two legislative chambers, which are set up differently and are not elected at the same time, by the relative over-representation of minorities, and by the existence of different parties, none with sufficient voting power to become dominant.

The tradition of respect for institutions and legality goes back to shortly after independence. While the 1973–90 military regime constituted a significant break, it was originally justified on the grounds that constitutional provisions had been violated repeatedly, and it came to an end within this tradition, as the result of losing an election.

In general, Chile's political and institutional framework makes possible the creation of stable and credible conditions for the involvement of private investors in public utility services, whether they are regulated by legislation or by specific contracts with the government or with government companies and bodies. In practice, both options are being applied.

the state became more active in a number of areas, and beginning with the Great Depression, it became involved in service production, especially in public utilities. The role of the state expanded during this period, reaching a high point between 1970 and 1973, a period when it concentrated the greater part of economic activity in its hands and imposed a wide range of price controls.

Since 1973, a large portion of public utility services has been transferred to the private sector, while the state has held onto the role of regulator in the areas where market imperfections were most apparent. The policy began during the military government (1973–90), which privatized the entire telephone sector and a great deal of electric power, mainly between 1985 and 1989. The policy of privatizing public utility services was partially continued by the administration that succeeded it in 1990 and by the current one. Neither of them has questioned the privatizations of the previous period and they have extended the policy to new sectors, such as concessions for roads, railways, and so forth. Regulation of the electric and telephone industries rests solely on laws and regulations. With regard to road concessions, regulation has been based on generally applicable legal provisions, and on contractual specifications for the particular conditions of each concession. For railway freight transportation, regulation is solely contractual.

The concern here is to examine the conditions and processes that led to the privatization of most public utility electric power and telephone services, and the particular conditions that explain why thus far the water industry has not been privatized.

Electric Power Industry

This industry began around 1880, through private enterprise. The first regulations were established in 1925. The state became directly involved around 1940 and took on the preponderant role, especially in power generation, although it existed alongside private companies until the latter were nationalized in 1970. Throughout the entire period, this industry has performed adequately, satisfying demand in quantity and coverage, generally at reasonably efficient costs.

The following are the main steps in the process that ultimately led to privatization:

- Return to real levels in rates, which had fallen sharply during the 1970–73 period, and drastic cost cutting. By way of illustration, the ENDESA payroll fell from 8,460 workers in 1973 to 4,270 in 1979.
- Restructuring of government companies in this sector, by separating generation from distribution and transmission. Distribution was divided geographically.
- Design of a new regulatory framework, which provided that rates would be set only for end users with less than 2000 kw of contracted power (around 60 percent of demand). Distribution companies would buy power to supply those users, in whatever proportion that they may do so. Rates were to be unrestricted for all other services.
- Transfer to the private sector began in 1980 with small companies, and culminated in 1988 with majority privatization of the main companies in the industry. The transfer of the larger companies included the granting of preferential options to the workers.

At the same time, the domestic capital market was deepened and the problem of the country's excessive foreign debt began to be resolved.

Privatization was not at all a response to an immediate emergency. It was carried out within a long-term development strategy that sought primarily to limit direct government involvement in the economy, free state resources for social purposes, improve efficiency through private management, and separate the roles of regulator and provider. Business groups actively supported the process. Groups of workers that could have opposed the process did not do so in view of the benefit represented by the preferential stock purchase options they were granted. Within the context of an authoritarian government, the opposition of other, primarily political, interest groups was not widely communicated and had little impact.

Toward the end of the military government, the goal of limiting the quantity of productive resources that were to be left to political officials to manage as they saw fit became particularly important, inasmuch as political authority was going to shift to what was then the opposition.

Some criticisms have been raised against the privatization of the electric power industry, primarily the following:

- The regulatory framework encourages competition in power generation, but ownership of transmission was left in the hands of the main generator.
- A significant number of water rights needed for developing fu-

ture hydroelectric projects was left in the hands of the main power generator.

- Control over the main generator company (ENDESA) and the main distribution company (CHILECTRA) is currently held by a single entity.
- The fact that the main companies in the industry have become highly profitable could erode credibility in the law and in the ability of the regulator to set rates that stimulate competition.
- The main companies have moved into real estate and highway concessions.

Recently, the arrival of natural gas from Argentina and the improvement in practice of the right of third party generators to have access to the trunk transmission system have lowered entry barriers and made power generation significantly more competitive.

Telephone Industry

Historically, the telephone industry developed in much the same way as the electric power industry. The differences were that direct government involvement began only in the 1960s and was initially limited to long distance service (with the creation of ENTEL), and supply clearly did not satisfy the demand (CEPAL calculated that in 1987 the gap was 23 percent). The upshot was long waiting lists for telephone connections; the average time period for obtaining a connection was 125 weeks—over two years—(mid-1980s).

In 1973, the industry was dominated by two government companies: one in local phone service (CTC, which had been nationalized during the government of President Salvador Allende) and another in long distance (ENTEL).

The process that led to privatization proceeded through the following steps:

- Recovery of real levels in rates, which had been cut drastically during the 1970–73 period, plus cost cutting. The secondary market for phone lines was made legal.
- Establishment in 1982 of a regulatory framework envisioning significant competition in local telephone service. In practice, regulation focused on requirements for interconnection, and did not

specify greater demands on levels of service, or establish mechanisms or criteria for setting rates.

- Regulatory changes between 1985 and 1987, which entailed specifying the obligations of concessionaires, establishing clear powers for the regulatory body, and defining a rate-setting procedure.
- Transfer to the private sector: CTC (local phone service) control was privatized in 1988 through an international bidding process that involved commitments to increase capital. ENTEL was privatized primarily through the sale of share packages on the stock exchange. In both instances, company workers were offered a preferential purchase option.

Privatization of the CTC was marked by the urgent need to provide resources and promote the development of a key industry that was a bottleneck for an economy whose driving force was export expansion. Privatization has meant a dramatic increase in investment in the industry, which has enabled the long-standing supply backlog to be resolved, but may also indicate that current regulations are stimulating some degree of overinvestment that ultimately is paid for by customers. Likewise, the opening of free competition in long distance service meant lower rates, noticeably below those that the regulator had previously set, which were supposed to have been the rates that would exist under competitive conditions.

Private Investors and Water Services

The legislation that went into effect in 1990 was clearly intended to create conditions for subsequently privatizing the water companies, by authorizing the government to sell its share in the two largest companies, EMOS and ESVAL. Privatization of other companies was limited to a 49 percent ceiling.

The main options for involving private investment and management are as follows:

- Granting concessions for new services. Since the legislation was promulgated, 34 concession requests have been presented, all by private companies, encompassing around 20,000 initial connections, with a goal of 80,000. Eight of the requests presented have been accepted, three were rejected, two withdrew, and the rest are under study or being adjudicated.

- Investment contracts with management for a predetermined period and transfer of the investments at the end of the contract (Build-Operate-Transfer contracts).
- Transfer of concessions. As of 1996, one instance of concession transfer had occurred. In the city of Valdivia (118,000 inhabitants) the state-owned ESSAL company awarded the concessions in question to the private company Aguas Décima S.A. through a public bidding process.
- Sale of the companies.

Investment contracts with management and transfer of concessions may include all phases of a service or a specific one.

The problem with transferring concessions for specific processes (such as sewerage treatment, for instance, which requires the greatest investment) is that the potable water distributor must bill users, leaving the concessionaires of other phases dependent for their revenues on the efficiency with which the distributor controls water losses and underbilling.[6] In view of the current widespread inefficiency in controlling losses and underbilling, the option of concessions for specific processes is regarded as unlikely until the problem is solved.

In order to bring in additional resources in phases requiring heavier investment, management contracts with investment offer an effective procedure that is now being applied in waste water treatment for the city of Antofagasta (Biwater, through a contract with ESSAN). The advantage is that the contract can incorporate specifications with greater detail than general legislation. When it is applied to a specific phase, however, the system does not resolve the management efficiencies displayed in a significant portion of government companies, and does not allow for effective separation between regulator and regulated.

The management contracts with investment approach encompassing all the concessions in a geographical area is being applied in the production and distribution of potable water and the collection and disposal of waste water for the southern coastal area of Region V (Aguas Quinta, by means of a contract with ESVAL). That system makes it possible to deal with management problems and has the advantage of allowing for the incorporation of

---

[6] The rate calculation procedure heavily penalizes inefficiency in controlling losses and under-invoicing, inasmuch as rates are calculated for standard levels.

detail specifications. One limitation, however, is that it makes service more expensive for users, both because it lowers the time period for repayment of investments and because it raises the costs of providing service by bringing in another relationship to be monitored: that between the concessionaire company and the contractor.[7]

Transferring the concessions of all the processes in one location is an option for involving the private sector fully in water service investment and management that enables companies to be restructured geographically. However, only in Valdivia has ownership in a service concession in a major city been transferred.

Since these cases of private investment and management have been operational for such a short time it is still too early to judge their performance and the degree to which they satisfy legislation and regulations. Indeed, they still do not appear in official statistics. The current government recently presented the legislature with a bill to improve regulation in this industry, with the explicit purpose of creating the conditions needed for adequately privatizing state-owned water companies in order to involve private financing and technology and improve management. This would "enable the state to concentrate its activity in priority areas where the private sector does not represent an efficient substitute" (message of the Executive on behalf of the bill).

The following are among the aspects taken up in the bill (see a breakdown and critical analysis of the law in Morandé and Doña 1997):

- It places restrictions on ownership of water companies (among others, that state ownership be at least 35 percent). The goal is to prevent horizontal monopolies in the real estate market, protect minority shareholders, and generate competitive conditions.
- It sets requirements for transparency in contracts and transactions with related companies.
- It bolsters the structure and powers of the regulatory body.
- It transfers to the state the water rights of the companies that would be privatized.
- It grants a preferential option to purchase shares in the companies to their workers for up to 10 percent of its capital.

---

[7] If the rates allow the subconcessionaire to obtain a market return by amortizing investments in a time period shorter than their useful life, it means they ought to be lower.

- It establishes a temporary obligation to provide help to potable rural water services.

In general, the bill presented by the Executive does not solve the main problems affecting the industry. For example, the requirement of a 35 percent minimum government share perpetuates the constraints on financing for needed investments and precludes a complete separation between regulator and regulated. Instead, the bill seeks to avoid problems perceived in the privatization of other public utility sectors, which either do not arise in the water industry or ought to be handled with specific tools. For example, the issue of transferring water rights to the state was apparently inspired by the privatization of the electric power industry. In that case, most of the water rights were granted to the main producer of power for short- and medium-term hydroelectric projects, thereby generating a monopoly position that could have been avoided. That problem does not exist in the water industry, however, and water rights are actually used for providing the service; indeed, when ownership is placed in an entity outside the company, responsibility for supply and developing sources of water is dissipated.

Privatization of Urban Water Service: Why Not?

Private investment and management have been slower to enter the urban water service industry than they have been in other public utility services for a number of reasons.

When Chile embarked on its economic liberalization program in the mid-1970s, the water industry was obviously behind in terms of organizational structure and regulations, compared to other public utilities. For example, the electric power and telephone industries historically were set up as companies and a regulatory framework existed as far back as 1925–30. Regulations had to be developed for the water industry from scratch, and an organization had to be created with its own assets obtaining revenues and producing profits by bringing together functions and responsibilities that had previously been spread out.

Moreover, there were no critical problems in the sector. State management performed adequately and the industry did not display any overwhelming shortage of capacity, as was the case in telephone service. Thus, there was no overwhelming need or pressure to privatize.

Box 5.7 Processes of Institutional and Operational Organization and Privatization in the Electric Power, Telephone, and Water Industries

	Electric Power Industry	Telephone Industry	Water Industry
Baseline, 1973	Two large state companies, both in distribution and generation. Low rates and high costs.	Two large state companies, one in local phone service and the other in long distance. Low rates and high costs.	Various state offices and agencies, overlapping in zones and responsibilities. Low rates and high costs.
Operational adjustment 1974–78	Rate increase. Operating costs cut.	Rate increase. Operating costs cut.	Rate increase. Operating costs cut.
Reorganization	Separation of generation, distribution, and transmission. Distribution divided along geographical lines.		Unification of the industry (1977) into one autonomous state body. Separation along geographical lines and establishment of companies under private law (1990).
Regulatory framework	Regulations modified (1978).	Regulations modified (1982). Regulations changed (1985–87).	Gradual application of long term self-financing rates (1990–94).
Privatization	1980–87: smaller companies. 1988: ENDESA, Chilectra, Chilgener, and Chilquinta.	CTC: 1988. ENTEL 1988–89.	Creation of a regulatory framework. 1994: Valdivia (1% proportion of whole country). 1994: Central coast. 8 concessions for new real estate developments. New privatizations subject to bill modifying legislation.

There was also less pressure from interest groups favoring privatization. The level of investments and volume of operations involved in the water industry is significantly less than in the electric power and telephone sectors. Investors have become interested in the privatization of the water industry relatively recently, since the creation of the companies in 1990.

On the other hand, there were interest groups opposed to privatization. Political actors whose ability to express themselves was constrained during the privatization of the electric power and telephone industries by the authoritarian government at that time were free to object in the case of water.

Investors and politicians are facing off in the current discussion on the conditions for privatizing urban water companies. The investor community wants rapid and complete privatization. Political actors argue that stricter regulation must be introduced to prevent monopoly advantages and reinforce oversight in order to avoid the problems they see in previous privatization processes. Workers have not expressed major opposition to the project, probably because they expect to be offered the preferential option to buy shares should privatization takes place. By and large, customers have not been involved in the discussion.

References

Ale Y, Jorge. 1988. "La Experiencia Chilena en el Estudio e Implementación de un Sistema de Tarificación a Costo Marginal en Agua Potable y Alcantarillado." Document presented to the Interministerial Commission on the Water Sector.

Corporación de Fomento (CORFO). Annual Reports, 1990–95.

————. 1993. "Gestión 1990–93: Empresas de Servicios Sanitarios—Filiales Corfo." Santiago, Chile.

EMOS S.A. 1993. "Relación entre la Metodología Tarifaria y la Optimización en el Diseño de Obras Sanitarias." Unpublished document.

Inecon Ltda. 1994. "Análisis Tarifario para Sistemas de Agua Potable Rural." Document prepared for the Corporación de Fomento a la Producción.

————. 1995. "Estudio de Valorización del Agua Cruda para Empresas Sanitarias." Document prepared for the Superintendencia de Servicios Sanitarios.

Ministerio de Hacienda. 1996. Proyectos de Ley de Presupuesto, 1990–96.

Ministerio de Obras Públicas. Annual Reports 1958–94. Santiago, Chile.

Ministerio de Planificación y Cooperación (MIDEPLAN). 1996. Unidad CAS, Depto. Información y Evaluación Social. Unpublished document.

Moncada, Alejandro. 1984. "Programa Nacional de Agua Potable Rural Chileno." Revista AIDIS (Asociación Interamericana de Ingeniería Sanitaria). 38 (5, 6).

Morandé, F. and Doña, J.E. 1997. "Los servicios de agua potable en Chile: condicionantes, institucionalidad y aspectos de economía política." Working paper R-308. Washington, DC: Inter-American Development Bank.

Morandé, F., Doña, J.E., and Casas, C. 1994. "Estudio de determinación de la tasa de costo de capital para el sector sanitario nacional." Paper prepared for the Superintendencia de Servicios Sanitarios. Santiago, Chile.

Servicio Nacional de Obras Sanitarias (SENDOS). 1977. "Plan Nacional de Coberturas. Primer Informe." Santiago, Chile.

_____ . 1977b. "Informativo Económico-financiero DOS (Dirección de Obras Sanitarias)." Santiago, Chile.

_____ . 1977c. Untitled presentation by the director of the DOS to the Third National Mayor's Conference Santiago, Chile.

_____ . 1983. "Reseña Programa Agua Potable Rural." Presentation at the Fifth Congress of Sanitary Engineering.

_____ . 1986. Organización Nacional del Sub-sector Obras Sanitarias. Mimeo.

_____ . 1988. Organización Nacional del Sub-sector Obras Sanitarias. Mimeo.

_____ . 1989. "Revisión de los Progresos del Decenio Internacional del Abastecimiento de Agua y del Saneamiento." Chile's presentation in the Working Group of Latin American managers in the Water Sector.

Superintendencia de Servicios Sanitarios. Annual Reports 1990–93. Santiago, Chile.

_____ . 1995. Memoria. Santiago, Chile.

_____ . 1994. "Análisis de Resultados Empresas Sanitarias, 1988–94." Unpublished document.

Superintendencia de Servicios Sanitarios: Departmento de Normalización y Control. 1995. Informes de Cobertura, 1991–95. Santiago, Chile.

Superintendencia de Servicios Sanitarios. Departmento de Tarifas. 1993. "El Sistema de Aportes de Financiamiento Reembolsables en las Empresas Sanitarias". Unpublished document.

_____ . 1994. Anuario. Santiago, Chile.

Troncoso G., Sergio. 1984 "Servicio Nacional de Obras Sanitarias." Revista *AIDIS*. 38 (5,6).

CHAPTER 6

Governance and Regulation: A Tale of Two Concessions in Argentina

Daniel Artana, Fernando Navajas, and Santiago Urbiztondo[1]

Traditionally, the water sector has been managed by the public sector in Argentina. However, in the last 10 years, Argentina has experimented with private participation on a scale and at a pace beyond other experiences in Latin America. The first two concessions granted in Argentina were in the province of Corrientes and the city of Buenos Aires. Each of the two concession processes, regulatory frameworks, and institutional contexts had relative advantages and disadvantages. These differences may have affected both the resulting performance of the two water companies and the post-contract negotiations. This chapter demonstrates the impact of the institutional and political context on the outcomes of concession arrangements, and highlights the strengths and weaknesses of the various actors involved in the process of improving water services with private sector participation.

In Argentina, as in most countries, the water industry traditionally has been managed by public companies. However, the wave of privatization over the past 10 years has crested over this industry too, forcing it to reconcile the advantages of private supply and the social demands typical of public utilities. Whether those advantages are capitalized upon depends on the design of the rate structure, the level of prices imposed on private operators, and how those prices are adjusted.

---

[1] Daniel Artana is Executive Director of the Fundación de Investigaciones Económicas Latinoamericanas (FIEL) in Buenos Aires, Argentina; Fernando Navajas is lead economist at FIEL; Santiago Urbiztondo is an associate economist at FIEL.

The first two potable water and sewerage concessions in Argentina[2] were in the province of Corrientes and the Greater Buenos Aires region. These concessions commenced operations in September 1992 and May 1992, respectively. They were followed by other concessions in the provinces that are still in the development phase.

The two cases share several common features. Both are concessions (i.e., they do not involve a transfer of assets) and both utilized the same method to select the winning bid. However, there are also major differences between the two: their regulatory designs, their institutional contexts, and their results thus far. Their common features are an advantage for comparative analysis, since they provide a control for certain variables and demonstrate the effect institutional differences have on the performance of each concession. Since the conclusions presented here are drawn from only two cases that were analyzed only three to four years after the concessions were granted, they must be viewed with caution. However, the information contained herein supports the modern theory of economic regulation. It can also help guide the study of other experiences to add to the stock of relevant case studies.

Both regulatory designs are flawed. With regard to the rate structure, which is a crucial factor for regulated public utilities to operate efficiently, the Corrientes concession has a better system than the Buenos Aires one. It is more transparent, has fewer cross-subsidies, and almost universal metering. The rate structure in Buenos Aires has kept the previous price structure nearly intact, giving the concessionaire, at least until now, no incentives to maintain or improve service quality. Instead, its earnings depend on its ability to collect, and on the real estate reassessment of the properties served.

With regard to the institutional design of the regulatory body, which is fundamental in determining the regulated companies' incentives to invest in sunk assets, the Buenos Aires concession is better than that of Corrientes. As an independent body, it is less subject to the meddling of those currently in political office and has a more specific and regulated mandate. In Corrientes, the regulatory body is under the direct control of provincial politicians in power, and there are few restrictions on interpretations and

---

[2] To put the cases into context, see a summary of Argentina's privatization experience in Artana, Navajas, and Urbiztondo (1997).

regulations.[3] The broader legal environment has gained increasing importance as a determinant of available and efficient regulatory options in other
contexts (Levy and Spiller 1994). At both the federal (Buenos Aires) and
provincial levels (Corrientes), the shortcomings of the courts highlight the
importance of defining the regulatory body's discretionary power, especially
in the case of Corrientes, where judicial power in the province is even more
dependent on the executive branch than its federal counterpart.

In short, given the two institutional characteristics considered—regulatory body independence and recourse to a politically independent judiciary—the Buenos Aires concession is better because it generates higher levels of investment, a requisite in both cases given the low degree of initial
coverage. Thus, the predictions regarding rate structure may prove to be
unfounded. It appears that regulatory and judiciary independence are more
important than the rate structure, since the behavior of the concessionaire
in Corrientes has been adversely affected by political changes that encouraged more opportunistic behavior on the part of the regulatory body. This
problem has not occurred in Buenos Aires, despite the downturn in the
economy, which could also have modified priorities for those in political
power.[4]

Performance Indicators Prior to Privatization

The first potable water service of Argentina was provided by Obras Sanitárias
de la Nación (OSN) in 1870 after the cholera epidemic that ravaged Buenos
Aires. Initially it served 30,000 people and coverage continued to expand
until 1960. That expansion ended in the 1970s, and in the 1980s, coverage as
a share of the population actually contracted. While in existence, OSN was
financed with grants from the National Treasury and the provinces.

---

[3] In the Buenos Aires concession, the regulatory body potentially has an even more important
link to the regulated company (Aguas Argentinas) than to those in political power due to the
way it is funded.

[4] Political changes had not occurred in Buenos Aires until 1996, when the first election for
mayor of the city of Buenos Aires was held. The winner was the Radical Party candidate.
Prior to that, the president (who belongs to the Justicialista Party) had filled that position by
appointment.

Until 1980, the basic features of government supply of potable water and sewerage services were the same throughout the country because the OSN provided all the service[5] and because institutional problems between the various provinces and the federal government stemmed from governments run by the same party at both levels. (During this century, oscillation between military and civilian governments has been much more significant than variations in political party labels during democratic periods.)[6]

The indicators of the OSN that depict the "low-quality equilibrium" characteristics of a public corporation are: a sharp decline in rates, uncontrolled expenditures (especially excessive payroll), and insufficient investment.[7]

In different studies of post-World War II utility rate cycles in Argentina (Núñez, Miñana, and Porto 1976), successive cycles in real rates of public utilities were found to reflect various factors. Attempts were made to use them as a nominal anchor, along with wages and the exchange rate, to stabilize prices for political ends and for the purposes of redistribution.

The public service most hurt by such policies was potable water and sewerage. An estimate of a double logarithmic ratio between public rates and overall price levels made by Núñez, Miñana, and Porto for the 1960–76 period for public corporations as a whole showed that the inflation elasticity of OSN rates was approximately 0.8, the lowest of all public utilities. Using SIGEP data, and 1960 as the base year (=100), it was shown that while the real level of public utility rates in 1976 was 123.8, the index for the OSN was 51.1 and had been even lower in previous years—the lowest of all public services. In other words, the real level of potable water rates fell by half in 15 years. The OSN represented the most extreme case of rate decline among government companies. This situation worsened throughout the 1980s and early 1990s. The last recorded information on SIGEP was in 1990. Figure 6.1

---

[5] The OSN's jurisdiction was nationwide until 1980. At that point, it was restricted to the Federal Capital and 13 districts of Greater Buenos Aires. Responsibility for service in the rest of the country was transferred to provincial governments.

[6] The difference may be due to the greater degree of coverage found in the city of Buenos Aires with respect to the national average, but that difference tended to vanish as the rest of the country came under the area served by the OSN (see FIEL, 1992).

[7] This feature is shared by all of Argentina's provinces. The level of investment made in water and sewerage during the 1980s was 43 percent lower in constant prices than it had been the decade before.

Figure 6.1
Real Rates for OSN and Other Public Corporations
1960–1990

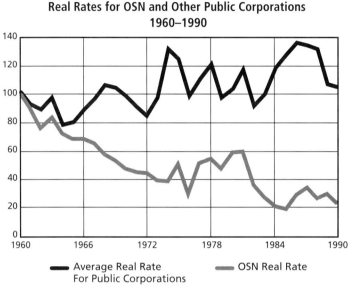

shows the decline in the real rate for water and sewerage services from 1960 to 1990 and its relationship to the general level of public rates.

While there may be reason to assume that the SIGEP index overestimates the decline in the real price of potable water and sewerage service—for reasons that may be better understood in section 5, which describes the workings of the rate system[8]—the evidence on rate decline is quite strong.

Table 6.1 provides some indicators of the low-quality equilibrium that characterized the OSN. Clearly, the rate decline is only one of many company indicators. In the early 1980s, the company had too many employees at low-wage levels, so much so that it ranked next to last on the public corporation pay scale, had the highest absentee rate among public corporations, and had very high labor costs as a percentage of total revenues. By the mid-1980s, the company had cut its staffing, but the average employee age was

---

[8] In estimating potable water and sewerage rates, SIGEP used the movement, over time, of what is called the K-coefficient, which is the main factor in rate adjustment, but only one component of the rate. Changes in other components, such as property assessment or in zone coefficients, may involve changes to the average price that are not captured by this calculation.

Table 6.1 OSN Performance Indicators: 1980–1990

	1980*		1985		1990	
Indicators	OSN	Other companies	OSN	Other companies	OSN	Other companies
1. Real Rate (1960 = 100)	58.9	103.1	19.6	128.1	24.1	105.0
2. Employment (000)	13.6	315.5	9.6	310.0	9.0	—
3. Real wage (1978 = 100)	100	100	164.1	124.1	nd	nd
4. Absenteeism (in %)	17.5	13.7	20.4	14.5	20.5	16.2
5. Labor cost Total revenues (in %)	63.8	41.4	57.0	25.6	60.0	30.0
6. Investment (1981 = 100)	100.0*	100.0*	67.8	68.7	19.5	55.4

*Data from 1981.
Source: Prepared on the basis of data supplied by SIGEP.

Table 6.2 Detailed OSN Performance Indicators: 1985

Total surface (subsequently, regulated area) (in hectares):   281,500
Surface with water service (in hectares):   50,900
Surface with sewerage service (in hectares):   37,400

	Fed. Cap.	13 Districts	Total
Population with water service (millions of inhabitants):	2.9	2.6	5.5
Population with sewerage service (millions of inhabitants):	2.9	1.7	4.6

Water production:	3,578,000 m^3 per day
Water connections:	1,002,176
Water meters:	148,354
Sewer connections:	665,347
Treatment:	97,080 m^3 per day
Employees:	9,600 (average age: 52)
Average consumption per person/day:	600 liters (equals 36 cubic meters per person every two months)
Age of the water system:	in Federal Cap.: 83% over 40 years and 55% over 60 years
Average delay for repair or handling leaks:	1 month in Federal Capital and 2 months in Greater Buenos Aires

over 50, thereby raising payroll costs and exacerbating absenteeism. These characteristics remained largely unchanged until 1990.

In general, the evidence shows that in the 1980s, the OSN suffered from low rates, low collection (cumulative delinquency was estimated to be around 85 percent), a bloated payroll, an imbalance in the quality of human resources, low investment levels, and deteriorated facilities. Information on company service for 1985 is spelled out in Table 6.2.

Privatization and Regulation: The Basics[9]

Privatization of potable water and sewerage services poses problems similar to those of other public utilities, but with some unique features:
- Economies of scale or scope mean there are few service providers;
- Sunk investment costs carry the risk of direct expropriation, or a more subtle type of expropriation through changes in contractual conditions that may be difficult to prove in court; and
- Residential consumers have low demand elasticity (hence the need to regulate the monopolist), and are also voters, thereby increasing the aforementioned risk of expropriation.

How is the regulatory body kept in check? How are conflicts resolved? How are company prices controlled? What are the entry rules for the service? Should there be cross-subsidies? These are the types of questions that must be considered when evaluating the regulatory design in this unique sector.

It is argued that sunk investments are more important in the case of water and sewerage service than in other public services. This is said to have led English officials to set up a regulatory framework in which a major portion of investments was financed with funds generated by the concessionaire.[10] It is also difficult for the consumer to determine service quality since adverse health effects from potential contamination are not always apparent to the eye, or are felt only over time. Such problems suggest that regulating rates through price caps is potentially more problematic than in other types

---

[9] For more details see Armstrong et al. (1994), Laffont and Tirole (1993), and Levy and Spiller (1994).

[10] See Armstrong et al. (1994).

of activities. Regulation through price caps is preferable to control by rate of return with regard to cost cutting, but is more problematic in assuring service quality and protecting sunk investments, hence the emphasis on the need to accentuate collection when designing the regulatory body and the tasks assigned to it. Specifically, efforts must be made to prepare a rather detailed contract in order to limit the discretionary power of the regulatory body as much as possible. That entails a potential cost passthrough, even if it partially undermines cost cutting—or providing clear guidelines for service quality—with credible sanctions to deter breach of contract.

Privatization of water and sewerage services presented some additional problems in Argentina:

- Country risk and, in the case of the Corrientes concession, risks associated with the provincial government, along with dependence of the judiciary on the federal or provincial executive branch posed a challenge in developing a reasonable framework that would encourage investment in the industry. This highlights the advantage of specifying the discretionary power of the regulatory body as much as possible and employing a system that limits the use of the judiciary.

- Delinquency in paying water utility bills was greater than in other privatized public utilities. Arguing that water is essential to public health, there were strong political pressures to prevent service from being cut off to residential users for nonpayment.

- Many families supplied their own water and sewerage services with pumps and pit latrines. Particularly in the case of latrines, where system coverage was low, individuals did not recognize the risks and assigned a low priority to receiving service through a system for which they would have to pay connection costs. The possibility of providing for oneself at a reasonable cost does not arise with other services for which the supply alternatives to the family are either nonexistent (telephone) or very expensive (liquid gas in lieu of natural gas).

- Rates were not set on the basis of consumption, but of property value, thereby contradicting the principles of efficient rate setting for public services.

- Lack of investment in the sector in the years prior to privatization had to be reversed. That posed a problem in designing regulatory frameworks, particularly in light of the first problem listed.

In developing a regulatory framework, a number of instruments were combined to achieve a regulatory context compatible with the institutional constraints of the country and region to be put up for concession.

The Regulatory Body

The design and role assigned to the regulatory body in both instances were extremely important for adequately protecting sunk investments without allowing the regulatory body to be captured by the regulated company. As already indicated, given the problems of the judiciary system, it was preferable to restrict its use for conflict resolution. In principle, there are several ways to respect that restriction. First, one can design the body in such a way that it has suitable incentives to "appropriately" interpret—in accordance with the general principles guiding the concession—the conflicts and regulatory adaptations that may not necessarily be foreseen at the beginning of the concession. Second, in the event that is not feasible to design an institution with such incentives, for example, in cases with accountability problems, precise language in the contractual clauses can limit cases in which interpreting an incomplete contract[11] effectively becomes an intervention.

The regulatory body for service in the Buenos Aires area is the ETOSS, Ente Tripartito de Obras y Servícios Sanitários (Tripartite Body for Water Works and Services), an independent entity created under the concession's regulatory framework (Decree No. 999). Under the regulatory framework (article 25), the ETOSS is financed by all the company's invoiced customers, who are charged a small fixed sum. As applied, however, this regulation has not achieved the goal of separating ETOSS funding from its own regulatory decisions in order to preclude its "capture" by the regulated company. This is because the regulatory body receives funding in proportion to the revenues of the regulated company, which equals 2.67 percent of billing. As a result, the budget increased 40 percent two years after the concession, and the provisions of article 25 of the regulatory framework were violated. In particular, the regulatory body was a budgetary beneficiary when it approved

---

[11] Naturally, this second alternative also requires (at least potentially) court intervention because in principle the regulatory body could obviate the restrictions placed on it by the contract. However, greater contractual specificity raises the visibility and therefore the cost of violating the contract, and thus constitutes a better solution to the institutional problem raised.

an extraordinary rate increase of close to 15 percent in 1994 (analysis of that decision is addressed in section 6). On the other hand, chapter 13 of the Concession Contract provides that fines levied on the company be set aside for customers through rebates on the first bill of the year.[12] Thus, fines do not increase the ETOSS revenue, unlike the regulatory body for natural gas (ENARGAS), which is explicitly allowed to receive income through fines. Clearly, the financial fortunes of ETOSS are directly related to those of the regulated company and there is no economic incentive to levy fines for wrongdoing. Together, these conspire against the regulatory body's objectivity and effectiveness.

ETOSS' decisions are subject to audit and legal monitoring by the Judge Advocate's Office of the nation, but there is no public hearing system for resolving conflicts or addressing significant regulatory decisions as is provided for in the regulatory frameworks for electric power and natural gas. Thus, ETOSS has a greater margin of discretionary power.

The makeup of the ETOSS board is highly political: it has six members, two each from the federal government, the federal capital, and the province of Buenos Aires. Moreover, members are appointed by the executive in each of these jurisdictions (Congress has no say in this sense), although once appointed, they may serve for six years, be reelected for another term, and may only be removed for just cause.

Finally, as is the nature of all regulatory bodies recently created in Argentina, the occupation of its members can be related to the regulated company's business. The only incompatibilities in effect are those that apply to government employment according to Law 22,140, which are entirely generic and provide no limitation in this sense. This suggests that the regulated company is an obvious potential employer when a member's term ends, a factor that can prompt a conscious or unconscious procompany stance on the part of the regulatory board.

In the Corrientes concession, the design selected for the regulatory body and its financing were highly unsuitable. The most noteworthy problems were:

---

[12] According to the 1994–1995 Annual Report and Financial Statement, they amounted to $464,000 in one year, equivalent to 8 percent of all ETOSS revenues.

- The AOSC, Administración de Obras Sanitárias de Corrientes (Corrientes Water Works Administration) is the regulatory body for water in Corrientes, but it continues to provide service in three cities—outside the concession area—performing two tasks that could cause conflicts of interest;
- The president of the board is appointed by the governor and can easily be dismissed;
- The monthly charge, all of which is set aside for financing the body, is adjusted according to rate changes. This ties financing only to the rate level, not to increased service coverage, which is what actually happens with the ETOSS in Buenos Aires; and
- The wages of agency staff are set according to cubic meters of water at the regulated price value, thereby introducing obvious problems with incentives against the consumer.[13]

An alternative that would have lowered the risk of politicizing the body would have been to create an agency with jurisdiction in several provinces, or to utilize the services of a national body. The Corrientes problem lies in that it was the first province to place water and sewerage services up for bidding at a time when such regulatory alternatives were not yet available.[14]

With regard to procedures in the ETOSS, the body has a very well organized structure, in which each department has to sign-off on a decision. There is even an outside ad-honorem commission that must pass judgement, thereby increasing the likelihood that rulings will be clear. In the case of Corrientes, the rules for the AOSC did not prevent it from consulting with the government inspector's office about economic problems when conflicts arose over contract interpretation.

In short, the regulatory agencies' design problems can create a framework that favors their capture by the regulated companies or politicization of

---

[13] Nevertheless, when the company requested a rate increase of almost 17 percent in 1993, it only succeeded (after two attempts) in obtaining one of approximately half that amount, when the increase in wages paid by the company was disregarded, even though this passthrough was envisioned in the contract. It could thus be inferred that there was a certain equilibrium between the counterbalancing incentives for the body, that is, being captured politically (political opportunism) and being captured economically (helping oneself by helping the regulated company through its rulings).

[14] In any case, the decision not to create an independent regulatory body whose financing and makeup would be different from the public sector in general was made by provincial officials.

their rulings. The contract in Buenos Aires specifies that any changes must be approved by the regulated company, and the appointment and dismissal of regulators in Corrientes is directly controlled by whoever is in office, thereby minimizing alignment with the company that arises from the nature of financing. Given this situation, the following biases are expected: the ETOSS tends to be biased toward the regulated company, and the AOSC tends to faithfully respond to the interests of whoever is in power politically. In fact, these turn out to be the biases that are actually at work in regulators' decisions.

Rate Structure and Contractual Adjustment Mechanisms

The objectives of the regulatory framework design are to stimulate investment, encourage adequate service quality, and charge efficient prices. What were the specific features of the regulatory frameworks of concessions in the city of Buenos Aires and the province of Corrientes, and how did they fare in view of these objectives?

Protection for Sunk Investment
In considering protection for sunk investment, the following issues are important:

Sale of Assets or Concession of Service

In both cases, the choice was made to grant the service through a 30-year concession rather than transfer ownership of the assets. The decision may have been based on the difficulty of assessing and precisely defining, at the time of bidding, the assets that would have been transferred (see World Bank 1996 and Price Waterhouse and Infupa 1990).[15] Moreover, if ownership of the company had been transferred, it would have been difficult to reduce

---

[15] Such arguments have had substantial political weight because, to the extent that there is a high degree of uncertainty about the status of the assets to be sold, participants in the bidding will likely compensate by offering a lower price for them. Should that be the case, and given the problems involved in making accounting sums reflect the true economic price of the assets, potential legal problems could arise for those responsible for the sale, who could easily be accused of "improper sale" of public assets. Other public asset bidding processes, such as that for the telecommunications company, required assessment by a government bank and by the investment banks advising the sale in order to establish a baseline value. The very uncertainty

the expropriation risk involved in the high amount of sunk capital stock. In the case of a water utility, assets are as, or even more, specific as those for transmitting and distributing electric power or natural gas.

Nevertheless, the decision to offer the concession rather than sell the company raises two problems:

1) The well-known problem of the final period. At the end of the concession, all assets return to the concession grantor, thereby creating an incentive to disinvest in later years. In principle, this problem is relatively minor in the case of Aguas Argentinas because the initially anticipated expansion was concentrated in the first 15 to 20 years of the concession, and because the water rates anticipate amortization of the investments during the concession period.[16] The problem becomes more serious in the case of Aguas de Corrientes because the winning bid proposes a sharp rate cut in year 15 when the discount, with regard to the base rate level, goes from 5 percent to 25 percent in year 14. While it is acceptable for a rate to be relatively high at the beginning of a concession to finance the required sunk investments and lower the expropriation risk vis-à-vis "regulatory opportunism," the magnitude of the reduction at the end of the concession is surprising, especially when compared to the 8 percent cut envisioned by the consulting companies. The winning bid involves a 17 percent rate cut for the 30-year average, but is concentrated in the second half of the concession. The bid was to be awarded to the company offering the largest discount, but was not limited to a particular time frame. A larger contractual guarantee ought at least to be required, even if a major discount in the middle of the concession could be justified as a way of financing initial investments. The required guarantee of $ 5 million amounts to only 25 percent of one year's billing (or

about assets in water has led the World Bank (1996) to suggest that short-term management contracts be granted for privatization in the provinces so as to more clearly specify the price of the assets to be sold. The problem with this suggestion is the possible asymmetry of information that favors the one operating the contract (either because it is directly involved in the bidding or because it sells the information to some bidders).

[16] With the exception of those made during the last 10 years of the concession, for which a residual value must be estimated. In the event the operator changes, that value must be paid back to the first concessionaire.

7 percent of the total investment thought to be made by the concessionaire),[17] and might not be enough to ensure this problem would
be overcome, should it arise. Neither case envisions the concession
continuing if the concessionaire is the winner in a bidding process
that occurs before the initial 30-year period expires. That procedure
has been adopted for the electric power concessions.[18]

2) The concession option increases the risk of opportunistic behavior
because it is basically governed by a bilateral contract between the
state and the concessionaire. In the case of an asset sale, in addition
to being spelled out in the transfer contract, the impersonal rules
that regulate other markets in the economy clearly dominate, and
are therefore harder to change for the sake of a particular company.
An asset sale would have caused fewer subsequent problems associated with renegotation, even though the political discussion would
certainly have been more intense.

Finally, in Corrientes, bids were accepted on concessions for service in
10 of the 13 cities served by the provincial public utility in order to make
privatization more attractive, and because shared management was expected
to inspire some cost savings.[19] However, the economies of scale when dealing with service in different cities are unclear. The decision may have reflected the desire to maintain a subsidy from the capital city to less populated areas since rates are equal throughout the concession area, and costs

---

[17] The World Bank (1996) calculates that the total investment to be made in the province of
Corrientes is US$ 75 million. Aguas de Corrientes has invested US$ 32.4 million in the first
four years of the concession. The initial rate level and metering requirements encouraged
much of the investment to be made at the outset. That being the case, it is contradictory for
the World Bank (1996) to speak of the problems that would have existed in Corrientes in
obtaining private financing for the investment.

[18] In any case, there would still be a risk of opportunistic behavior on the part of the regulator
because the value of the concession is affected by its decisions. However, because their effects
become visible in the bid amount, protection of the company's sunk investment is potentially
greater. Using an alternative system in which the government pays the company the accounting increase on its assets incorporated during the concession resolves the problem of regulatory opportunism, but raises another problem—namely, accounting values, where opportunistic behavior may again be manifested (although perhaps to a lesser extent).

[19] See Price Waterhouse and Infupa (1990).

are presumably higher in smaller cities.[20] Thus, a further burden is placed on the regulatory body because the company clearly has an incentive to expand or improve service in the areas where rates exceed costs, and to neglect cities where the average price does not cover costs. A political decision to subsidize particular locations by means of a direct charge to the provincial budget would have caused fewer problems while keeping rates in cities with lower costs in line with those costs.

Popular Capitalism

Allocating 10 percent of shares to workers through the Program for Shared Ownership was intended to "buy" the consent of former OSN workers for the concession and has been a common practice in other privatizations undertaken by the federal government. Of course, it is difficult to argue after the fact, once privatization has occurred successfully, that this was a necessary or excessive price for its political viability. But the conditions at the time of bidding were propitious for labor unions to accept the transfer of management to the private sector. For one thing, employees knew that no investments had been made for a decade, and that the company was on the brink of collapse. Moreover, the initial wage level was quite low and the average age of employees was very high, thereby making the voluntary retirement program offered by the OSN very attractive in the context of an open economy with low unemployment. Moreover, the labor union was involved in the privatization from the beginning (it had a representative on the Privatization Committee), and its good relationship with the company has lasted through the present.

In Corrientes, privatization provided 2 percent of shares, and 15 percent of profits, to employees. Here again, this device was clearly used to reduce the opposition of employees who were losing job stability.

Neither case provided for a portion of the share package to be distributed among small investors. Instead, the remaining shares were assumed by the operators—in both cases well known international companies—and by local or foreign companies.

---

[20] Studies conducted by consulting firms charged with the privatization suggest that costs are higher in the three cities not included in the concession area.

Bidding Procedure

The method for choosing the concession operator was appropriate in both cases. In Buenos Aires, the expansion and quality requirements could not be changed during the first five years of the concession. Expansion plans for subsequent years could be changed on the basis of well-founded arguments, as long as the concession's principle of "company risk" was not changed. Consequently, the company could not be penalized for, or benefit from, actions prior to granting the concession and rates could only be reduced during the second five years. The rate system could not be changed during this time either,[21] and no royalty would have to be paid for the use of current assets. Firms that were qualified as technically and financially competent to meet these obligations competed for the concession on the basis of the lowest water rate they were willing to receive.

Since the competition was based on such a crucial aspect of the concession's financial conditions as the rate level, the bidding process would not make sense if the contract were to be renegotiated immediately after the concession began (see Spulber 1991). The process would be equally flawed if the bidding participants' ability to evaluate the company's condition and the problems to be faced in meeting contractual requirements were limited by the speed of the transfer process and unreliable information.

In Corrientes, goals were set for service coverage and specific construction works (waste plants) and the concession was awarded to the company offering the lowest average service rate.

Awarding concessions on the basis of the lowest rate has been criticized for encouraging only a modest expansion of coverage in relation to the service coverage prior to the bidding process. It could also mean a price cut for users who had historically received subsidies from the central government. Both arguments are mistaken.

First, there is an inescapable relationship among the three major variables that define a concession's feasibility: investment, rates, and concession fees. The government can only determine two, because the third is deter-

---

[21] In connection with this, article 17 of Appendix VII to the Concession Contract provides that changes in the demarcation of each geographical zone for calculating the fixed component of the rate must be billing neutral for the concessionaire.

mined by those interested in participating in the bidding process. If a more ambitious investment plan is chosen, lower income from fees or higher service rates must be accepted. In Buenos Aires, the fees had been set at zero, and therefore increased investment would lead to higher rates. Second, the strategy of having an extremely ambitious investment plan led participants to offer bids with higher rates. This was very risky because many users were accustomed to not paying their water bill, and because there was strong political pressure against charging "excessive" prices for an essential service. To ignore these characteristics would have unnecessarily raised the "expropriation" risk on sunk investments. Setting up the bid for the lowest rate reduced the risk of ending up with a low-quality equilibrium.[22]

The natural monopoly in supplying water and sewerage in the city of Buenos Aires was legalized through an extension of the OSN Organic Law (Law 13,577) by demarcating the regulated zone and prohibiting users within the borders from receiving service from neighboring concessions. The intention of this concession, contrary to the argument made in the transfer of ENTEL and Aerolíneas Argentinas, was not to "collect and deposit the money," as was evident in the decision not to charge concession fees for using the pre-existing assets. Thus, the prohibition of cross-border competition can be understood as an additional tool for lowering the average service rate offered in the bidding.

Service Cut-off of Delinquent Accounts

Article 75 of the Buenos Aires Regulation for Users provides for cutting off service to delinquent accounts for failure to meet three successive payments (art. 38 of Law 13,577 already contemplated it for the OSN). A tem-

---

[22] In the case of the province of Tucumán, for example, there were serious problems at the beginning of the concession. In keeping with an ambitious expansion target, the price set for a cubic meter of water was several times higher in that province than in Buenos Aires and Corrientes. Likewise, the alternative of setting the rate and the fees, and awarding the bid to the company offering the largest amount of investment raises the problem of generating efficient costs because competition takes place in a realm in which real resources can be wasted. Moreover, it is hard to compare bids, and hence the process becomes less transparent. To illustrate the problem of rent dissipation when bidding is based on investment plans, see Nellor and Robinson (1984). The problem of the lack of transparency in the case of bidding on the water service for the city of Buenos Aires on the basis of investment plans is mentioned in Gaggero et al. (1992).

porary exception may be made at the request of the ETOSS or the Ministry of Health and Social Action, but it is not specified who is to pay while exceptional treatment is in effect. While this may seem natural in light of the health aspects and priority of water services, the concessionaire runs the risk of expropriation since no limit is placed on the state's power to prevent service cutoffs. It would have been more appropriate for the state to compensate for a portion of the cost for services provided and not charged; it should be only a portion so that there would be no serious moral hazard for either party.[23]

Article 44 of the Aguas de Corrientes contract provides for service to be cut off for failure to pay. It should be noted that cutting off service is the only short-term tool available because attaching property to collect what is due has to be pursued through the ordinary channels of justice and usually takes several years.

The Concession as a Monopoly and Tax Stability

Aguas Argentinas has been able to maintain a monopoly because all customers, residential and nonresidential, are required to have a connection, and therefore, "home service" (defined in article 10 of the regulatory framework) refers to any service with indoor facilities for users. It is therefore mandatory that residential, business, and industrial customers be connected, and that any alternative source be blocked (i.e., made unusable), although nonconnection or disconnection may be requested for an uninhabited property (art. of the Regulatory Framework). Article 6 of the Regulations for Users refers to the obligations of inhabitants in the service area.[24]

In Corrientes, service may also be provided to anyone who requests it and property owners are obligated to install water and sewers at the discretion of the company. The user must pay for the connection and must close

---

[23] According to company information, cuts in service occur all the time for all types of customers, although some have been suspended at the request of the ETOSS (users really unable to pay), in which case the company has gone to court as plaintiff. On the other hand, 90 percent of government customers pay for the service, although only 60 percent do so on time with no collection actions taken.

[24] This differs from England where business and industrial users are not obligated to close off other sources of water supply. See Armstrong et al. (1994).

wells, although compliance with this requirement apparently has not been strict.[25]

Government also has the power to charge taxes after the concession has been granted. Article 42 of the Aguas de Corrientes contract provides for the service rate to reflect the impact of changes to the VAT and the provincial gross revenue tax. That protects the company from subtle "expropriation" by means of changes to indirect tax pressure. However, there is no similar protection for property taxes.

Billing Efficiency

One of the most problematic aspects in providing potable water and sewerage in Argentina has been the lack of a framework that allows water rates to cover the opportunity costs of providing it, offers incentives for rational water use, and enables financing of expansions efficiently and fairly (see, for example, Guadagni 1973). The main features of billing "technology" remained unchanged during the industry's reorganization after the Aguas Argentinas privatization, although the groundwork had been laid for the (as yet undefined) shift toward the use of meters. In the case of Aguas de Corrientes, it was changed when it became clear that consumption by all users would be metered by the end of the third year of the concession.

An analysis of the rate design adopted in both concessions and the consequences of successfully handling institutional change after privatization illustrates the various consequences of inefficiency—notably the lack of metering and the absence of a positive marginal price—and the implications that the potable water supply has on the political economy. This framework is then applied to a simple case to evaluate the recent decision to revise water rates in exchange for increased investment or investing ahead of schedule.

Rate Design in Concessions

For Aguas Argentinas, the rate structure prior to the concession generally preserved the previous situation. Commercial and industrial users are to

---

[25] It should be noted that for environmental reasons, the obligation to close existing services seems more reasonable with respect to sewerage than potable water.

be metered, as was previously the case for all but a few exceptions that were supposed to be eliminated during the first two years. Residential users still without meters at the time of the concession (approximately 95 percent) would be metered at the discretion of the concessionaire, or at the user's request—in which case, the user would pay for the meter and its installation.

Thus, the envisioned transfer to a metered system is slow and inefficient. It is slow because the choice can be made only once, and users are discouraged from doing so because they do not know how much water they consume and therefore cannot determine the relative attractiveness of each system. Residential users may only change their minds once if, as a result of metering, the cost of the service changes by over 20 percent. The company must then compensate users if it wants to meter service by a sum equal to the cost of replacing and installing the meter.[26] It is also inefficient because the fixed charge in both systems depends on the characteristics of the property served, while the cost of the meter and its installation does not. That creates a situation where the owner of an expensive piece of property, with inelastic water consumption, is more likely to request metering while the owner of a less expensive plot, with elastic consumption, does not. From the standpoint of productive efficiency, such differentiation should not occur because for society it is preferable for customers to have metering when the savings in water consumption as a result of metering, assessed in terms of its production cost, is greater than the cost of the meter itself.

Reference values were also set for connection and infrastructure charges, which apply to customers whose service is being expanded within the regulated area.[27] Moreover, cross-subsidies, a rate feature distinctive to this service, are explicitly allowed (article 43, section 3, of the regulatory framework), whereas subsidies are explicitly prohibited for both electric power and natural gas. Specifically, the selected rate structure contains a

---

[26] Indeed, thus far (according to information provided by Aguas Argentinas) the number of residential users who have requested metered services is minimal.

[27] A connection charge must be incurred whenever the user is connected to the system if, under some circumstances (e.g., a home is abandoned) the customer decides to be temporarily disconnected. In contrast, the infrastructure charge goes into effect when service is available at the respective property, regardless of whether or not actual network connection has been made.

subsidy from those customers who already have service to new customers in expansion areas because the infrastructure charge is not high enough to cover the full cost of incorporating new customers.

In principle, the rate adjustment criterion is like a ceiling price. Nevertheless, article 11.11.1.3 of the contract provides exceptions for ordinary (or periodic) and extraordinary revisions. Ordinary revisions—to expansion plans and improvements according to five-year plans, for instance—are based on contract enforcement. Extraordinary revisions refer to rate changes that arise from modifications of the concessionaire's costs by more or less than 7 percent, or changes in expansion plans, quality requirements, exchange rate, and taxes. In other words, there is an adjustment clause that should neither reward nor punish the company (passthrough). On the other hand, there are numerous references to the economic and financial equation and regulatory framework authorizations that the concessionaire must contract services for sums over US$ 10 million through a bidding process. This sends contradictory signals that introduce a degree of "noise" and lend themselves to interpreting the spirit of regulation as "rate of return," thereby creating a problem of consistency in regulation by fixed price with passthrough.

Finally, article 47 of the regulatory framework states that the variable for rate regulation is average revenue, whereas article 11.4 of the contract states that (each of the) regulated prices must be understood as maximum prices. The concession grantor may offer discounts without discriminating between customers in similar situations, assuring that the resulting discounts will not allow for rate changes among customers. The decision to regulate only by average rate and not delegate the choice of rate structure to the company—even in the case of a natural monopoly in all areas of its operation—is justified by strong health externalities associated with water service. These externalities would not be taken into account in the Ramsey prices that might be chosen by the company.

In Corrientes, regulation is designed on the basis of a ceiling price criterion with passthrough of some costs (wages, aluminum sulfate, and electric power). But, as in the case of Aguas Argentinas, article 7 of Decree 5118 (1990) says the rate must be fair and capable of covering costs while providing a reasonable profit. This indirectly introduces the idea of regulation through the rate of return. In addition, the contract itself provides for renegotiating the rate every three years if costs change. Partial passthrough of some costs presents an obvious problem of moral hazard since the company is involved in negotiating wage agreements. With regard to the market price of aluminum sulfate, the company's consumption is so crucial to total demand that it can affect that market price.

In Corrientes, the rate schedule is the same for residential and non-residential consumers. This structure is better than that envisioned for Aguas Argentinas (where the residential rate is lower), because presumably the cost of dealing with a residential customer will not be lower than that with other customers. Likewise, with regard to the fixed charge, there are no varying "elasticities of access," since all customers must pay. (There could be different elasticities of water consumption that would justify higher variable charges to industrial customers from a Ramsey price standpoint).

Problems Setting Rates

Basic Formulas for Metered and Unmetered Systems

The rate-setting system for potable water in Buenos Aires follows a cadastral system in which each property's area, location, and age are used in a complex way to determine charges that maintain a rather unclear system of cross-subsidies. As a result, charges are completely unrelated to the volume of water consumed. In addition to the issue of measuring consumption, which has dominated much of the discussion regarding reform, other aspects of the system seriously complicate the political economy of providing service.

Water service rates are broadly divided into two categories: residential or family (which includes a portion of small businesses), and commercial or industrial. Each of these, in turn, can be either unmetered (the main category in terms of both physical volume and revenue) or metered service.[28] To understand the rate system, it is useful to start with the description of the formula for unmetered service, and then describing that for metered service.

---

[28] From the revenue structure of the OSN company at the time of privatization, it is apparent that only 10.5 percent of revenue came from metered water supply, equally divided into residential and commercial/industrial categories. The unmetered residential category contributed 57 percent of total revenue (of which 41.5 percent came from the Federal Capital—with full coverage—and 15.5 percent from the districts of Greater Buenos Aires supplied by the company—with average coverage of 48 percent for water and 33 percent for sewers). The relationship between the physical number of meters and connections was 14 percent for the Federal Capital and 22 percent for Greater Buenos Aires. Somewhat over 13 percent of these meters were out of service.

The basic formula for the unmetered service rate (P) is as follows:

$$P = T \cdot K \cdot Z \cdot (Sc \cdot E + S /10) \tag{5.1}$$

where T is a basic or general rate, K is the adjustment coefficient, Z is a "zone" coefficient that discriminates by district, Sc is the surface covered by the property, E is a coefficient of the dwelling quality which depends on the age and type or category of building, and S/10 is a tenth of total property surface (whether covered or not). Given the base or general rate, and the cadastral structure that defines the other components of the formula (5.1), the companies that competed in the bidding for the utility concession offered the lowest possible value for the K coefficient.

There are several aspects to this formula. First, the P rate can differ according to class of user. Second, it can also vary by the zone classification adopted (historically, the Z coefficient could range between 0.8 and 3.5). Third, it can differ by variations in the E coefficient (which historically ranged between 0.6 and 2.6). Fourth, it can vary by changes in the declaration of cubic meters of a particular property that are covered and not covered. The result of all these factors is a complex web of unclear cross-subsidies, since the resulting charges have no relation whatsoever to the volume of water consumption nor to the costs of servicing the property.

The rate system in the province of Corrientes is designed better because the fixed charge does not depend on any property feature and is the same for residential and nonresidential customers. The system is therefore more transparent. However, some problems that were not corrected at the time of bidding persist. For example, because the concession includes 10 cities in the province with the same rate schedule but markedly different housing densities per sector, there are some distortions where the prices paid by consumers do not reflect the opportunity costs of providing the service.[29]

---

[29] The incentive to the concessionaire to reduce investments in areas of lower population density does not lead to an optimal solution. True, the company's natural response to invest less goes in the "right" direction (in the sense of adjusting the regional investment pattern to its marginal yield, which presumably is lower in areas of lower population density). But there is no guarantee that optimal capital expansion will occur in every zone (utilizing concessions as a tool to obtain efficient capital allocation is a strange way of solving the problem of moral hazard). Moreover, the regional price pattern is distorted in relation to the optimal pattern, and that produces welfare costs that could be reduced with rates that better reflect costs.

Additionally, the investment cost per sewer connection in this province would be approximately double that of water given the need for larger diameter pipes and waste treatment plants, whose cost is higher than that of water intake. Nevertheless, the connection fees would not reflect this cost differential. However, the possible positive externality toward other customers who would thereby have sewers instead of pit latrines could justify charging a lower connection fee.[30]

Even if this externality were significant, the rate system introduces some distortions because the company is not encouraged to invest in waste plants and sewerage systems. Therefore, the regulatory body needs to monitor carefully to prevent that bias from being realized. While setting coverage goals for each location's population should restrict this moral hazard problem, in practice, expansion by region and service occurs in a way that best serves the company's interests. A more efficient alternative for solving the externality problem is to subsidize the rate paid by the customer by reimbursing the company's cost differential. [31]

In contrast to the unmetered rate, Aguas Argentinas has a metered rate (PM) that is defined as one-half of the unmetered rate plus a variable rate that depends on the amount used above a pre-established consumption level:

$$PM = P/2 + K \, pm \cdot (X - Xb) \tag{5.2}$$

where PM is the price per cubic meter applied when consumption X exceeds basic consumption, Xb. The average rate then turns out to be a three-part rate: a fixed charge, P/2; a block of free consumption up to Xb, where the marginal price equals zero (Xb equals 15 m³ per month) and the average price is declining; and a block where the marginal price equals PM and the average price is rising or falling depending on the system design. The price,

---

[30] This justification of a lower connection fee for sewers does not lead to the conclusion that the current rate is socially optimal because there is no proof that the value of the externality coincides with the differential between charges and connection costs.

[31] It should be mentioned that the most important expansion plans are discussed with each municipality, since they supply the employees and, in some cases, materials. Thus, the company may impede expansions in areas where, from its standpoint, it is less desirable for it to do so.

PM, the fixed charge and the unmetered rate are doubled if the user receives sewerage service along with potable water.[32]

In the case of Corrientes, there is also a three-component rate for metered service (which should soon apply to all customers). It includes a fixed charge of 3.75 m³ of water (presumably to cover the cost of the meter rental, reading, and maintenance services), and an average price per cubic meter. However, beyond 10 m³ per month, there is a declining average price.[33]

Implications for Consumer and Company Decisions

Much of the discussion surrounding the potable water rate system has involved evaluating possible incentives for consumers and companies to go from an unmetered to a metered system, where meter installation costs are factored in. This discussion emphasizes incentives for voluntarily accepting micrometering by comparing formulas (5.1) and (5.2). (See, for example, World Bank 1996). As a rule, however, it does not cover all the consequences an unmetered system may have on company incentives, particularly the rather unclear manner in which the system (5.1), supposedly the basis for "negotiating" a transition toward the metered system, is defined.

Starting from an unmetered system such as (5.1), consumers are assumed to have a utility function in which water consumption can be separated from other goods, and the company has a cost function that depends on the amount of water produced, its quality, and a given capacity. From this a set of implications relating to consumer and company incentives are derived. This exercise was carried out in Porto (1991) and leads to the following predictions or expected results:

First, given that the consumer faces a marginal price equal to zero, consumption is set at the partial saturation point for water, that is, when marginal utility equals zero. Second, because connection is mandatory (the consumer cannot disconnect) and the water rate has property tax features,

---

[32] With regard to the technological aspect of supplying water and sewerage service jointly, the economies of scope are significant for commercial service (billing): if water alone costs a user $1.00, the cost to a user with water and sewerage is approximately $1.50. This suggests that the decision to double the bill when sewerage service is also offered is not very justifiable.

[33] Current average consumption is somewhat over 11 m³ per month, which suggests that a significant portion of residential customers is not included in the second segment.

the company may individually extract sums higher than the consumer's surplus. In other words, there are levels to the parameters in formula (5.1) that may imply that consumers are required to pay more than they are willing, and yet they may not opt out.[34] This problem also exists in Corrientes, although the obligation to be connected is not universal.

There are incentives for the company to minimize costs, if it limits passthrough and uses formula (5.1) as a ceiling price; but it also has to lower the amount produced, since marginal revenue for producing and selling an additional cubic meter is zero. There are also incentives for the company to reduce system losses by improving macrometering—including detecting losses from unmetered customers. This problem is less acute for Corrientes since 100 percent of customers have to be metered, but it does occur with a significant number of consumers whose monthly consumption is less than $10 \, m^3$.

Another major problem with this kind of system is that the company has no incentive to improve service quality. This problem is not as serious in Corrientes.

There are incentives for the company to concentrate its efforts on influencing rate system components by adjusting not only the K coefficient, but pushing for change along three lines: the "zone" structure or the Zs, the "quality of residence" structure or the Es, and the reclassification of properties by updating the proportion of covered to uncovered surface. These changes can take place in a relatively concealed manner, given the obscure nature of the rate-setting system. The political economy connotations of this last point for Aguas Argentinas can be quite significant, because these coefficients, in fact, determine the level and rate structure for water.

Since it is related to the property registry system, the rate-setting problem may be associated with determining the real estate or property tax. There are incentives for the company to have property assessments adjusted to account for home improvements, as is normally sought with changes in the real estate tax. This is not the case in Corrientes, however, where rates only differ between developed and undeveloped properties, although there is a

---

[34] The regulatory framework governing Aguas Argentinas allows the customer to stop paying for service when the property is unoccupied. However, this freedom is diminished, not only by the fact that its use is inevitably restricted to those who have at least two properties, but by the difficulty in proving to the Regulatory Agency that no one is, in fact, occupying it.

clear rate schedule. The problem here results from the passthrough of some costs in a poor design that exacerbates incentive problems, and from the aforementioned cross-subsidy.

Compensatory Rate Adjustments and Rate Renegotiation

Profits (p) for the company providing water services in the city of Buenos Aires come from the difference between revenues (R) and Total Costs (TC), which can be defined as

$$
\begin{aligned}
p = {} & R\,(a, T, K, Z, E, Sc, S, pm, X, Xb) - TC\,(Xp, q \cdot S) \\
= {} & \Sigma\Sigma\Sigma\,\{[(a + (1\text{-}a)\,/\,2].[T \cdot K \cdot Z \cdot (ScE + S/10] + \\
& + ((1\text{-}A)\,/\,2.k.PM.\,(X(pm,q) - Xb))\} - TC\,(Xp, q, \Sigma\,X),
\end{aligned}
\tag{5.3}
$$

where a denotes the percentage of unmetered customers, Xp denotes the volume of potable water produced, q denotes its quality, Σ denotes the sum over the total set of customers served, and the remaining terms denote previously defined variables.

Thus, revenues come from: unmetered sales (in proportion a), metered sales (proportion 1-a), and the parameters of the corresponding rate systems. The triple sum indicates variations between classes of customers, zones (Z), and types of housing (E). Costs depend on the water produced, its quality, and a measure of capacity or coverage in relation to the total surface of residences served (Σ S).[35]

Formula (5.3) shows that company revenues are unit elastic with respect to the K coefficient because the latter enters all its components linearly. That is, a 1 percent increase in K raises sales revenues in the same proportion. Hence, when production costs remain constant, an increase in K causes a more than proportional increase in earnings.[36]

---

[35] This formula omits other revenues (connection, infrastructure, bulk sale of water) in view of their relevance to the rate issues being addressed.

[36] The equivalent formula for Corrientes is much simpler: all customers are measured in the same way; residential and nonresidential customers all face the same rate pattern, with no distinction made on the basis of property characteristics, except for unoccupied land. Nevertheless, Aguas de Corrientes revenues also have a unitary elasticity vis-à-vis the K coefficient.

Therefore, the rate adjustment that would compensate the company for increasing capacity or quality by raising the K coefficient, while it keeps its earnings constant, will depend on the elasticity of profits to such a capacity/quality increase. It is easily shown that it will never be in the same proportion.[37] That is, even though revenues do not rise as a result of the expansion plan (which is not the case in the example posed because revenues rise with S), under no circumstances should K rise in the same proportion as S. In this regard, it is strange that the 1994 rate renegotiation that increased capacity by advancing the investment program has established (at least so it seems) a proportional relationship between the increase in the K coefficient and the increase in investment. It is difficult to specify the quantification that would justify such a step, especially because company revenues are not expected to be neutral with respect to investment. On the other hand, the more these investments are aimed at improving service quality, the less impact they would have on revenues (due to the rate system) and the less inappropriate the measure adopted would be.

Further Implications and Possible Lines of Reform

Thus, there are disadvantages to the property assessment system on which potable water rate setting is based, especially in the case of Buenos Aires, because it feeds into a political economy already conducive to socially nonproductive negotiations hidden behind a murky system. Discussions of reform have generally focused on the possibility of introducing metering and incentives for negotiation between the parties (consumers and company).

These negotiations can depend on, or be conditioned by, earlier developments in rate adjustments that modify the parties' incentives to accept

---

[37] For example, if, in order to simplify notation, formula (5.3) is reexpressed as $p(k,S) = I(K,S) - CT(S)$, the percentage increase in K that leaves profit p unchanged in the face of an increase in surface served, S, is obtained by entirely differentiating this formula, and results in $(dK/K)/(dS/S) = - (dp/I)/(dS/S)$ (for this result, the unit elasticity of revenue with regard to K must be kept in mind). Given that $I = p+C$, the term on the right side is less than $- (dp/p)/(dS/S)$ (i.e., the absolute value of the surface expansion elasticity of profit). Likewise, in the worst case scenario, $dI/dS = 0$, that is, serving more areas does not generate further revenue. (For example, if a service is uncollectible, or if the expansion in question is a quality improvement for customers with unmetered service.) Then the surface expansion-elasticity of profit would be -1 (maximum absolute value), thereby proving that $(d/K/K)/(dS/S)$ is, in all cases, less than one.

metering. In a recent study, the World Bank (1996) examined possible incentives that encouraged consumers to voluntarily go to a metered system.
It noted that the relative advantage depends on the set of unmetered rate
parameters (like Z and E) compared to the "quasi-tax" portion of it. This
study speculated as to the values that generate incentives to accept metering,
but downplayed the complex web of differentiated coefficients and the possibility that the company or pressure groups would change those values. For
example, consumers of potable water cannot lower their charge by reducing
consumption in the unmetered system and wind up paying sums higher
than their demand. However, they must be wary lest changes in the rate
components through utilization of quasi-tax changes that increase consumer
demand be used later to force metering. The best recommendation seems to
be to discontinue the property assessment classification system as soon as
possible, perhaps at the end of the first five-year period of the concession to
avoid violating the contract clause and introduce "legal insecurity." This elimi-
nates incentives to reclassify consumers while it protects the company from
being pressured into changing the distribution of charges.

The three-part rate systems implicit in the two concessions analyzed
here also focus on equity. It has been argued (World Bank 1996) that this
rate design is equitable because it "limits" the decline of average water price
to an assigned range. Depending on how the system is designed, the average
price may rise beyond basic consumption. This result is not immediate. On
the one hand, note that formula (5.2) is not in two parts but three, and that
the middle block operates with a falling average and marginal price equal to
zero; that is, it is a locally regressive arrangement (which is why the report
mentions limiting average price growth).

Given the fixed-price features, and assuming that the poor consume
less, equity-oriented reform would lower slightly the fixed charge and increase the marginal price of the next segment. In the case of a three-part
rate, it is unlikely that a suitable design would leave a high fixed charge and
lower the marginal price of the next segment to zero.[38] On the other hand, a
marginal price of zero in the bottom layer of a three-part rate may be consistent with the definition of a priority potable water and sewerage service,

---

[38] The telecommunications industry has proposed social rates that involve a lower fixed cost
and a higher marginal price. See Artana et al. (1995).

that is, one where health officials want to encourage families to consume an indispensable minimum of potable water to avoid greater social harm (i.e., externalities, such as infections, epidemics, excessive Public Health expenditures, etc.).

On the other hand, from the standpoint of both efficiency and fairness, the cross-subsidy that exists in both concessions, from current to new customers, merits analysis. In this regard, the World Bank (1996) estimates that current Aguas Argentinas customers are subsidizing the expansion of service to new customers by a present value of $ 480 million (for 30 years of concession at a temporary discount rate of 10 percent a year).[39] While this calculation may overestimate that subsidy, there is no doubt that it exists and is quite large.[40] In terms of efficiency, it can be argued that this subsidy acts as a disincentive for Aguas Argentinas to expand (World Bank 1996). However, this conclusion can be challenged. First, expansion was not left to the economic interests of the concessionaire, but was established as part of a contract, and should be interpreted as a counterpart to the rate level offered in the bid. The company's ability to determine the speed of expansion (below the concession requirements) is therefore reduced. Second, without a cross-subsidy, it is unclear whether new customers, who are typically low-income and located in the districts of Greater Buenos Aires, would be willing or able to make higher payments. In this case, there would not only be no incentive to expand, but the financial balance of the company could be jeopardized. Indeed, the company would prefer to raise the cross-subsidy by lowering the infrastructure charge and financing the reduction with higher rates to existing customers (a rebalancing to eliminate the need to deal with new customers in the southern and eastern areas of the concession who are unable to pay). This year, for example, out of a projected $50 million in revenues from an infrastructure charge, it is now estimated that only between $10 million and 20 million will be collectible. That would also be

---

[39] The calculation method, however, is not clear. The cost for connecting water and sewerage service is a per capita $47.60 per year (with 10 percent discount, assuming five persons per connection), which implies a present value of $520 per person, or $2,600 per connection. If that were the case, the subsidy would actually be high (80 percent) because a connection cost $450 prior to ETOSS Resolution No. 83/95.

[40] In view of the investments required in the First Five-Year Plan and according to estimates by Aguas Argentinas itself, the expansion subsidy is approximately 60 percent.

"fair" because "expansion" is more redistributive than present service, since the new areas typically consist of populations whose incomes are lower than those in the federal capital and other areas presently served. Finally, from the standpoint of intragenerational transfers through potable water service financing, given the deficits of the OSN in the past, and investments financed as outright grants by the National Treasury and the provincial government of Buenos Aires, initial customers contracted an unrecorded debt to future customers within the regulated area. The latter also paid taxes, which went toward the financing, but never received the service. This constitutes another reason for including expansion costs in the usage rate. Note that the regulatory framework explicitly allows for such mechanisms, contrary to that for gas and electricity.

In conclusion, there is a disincentive to expand that could be remedied if the company were to be rewarded for expansion only after it was completed, with the regulatory body holding funds contributed for this purpose from customers who already have service. That way the company would perceive a "subsidy-free" price structure even though cross-subsidies would continue to exist.

Contract Performance

How effective are the regulatory frameworks in assuring reasonable investment flow and high quality service? The main problems arise from the decision to establish concessions rather than sell assets and the distortions created by the rate systems (due to the lack of metering in Buenos Aires and cross-subsidies in Corrientes), which make it more likely that contractual issues will be renegotiated. This in turn may result in a procompany bias or a bias toward expropriation due to design flaws in the regulatory agencies. In spite of this, other instruments were used to provide some guarantee in awarding the concession. These include allowing delinquent users to be cut off (although the rule is less rigid in Buenos Aires), granting strict monopolies, introducing price control features through rate of return by accepting some cost passthrough, and establishing investment goals for Buenos Aires, and service coverage goals for Corrientes.

The following observations offer partial evidence to conclude that Buenos Aires has experienced a degree of procompany bias. In Corrientes, however, design problems combined with a difficult political context had the opposite effect: discussions between the company and the provincial executive were highly politicized and led to a concentration of stock holdings in the hands of local investors.

The performance results for both concessionaire companies are consistent with expectations based on the above conclusions. The expansion goals envisioned in Buenos Aires were met (the first three years of the concession were evaluated). In the case of Corrientes, as the political situation grew more complicated, the company fulfilled the contract less and less.

Behavior of the Regulators

Buenos Aires

With regard to Buenos Aires, the regulatory design displayed both positive and negative features. Regarding the incentives of the main "players" (i.e., the ETOSS and Aguas Argentinas), the regulatory body, while supposedly political in identity, receives its financing in direct proportion to company billing and cannot benefit economically from the application of fines. Board members also enjoy stability in their positions, while the regulated company enjoys a strong monopoly, with incentives to maximize benefits more through property reassessment than by cost cutting or quality improvements. Moreover, decisions by the ETOSS are subject to only limited oversight, given the complexity of the rate system, and the absence of public hearings to discuss its future rulings. This enhances its discretionary leeway. Due to contract specificity and the consequent need to rely on the knowledge of the regulated company, combined with the aforementioned nature of financing, decisions are biased toward the company.

A discussion of various ETOSS decisions suggests there was bias toward the regulated company. This is only a presumption, since verification beyond any doubt is beyond the scope of this work. Section 6.2 presents company performance indicators of private management over the past three years. The attainment of various goals and high profitability—which according to *The Economist* (February 24, 1996) is quite unusual on a global scale—makes it hard to argue that the bias is anything but procompany. Only recently have some ETOSS decisions been questioned. For salient aspects of the requests for information that lawmakers have made to the executive branch, see Artana, Navajas, and Urbiztondo (1997).

ETOSS Rulings Included in the Customer Regulations

As stated in article 66 of the Customer Regulations, residential users have a one-time option to have metered service, except when the service cost increases by more than 20 percent as a result of metering. In that case, if the company had sought the meter, it must compensate with a sum equal to the meter replacement and installation cost. Of course, after a change of mind, the company would be in the best position to make the decision for metering itself, since it would undoubtedly be profitable to do so. In that sense, the protection of the customer's right to choose could have been improved by further restricting the company's power to meter after a customer who had requested metering changed his/her mind.

According to an ETOSS ruling, the installation cost for any metering device with a diameter less than or equal to 50 mm is $99 for the work plus a unit price ranging between $31 for 15 mm diameter devices, and $219 for 50 mm devices. The sizable price difference occurs for 20 mm–25 mm devices, whose price jumps from $36 to $112. In Corrientes, the cost of small meters (with a capacity of less than 3 m³, used by 95 percent of residential customers) is $15, and the more expensive ones (capacity over 10 m³) are $30. Note that the ETOSS ruling setting meter prices for the city of Buenos Aires was made after the bidding process and constitutes postcontract protection for the company, given the high prices compared to other countries, and to prices set in Corrientes.

The Customer Regulations procedures for conflict resolution are also inadequate. For example, when a meter error occurs and the user asks that it be checked, it is done by the concessionaire. If the concessionaire says the meter is working properly, the user must pay the inspection cost. Thus, there is a problem of moral hazard; it suits the company to say there are no problems when its metering produces overestimates (see art. 26).

1994 Rate Increase (ETOSS Ruling No. 81/94)

The company requested a rate adjustment in order to achieve expansion and quality goals ahead of schedule (incorporating the shantytowns into the Municipality of the City of Buenos Aires, which made the request). The estimate by Aguas Argentinas of higher costs was subjected to outside auditing, and the Ministry of the Economy and Public Works and

Services authorized a correction. The decision of the ETOSS Board was unanimous.

Planned improvements and expansion required investments totaling $122,085,000 over a two-year period, divided as follows:

- Replacing water with nitrates: $31,845,000
- Increasing investment goals
  a. Expanding Gral. Beltrano stabilizer: $14,000,000
  b. Extending distribution systems (300,000 inhabitants, primarily in the districts of Lomas de Zamora and Tres de Febrero,[41] representing an increase of approximately 6 percent in the number of customers): $66,440,000
- Installing water and sewers in shantytowns, MCBA (Municipality of the City of Buenos Aires): $9,800,00 (i.e., this is the least significant change, but it is always mentioned first in justifying the decision).

The rate adjustment was approved as follows:

- Rates linked to consumption (by the adjustment factor "K"): 13.5 percent increase;
- Rates for service reconnection and cut-off (art. 38 and 39): 13.5 percent increase;
- Charge for water infrastructure (residential system): 38 percent increase;
- Charge for sewer infrastructure (art. 40): 45 percent increase;
- Charge for service connection (water and/or sewers, art. 36): 42 percent increase;
- Charge for treatment of industrial effluents (art. 43): no change.

An initial conclusion would be that the balance shifted heavily against new users (although from the outset, the cross-subsidy for expansion was not reversed), and that the average rate increase was over 13.5 percent (according to Aguas Argentinas officials, the average increase was close to 15 percent). Public opinion paid little notice to this and there was very little protest, suggesting two possible explanations. First, since they were only "potential" or "future" users, the new customers did not recognize the 42 percent rise in the price of connections and infrastructure charges. They realized it when it came time to pay, but not when the decision was made (see

---

[41] Note that the current governor of the Province of Buenos Aires, whose representatives make up a third of the ETOSS Board, was mayor of Lomas de Zamora.

Ambito Financiero, February 23, 1996, p. 8 and *Clarín* April 24, 1996). Second, existing customers did not perceive the service as expensive, so they accepted a price increase. The increase for them was less than for new users anyway.[42] This is quite different from what happened when an attempt was made to increase telephone rates.

How was the 15 percent increase calculated? Reliable information to answer this question is not available, but some speculations can be made. The 1994–95 ETOSS Annual Report (pp. 48–49) stated the timetable for goals had moved up. This was interpreted to mean a 13.8 percent increase in the investment program for the first 10 years of the concession[43] and a $243.3 million increase in operating costs, equivalent to about 15 percent of previous operating costs. Thus, the 15 percent cost increase (including presumably greater cumulative costs) led to a corresponding 15 percent rate increase.[44]

Putting aside the adjustment for higher costs, it is tempting to assume that the 10 percent cost increase resulting from moving up the investments[45]

---

[42] The average bimonthly bill for water and sewerage services is $13.80 while the average bill for telephone, gas, electricity, and cable TV is approximately $45 each. This also contributes to the absence of major complaints about service.

[43] Investments total $333 million. Their composition is not spelled out, but surely contains a rate adjustment of approximately 5 percent for the cumulative cost variation from the time of the concession to that date. According to the contract, when cost increases reach 7 percent, a rate adjustment was to be made (in principle, for the same amount). Thus, when the investments were moved up, the extraordinary revision that would have been made in late 1994 (when the costs would have risen by 7 percent) occurred earlier. Hence, of the 15 percent average increase, 5 percent would be for higher cumulative costs from the time of the bid to the time of the revision. The Ruling states further that the reference date of the next extraordinary rate revision will be May 1994, when it will be reviewed. From that time, up to a year ago, the cost increase approached 7 percent, but is now approximately 5 percent, and the company has received no additional rate adjustment.

[44] Page 49 of the ETOSS Annual Report, in the section entitled "Extraordinary Revision" seeks to explain the calculation method. It involved keeping the debt level for year 10 of the Concession constant, and raising revenues during years 2 to 8 of the Concession. This explanation is not inconsistent with the hypothesis proposed here, and it should be noted that the economically appropriate criterion is not to hold debt constant, but to keep earnings constant. In any case, the increase seems excessive and there is no explanation for how $122 million in improvements and expansion become the $333 million used in the calculation.

[45] The sum total of anticipated investments, $ 122 million, distributed over 8 years and assuming an average financing cost of 10 percent, generates a cost increase of $16.8 million a year in the first 10 years, which equals approximately 5.6 percent of annual costs at this time. To reach 10 percent, higher operating costs due to greater coverage must certainly have been included, but that could not be confirmed.

caused rates to increase in a similar manner. If the calculation was actually made in this way, the critical comments below are in order.

If earnings are positive, revenue and cost increases in equal proportion mean greater returns, and if returns are highly positive, there is no reason to reward new capital in the same way as the extraordinary return for existing capital. This is because such a change does not account for greater current revenues (due to greater consumption resulting from a near 6 percent increase in the number of customers) accompanying greater current costs.

Being unable to specify whether or not these sums are reasonable, we should point out that the ETOSS annual report offers no clear information on such an important topic. Also, article 11.11.3 (Ordinary Revisions) of the Concession Contract refers to ordinary revisions as those having to do with rate changes due to adjustments in goals and/or capital disbursements envisioned in the Five-Year Plan for Improvements and Expansion. It goes on to state that this refers only to revisions involved in presenting the Second Five-Year Plan, and those following it. In this sense, moving up investments before the first Five-Year Plan has ended would not be in agreement with the terms of the Concession Contract.

Determination of the Infrastructure Charge (ETOSS Ruling No. 83/95)

Article 40 of the Concession Rate System set the reference value for the infrastructure charge for both residential potable water and sewerage systems. These values were then modified as indicated in the aforementioned ruling, but were still used as reference values. Therefore, the definitive (as opposed to the reference) value for the infrastructure charge was then set for potable water service (there is no mention of sewerage service).[46]

Consequently, a water service infrastructure charge was approved that could vary in accordance with this formula:

$$ICi = LSi \cdot Km \cdot Pds + Pc,$$

---

[46] Since this constitutes a change in the rate system and a company proposal was not mentioned in the justification of the ruling, article 11.11.1.1. of the Concession Contract requires the Ministry of Economy to give prior approval. The ETOSS does not say it received the necessary approval (Application Authority).

where ICi is an infrastructure charge on the property; LSi is the land surface of property; Km is a coefficient based on the type of soil and percentages of road and pavement work for each specific project (with a maximum range of approximately 100 percent difference, because the minimum value is 0.6944 and the maximum is 1.3713); Pds is the price of the "distribution network" component, which equals $0.97/m² of the land surface of the property; and Pc is the price of the "connection" component (equals $208.13 up to 22 mm diameter, $266.22 from 21 mm to 33 mm, and $297.40 from 34 mm to 41 mm).

According to an article that appeared in *Clarín* ("Notifications of Water Connection Suspended," April 24, 1996), this charge varies between $400 and $600, and hence on (linear) average, seems to be higher than the $450 indicated by ETOSS Ruling No. 81/94. Still, we should remember that the system is being expanded in an area that has seen fewer improvements on average.[47]

According to the explanation given by Aguas Argentinas, this calculation is correct. On average, the infrastructure charge rises for each user (except for those owning very small plots of land) because the reference value specified in the contract was calculated on the basis of a cost estimate for connecting a block, assuming there would be 40 lots (i.e., lots of 250 m²). However, the expansion zone is less dense (i.e., the typical lot has a surface area that exceeds 250 m²). Thus, the higher infrastructure charge each connection receives as a result of Ruling 83/95 generates the same total revenue for the company as the previous reference charge that referred to a higher estimated density.

Note, however, that the company should have anticipated that the expansion area is less densely populated, and accordingly, have specified as

---

[47] In any case, we can perform the following exercise: property measuring 400 m² (a typical 10 m x 40 m lot in the metropolitan area) with a low installation cost (softer soil, with no pavement or roads) and a small diameter connection must pay $476.70. This is higher than the previous uniform sum of $450 (which includes the 45 percent increase mentioned earlier). In Corrientes, it costs $17 to be connected to the existing network. This sum cannot be directly compared to that in effect for Aguas Argentinas because it is only valid in circumstances where the customer has the system at the door of his/her house, and requires only the connection (which he/she must then pay for). There is no connection cost in Corrientes for zones requiring construction of the street system because these investment plans are negotiated with each municipality, which in many cases make contributions in kind (labor or materials).

much in their quote during the bidding process. Therefore, the ETOSS could have argued that the average user charge should remain unchanged, and the company's revenue loss, due to a lower density than initially anticipated, would have been treated as a business risk.

In conclusion, the infrastructure charge is related to cost, and since the demand elasticity is minimal, efficiency considerations are out of place because they tend to eliminate cross-subsidies from unimproved to improved properties. Nevertheless, the initial evaluation of the ruling is negative for the following reasons: it maintains a regressive cross-subsidy between properties under a single expansion project[48] and; it never seems to be the case that no customer would be better off, since even those at a lower cost must pay a higher charge than the prior reference charge. Since processing a new infrastructure charge within a particular time frame does not appear inevitable under the contract, and although additional information is needed to render the specifics of this assumption (i.e., average surface area of new users, average soil characteristics, degree of road paving, and the existence of access roads), the ETOSS ruling seems to have favored Aguas Argentinas unilaterally.

Rate Classification Adjustment (ETOSS Ruling No. 20/ 93)

In evaluating the reclassification of residential to nonresidential customers, who pay double the previous fixed charge and do not have unlimited consumption, the ETOSS granted the company a two-year extension in meter installation for the new nonresidential classifications. Customers have the option to request metering (cutting the fixed charge in half) or to wait for the company to do it. In any case, they are immediately classified as nonresidential (article 11.13.2.1 of the Concession Contract), and customers are responsible for paying meter installation costs (article 25 of the contract).

The decision is consistent with the specifications and the contract. According to article 45 of the Specifications, the ETOSS had the authority to make such an extension and agreed to grant it on the grounds that it was

---

[48] The paving characteristics are those of the average property. Thus, to the extent there is a positive correlation between paving and the wealth of their owners, there is a subsidy from those who are without improvements toward those with them because as the average degree of improvements and paving increases so does the infrastructure charge.

technically impossible for all the reclassified customers to be metered immediately. However, why was no thought given to transferring the company's economic benefit from that extension to consumers in another way?[49] It should be noted that the customers in question were certainly businesses and professional people, whose water consumption is low, and hence, it is in the company's interest that they continue to pay a higher fixed charge without metering.

It is also interesting to note that article 1 of ETOSS Ruling No. 66/95 further requires Aguas Argentinas to install and/or repair 80,000 water meters a year from May 1, 1995, to April 30, 1998. If it is referring to clause 11.12.1 of the contract, why does it not mention which event of noncompliance on the part of the company allows the regulatory body to place a further requirement on it. Noncompliance entails levying fines, and the obligation to install meters, which the regulated company would do in any case, is not an acceptable substitute.

Billing to Consortiums (ETOSS Ruling No. 12/94)

In general, it is technically impossible to place individual metering devices in condominiums. Consequently, the ETOSS allowed the company to measure the water consumption of a group owner (i.e., using only one meter), and made it responsible for assuring that each of the functional units pays its share. Even though this power had been granted to the previously existing OSN in its Organic Law (art. 72, Law No. 20,324), the following should be noted:[50]

- Since the "fixed" charge on metered service is a "quasi-tax" proportional to the property surface served, the joint (group) "fixed" charge is equal to the sum of the fixed charges that the functional units would have been billed if they were individual. Thus, it is clear that this type of fixed charge is irrational;

---

[49] On the other hand, no deadline is set for the company to install the meter when requested to do so by the customer (ETOSS Ruling No. 44/93 sets a limit of three months and the only penalty is that the customer only pays half of the fixed fee).

[50] This revision did not conflict with the OSN, however, since there were about 4,000 metered ownership associations at the beginning of the concession, surely for lack of metering incentives under public ownership. In contrast, there is currently a court order suspending installation of meters on collectively-owned properties as the result of a case filed by the Ombudsman.

- Jointly metered apartment houses do not resolve the "free ride" problem, and therefore price-elasticity of demand is very low. These are the customers that the company is most interested in metering; and
- The decision also preserves the concessionaire's obligation to inform each functional unit about the charge to that user. This constitutes a duplication of tasks because, in fact, the management group will have to do that itself. If that concessionaire obligation were abolished, the savings could be passed on to consumers in the form of a lower fixed charge.

Corrientes

Determination and completion of the water and sewerage service concession for the 10 main locations in the province of Corrientes occurred during Governor Leconte's term (1987–91). The governor decreed the privatization on the basis of the provincial law that had followed the National Law on Reform of the State. The process was hastened by the absence of any discussion in the provincial legislature.

Provincial politics has been dominated by the PAL (Pacto Autonomista Liberal-Liberal Independence Party), which has been in power from 1983 to the present. Its only break in power was the 1992–93 period when the federal government stepped into the province after a tie had occurred in the Electoral College chosen in the 1991 elections. Nevertheless, political risk in the province has increased due to serious internal rifts within the PAL, which first became public in 1994 and finally exploded in 1996, when one faction of the party opposed the fiscal adjustment program championed by Governor Raul Romero Feris.

According to political analysts, the province has no strong labor unions, the church is not united in its position, the justice system—linked to the PAL government—is immersed in the political crisis, and the main media outlets are owned by the PAL and opposition political leaders. Moreover, the province's deteriorating financial situation produced a higher risk of expropriation of sunk investments. For example, politicization of public utilities could compensate for the need to cut back on payroll spending. In 1995 and 1996, the province adjusted payroll spending and took steps to lower the social security deficit.

This was the political and economic context that suggested the water and sewerage concession in Corrientes was heading toward a low-quality service equilibrium in early 1996. Clearly, there was a greater risk of covert expropriation by the provincial government. The makeup of shareholders in the private company changed during that time, which has at least partially reversed the situation.[51]

Article 39 of the contract envisions rate modifications should any of the following costs vary by more than 5 percent: (a) the electric power price (set by the provincial government); (b) basic labor agreement wage; and (c) aluminum sulfate prices. In July 1993, the company requested a 16.84 percent rate increase, and the regulatory body authorized one of only 6.04 percent arguing that cost indexation was prohibited within the framework of the Law of Convertibility passed by the federal government in April 1991. It did agree to adjust the rate as a result of the change in the electric power price charged by the provincial electric company, however.[52] This is a peculiar interpretation of the Law of Convertibility because that law eliminated general rate indexation, but not relative price changes, even if they should be the result of cost changes. Indeed, the federal government admits that changes in generation costs or costs to natural gas producers are subject to passthrough to final electric and natural gas bills, even though adjustments based on wholesale or retail general price indices in the distribution margins of both products are not allowed. It does, however, recognize dollar inflation.[53]

In September 1994, a provincial judge declared it unconstitutional to cut off water service for delinquency in payment. The provincial government stated its intention to comply with the contract. According to the regulatory body, the concessionaire is cutting off service for customer failure to

---

[51] See Esfahani (1996).

[52] In November 1993, it authorized another 2.65 percent increase for the same reason: a rise in the cost of electric power.

[53] It could be argued that measures taken by the regulatory body moderate the incentive problems caused by allowing cost variations to be transferred to the rate. Even though a decision to move toward a ceiling price with fewer cost passthrough aspects may in itself be reasonable, the text emphasizes that the decision adopted in July 1993 subtly changes the concession contract, because article 39 authorized transfer of these cost variations. Also, previous clauses in the regulatory body ruling cite as justification a report by the State Inspection Office, which suggests that wage hikes should not be recognized. (The Inspection Office comes under the executive power in the province).

Table 6.3 Fines Imposed by the Regulatory Body on the Aguas de Corrientes Company

Period	Number of fines	Amount (in m³ water)	Average fine (m³)
1993	6	32,000	5,400
1994	9	94,000	10,400
1995	12	151,500	12,600

Source: AOSC (regulatory body for water and sewerage service in Corrientes).

pay in accordance with its plans.[54] Hence, there is the possibility of political pressure to delay cutting off service to more sensitive users. In practice, service has been cut off, but never on a broad scale, and around 20 percent–25 percent of billing is noncollectable. About half of what is noncollectable is said to be that of the provincial government itself.

There have been problems with the labor union, in a province where labor union power is weak. For example, in 1995, the labor union sought to have the concession contract canceled because no board member represented the unions and because of effluent treatment problems. It also cited failure to comply with placing meters and breach of the collective bargaining agreement. (*El Litoral,* July 25, 1996).

The regulatory body raised the number and amount of fines imposed on the concessionaire for a variety of problems. Table 6.3 indicates sums for the 1993–95 period.

A number of politicians have questioned the contract and asked that it be canceled due to water quality problems (*El Litoral,* February 24, 1996). A PAL senator asked that the judicial system intervene on the issue of cutting off water because "the state's responsibilities in social matters are absolutely mandatory, and in the history of great epidemics in the country and in the world, this obligation has outweighed the mere legally binding nature of contracts" (*El Litoral,* June 13, 1995). At the request of this senator, on September 1995, the Provincial Senate gave half passage to a law creating a mixed commission composed of legislators and the company to review which

---

[54] Regulatory body responses to a questionnaire submitted by FIEL.

delivery cutoffs could actually be made. Passage was completed in 1996. Another law was passed that required the regulatory agency to revise interest charged on overdue payments collected by Aguas de Corrientes in line with those established (sic) by the Law of Convertibility.[55] This could force the company to return excess sums received.

In 1995, fulfillment of the physical service goals began to slow. Interestingly, the gap arises for two reasons: (a) the population growth rate in the concession area proved to be considerably higher than that envisioned in the specifications, and meant an automatic increase in those goals; (b) the company did not satisfy its obligation to install three purification plants. With regard to the plants, the company claimed that local and provincial officials delayed transferring the land on which they were to be installed, but regulatory officials recommended the contract guarantees be enforced. No final decision has been made on this conflict. With regard to the higher-than-expected growth rate, Figures 6.2 and 6.3 prepared by the regulatory agency show that political problems were at their height in 1995 and 1996, the same period in which the water and sewer connection plan was not being fulfilled.

Finally, in early 1996, the principle shareholder in the company sold its holdings to local shareholders, who presumably were better able to deal with the pressures of the provincial government.[56] It could be argued that in a high-risk province, the manner in which the company's shareholder capital was set up could have led to these events, and a company could have been established primarily with local capital. However, there are several reasons as to why that did not happen in 1990. At the time of privatization, the provincial political horizon was relatively stable and it was hard to foresee fighting within the governing party. In the bidders' prequalification, importance was given to technical requirements such as prior involvement in metering, billing, and payment; managerial and business capability (17 percent of the total number of points); background in providing public utilities in water and sewerage services (23 percent of the total); and shareholder net worth of over $15 million (22 percent of the total). Taken together, these requirements reduced the likelihood that a company made up primarily of capital from Corrientes would be successful.

---

[55] The Law of Convertibility does not set ceilings on interest.

[56] For a theoretical discussion on the dispersion of shareholding trends in public utility company stocks in the United States that supports this point, see Kahn and Urbiztondo (1991).

Performance Indicator Trends

Aguas Argentinas

As seen in Table 6.4, performance indicators have moved in a positive direction. With regard to surpassing water and sewerage connection goals, the company provided the information. However, the positive performance is not apparent with respect to the Specification of Terms and Conditions, because the expansion goals were set as percentages of the population in the concession area defined by five-year periods. Compliance depended not only on the number of new connections, but also on the area's population growth, and no annual goals were set. Therefore, the population growth assumptions used are crucial when comparing those goals to connections actually made. For example, at the start of the concession, 6 million people (70 percent of the total population of the concession area) were served with water. The coverage goal to be reached in year five of the concession is 82 percent of the total population, which translates into 205,000 persons per year if there is no population growth, and 351,700 persons per year if the population grows at a 2 percent annual rate. Actual annual expansion during the first three years of the concession was around 594,700 people. That is consistent with a population growth rate of around 1.3 percent, which is average for Argentina. Actual expansion is clearly not far from that estimated at the beginning of the concession.

As shown in Table 6.5, the Aguas Argentinas financial indicators are excellent. Company profits were negative the first year, but that was reversed immediately. The company achieved a net rate of return on equity of over 40 percent in the third year of the concession, basically due to the substantial increase in revenues for services annually (especially in the second year of the concession).[57]

---

[57] The structure of real revenues (in millions of current dollars) unfolded as follows:

	Year 1	Year 2	Year 3
Residential	169	198	210
Nonresidential	93	124	126
Quilmes	8	9	11
Other	9	20	39
Infrastructure charge	0	0	14
Total	279	350	400

Table 6.4 Trends in Aguas Argentinas Performance Indicators

Increased population served with water	844,00 inhabitants (115 percent of goals as reported by the company)
Increased population served with sewers	386,000 inhabitants (340 percent of goals as reported by the company)
Repair of water pipe system	634 km (155 percent of goals)
Water not accounted for	31 percent (goal for year 15 attained) initially (in the specifications) the loss was 43 percent
Meter installation	92,500 (116 percent of goals according to ETOSS Ruling No. 66/95)
Increase in productive capacity	37 percent (24 percent due to rehabilitation of pre-existing plants)
Water Pressure in Federal Capital	
• Percentage of connections with over 8 meters pressure	From 15 percent (year 1) to 97 percent (year 3)
• Percentage with pressure under 2 meters	From 2 percent (year 1) to 0 percent (year 3)
Water Pressure in Greater Buenos Aires	
• Percentage of connections with over 8 meters pressure	From 13 percent (year 1) to 54 percent (year 3)
• Percentage with pressure under 2 meters	From 4 percent (year 1) to 1.7 percent (year 3)
Hours of delay in resolving water complaints	From 70 in 1993 to 50 in 1995
Hours of delay in resolving sewerage complaints	From 70 in 1993 to 25 in 1995
Collection within 6 months	Rose from 86 percent at the beginning, to 89 percent by the end of the third year
Investment	$625 million ($145 in year 1—$127 for upgrading the company—$210 in year 2, and $ 270 in year 3—$157 in expansion, $50 in rehabilitation of existing assets and $64 in upgrading the company)
Staff	Initially 7,365; first year 3,800; since then, growing at 2 percent/year
Jobs created by investments	2,100 the first year; 5,300 the second; and 8,200 the third (including contractors of works and services, according to the company)
Growth in average gross salary (contract staff)	46 percent increase in 3 years

Table 6.5 Trends in Aguas Argentinas Financial Indicators
(In millions of current dollars)

Year	1993	1994	1995
Net Worth (NW)	95	131.9	185.4
Net Profit	−23.2 (19 percent of capital contribution)	26.45 (25 percent of capital contribution)	53.6 (41 percent of capital contribution)
(Net) revenues for services	163.3 (with 8 months of operation)	305	360.8
Total Costs		303.2	341.45

In conclusion, the concession has moved in a satisfactory direction, both in terms of meeting expansion and improvement goals and in the bottom line achieved by operations. Thus far, there has been no fluctuation such as that seen in the Corrientes concession, which is discussed below.

Aguas de Corrientes

The private company took over water and sewerage services beginning in September 1991. Table 6.6 shows the results under private management for the 1991–95 period. In four years, the number of water connections rose by 22 percent and the number of sewerage connections by 50 percent, thus attaining greater service coverage (an additional 7 percent of the population with water, 12 percent with sewerage). Between September 1995 and March 1996, the number of connections will have risen even more rapidly (7.2 percent for water and 31.6 percent for sewerage). Figures 6.2 and 6.3 illustrate the degree to which goals were met during the period between August 1994 and June 1996.[58]

---

[58] These figures, prepared with information provided by the regulatory body, should be interpreted with caution. For example, the jump in the number of sewer installations noted in Figure 6.3 is due to the AOSC's acceptance of homes where the system comes to the door but is not connected as counting toward goal fulfillment. This company claim was accepted after most of the capital stock had been transferred to business people in Corrientes.

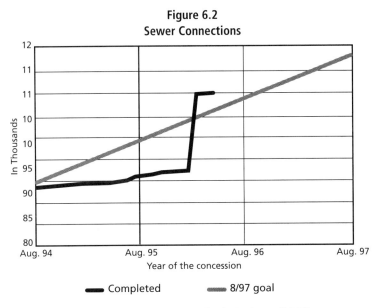

Figure 6.2
Sewer Connections

Source: Administración de Obras Sanitarias de Corrientes (AOSC).

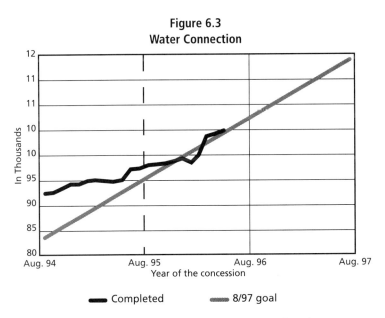

Figure 6.3
Water Connection

Source: Administración de Obras Sanitarias de Corrientes (AOSC).

Table 6.6 Performance of Aguas de Corrientes S.A.

	To Sept. 1, 1991	End of 1995	May 1996
Num. of water connections	80,000	97,954	104,974
% of population in water system	66.14	72.96	76.31
Number of sewer connections	35,939	53,908	70,962
% population with sewers	29.63	41.60	50.58
Daily consumption per inhabitant	471 L/day	421 L/day	377 L/day
Employees/1,000 water connections	7.38	2.55	2.59
Rates ($/m³ of water)	0.3275	0.355	0.355
Investment (millions of US$/year)	1.4(*)	11.5	nd
Billing (US$ million/years)	28.3(*)	21.4	nd
Water production (millions of m³)	61.5(*)	55.1	nd
Estimated loss (% of prod.)	60.7	45.0	nd

*First year of concession.

Increased micrometering made it easier to lower average water consumption during the first years of the concession from 471 liters/day in 1991 to 377 liters/day in May 1996.[59] There was also a notable increase in the productivity of employees, the number of which fell from 590 at the beginning of the concession to 250 in September 1995. There were only 230 employees by the end of that year, although information from the regulatory body reports that it increased to 270 in 1996. The number of employees per 1,000 water connections thus fell from 7.4 in 1991 to 2.5 in 1995–96. Water loss was also reduced from 61 percent in 1991 to 45 percent in 1995.

In short, performance by Aguas de Corrientes has been reasonable, although its inability to collect for service has hindered its development. It does not seem accidental that company ownership has been transferred to local partners in order to avoid a low-quality equilibrium such as began to appear in late 1995.

---

[59] The company does not read 100 percent of the meters as specified in the contract. At the end of 1995, the reading percentage was somewhere above 80 percent.

Conclusions

The regulatory framework in Corrientes is better than that of Buenos Aires, although the two share many similarities. One major exception is the design of the regulatory agency, which is under the executive branch and whose salaries are based on the water rate. There are no major "fissures" to suggest a design problem that later led to opportunistic behavior on the part of the government. The exception is the design of the regulatory body and the transfer of service by concession, which opened considerable possibilities for re-negotiation since each change in assets required approval. Nevertheless, the problems that did arise did not stem from this weakness in the contract. They were rooted in the significant change in the attitude of local political leadership when macroeconomic conditions changed. This impacted on the provincial treasury, thereby creating pressure not to collect delinquent accounts, even though the regulatory framework explicitly allowed for it.

Initially, the contract was appropriately applied in Corrientes, given the political context. In 1994, as the governing party was torn by political infighting, opportunistic behavior reduced the credibility and completion of the coverage plan. Majority stockholders even sold their shares to a local businessman who was more prepared to prevent expropriation as would be expected on the basis of a simple model of political economy. It therefore became clear that the contract was flawed, since its implementation is highly sensitive to the prevailing political context.

A decisive factor in the Corrientes concession problem was the high proportion of noncollection—much higher than estimated at the time of the bidding. The legal and political context made it very difficult to collect debts. An alternative for future concessions in other provinces could be to share collection on delinquent accounts above a certain billing percentage with the regional government in order to generate an extra revenue flow to the provincial government.[60]

In Aguas Argentinas, the property assessment system remained in effect, limiting options for metering. Reassessments rather than efficiency improvements (improved quality, for example) were seen as the way to maximize profits. This decision may have been made to avoid redistribution problems: going to a metered system would have further raised the rate for

---

[60] In other words, the fixed monthly concession fee would be replaced by one tied to the concession's ability to collect.

the least expensive properties, which today are favored by the assessment system. In any case, the use of public utility prices as a way to distribute income is open to criticism and has not been adopted by the federal government in selling electricity and natural gas.

In Buenos Aires, funding of the regulatory agency is, in practice, tied to the revenues of the regulated company (notwithstanding a design to the contrary). Moreover, it cannot reap any economic benefit from penalties imposed on the concessionaire for breach of contract. This introduces a potential procompany bias into the ETOSS. Its effect is just the opposite of what might be expected from the design adopted for constituting its policy board, as compared to other regulatory bodies at the national level.

There seem to be more labor union problems in Corrientes than in Buenos Aires. Perhaps the postconcession government in Corrientes handled labor unions in a more political manner.

In Buenos Aires, the rate balance shifted in 1994, aided by its low visibility—it hurt new users with delayed temporary effects—and/or because the service had little impact on user revenues as a whole. This regulatory environment contrasts sharply with the current situation in the telecommunications industry where such shifts are prohibited for their visibility and their damaging effect on current users.

Furthermore, water rates are not transparent, and the shift occurred at a time when consumer groups and the public defender were not yet strongly organized, the economy was booming, and inflation was low. In short, when everything was more tolerable than during a recession and deflation (1995). Pressures in the opposite direction appeared in 1996, aimed at lowering the infrastructure charge and checking the company's monopolistic behavior.

In conclusion, the design of the regulatory body and methods for monitoring it are important (with regard to economic independence, political dependency, etc.). In Aguas Argentinas, its design disregarded funding provisions. In Corrientes, the regulatory body was kept under the government's regulatory scope and seems to have been used as an instrument of political harassment. The political and media context was also important. Pressure by regulated companies and pressure groups initially seems focused on problems of bill collection. In the case of Buenos Aires, the focus is on real estate reassessment of properties owned by utility customers. Once this pressure is lifted, the problems will likely spread to those regulatory areas that are susceptible to varying interpretations.

References

Aguas Argentinas. 1993, 1994, and 1995. Annual Reports.

Armstrong, M., Cowan, S., and Vickers, J. 1994. *Regulatory Reform: Economic Analysis and British Experience.* Cambridge, Mass: MIT Press.

Artana, D., López Murphy, R., Navajas, F., and Urbiztondo, S. 1995. "The Shift in Telephone Rates." Working Document No. 48. FIEL.

Brown, S. and Sibley, D. 1987. *The Theory of Public Utility Pricing.* Cambridge, Mass.: Cambridge University Press.

Esfahani, H. 1996. "The Political Economy of the Telecommunications Sector in the Philippines." In: B. Levy and P. Spiller, editors. *Regulations, Institutions and Commitment: Comparative Studies of Telecommunications.* Cambridge: Cambridge University Press.

ETOSS. 1993/1994 and 1994/1995 Annual Reports.

FIEL. 1992. *Infrastructure Capital in Argentina. Public Management, Privatization and Productivity.* Buenos Aires: Ed. Manantial.

Gaggero, J., Gerchunoff, P., Porto, A. and Urbiztondo, S. 1992. "Some Thoughts on OSN Privatization." *Estudios.* October.

Guadagni, A. 1973. "Economic Aspects of Urban Cleanup in Argentina." *In Problemas Económicos Argentinos: Diagnóstico y Política.* Buenos Aires: Ed. Macchi.

Kahn, C. and Urbiztondo, S. 1991. "Ownership Dispersion, Expropriation, and Majority Rule." Mimeo. University of Illinois.

Laffont, J. and Tirole, J. 1993. *The Theory of Incentives in Procurement and Regulation.* Cambridge, Mass: MIT Press.

Levy, B. and Spiller, P. 1994. "The Institutional Foundations of Regulatory Commitment: A Comparative Analysis of Telecommunications Regulations." *The Journal of Law, Economics and Organization.* 10 (2).

Navajas, F. and Porto, A. 1990. "The Quasi-Optimal Two-Part Tariff: Efficiency, Equity and Financing." *El Trimestre Económico*, LVII (4), No. 228.

Nellor, D. and Robinson, M. 1984. "Binding Future Governments: Tax Contracts and Resource Development." UCLA Department of Economics. Working Paper.

Ng, Y. and Weisser, M. 1974. "Optimal Price with a Budget Constraint. The Case of the Two-Part Tariff." *Review of Economic Studies*, Vol. 41.

Nuñez Miñana, H. and Porto, A. 1976. "Analysis of Price Changes in Argentine Public Corporations," *Desarrollo Económico*, 16 (63).

Porto A. 1991. "The Rate Structure in Unmetered Federal Sanitation Works." Mimeo. Instituto Torcuato Di Tella.

Price Waterhouse and Infupa. 1990. "Report on the AOSC." Mimeo.

Spulber, D. 1990. "Auctions and Contract Enforcement," *Journal of Law, Economics and Organization.* 6 (2).

World Bank. 1995. "Argentina: Managing Environmental Pollution: Issues and Options." Vol. II. Technical Report No. 14.070-AR.

World Bank. 1996. "Argentina: Reforming Provincial Utilities: Issues, Challenges, and Best Practice." Mimeo. Washington DC.